COUNTRYWOMAN'S COOKBOOK

Compiled by
Carol Odell

Photographs and illustrations: JIM GULLY

RIGBY

ACKNOWLEDGMENTS

Grateful acknowledgment is made to Mary Gully for preparing the food shown in the photographs; to June Tanner for allowing her homestead, Kipsy, to be used in the photographs; and to Farmer Jones Meat Market, Norwood, South Australia, for help and advice with the meat used in the photographs.

National Library of Australia
Cataloguing-in-Publication entry

Countrywoman's cookbook.
    Originally published as: The Australian countrywoman's cookbook. Adelaide: Rigby, 1977.
    Includes index.
    ISBN 0 7270 1471 4.
    1. Cookery. I. Odell, Carol. II. Gully, Jim. III.
    Title: Countrywoman's cookbook.

641.5

RIGBY PUBLISHERS LIMITED • ADELAIDE
SYDNEY • MELBOURNE • BRISBANE • PERTH
NEW YORK • LONDON • AUCKLAND
First published 1977
Second edition 1981
First Impression 1984
Wholly designed and typeset in Australia
Printed in Hong Kong by South China Printing Co.

Editing and additional material by Deirdre Adamek
Designed by Jim Gully

Contents

The Pleasure of Cooking Country Style

Even to those of us brought up in the city, there is something about the thought of a farmhouse kitchen that breathes comfort, peace, and security. Anyone brought up in the country, especially the country before the Plastic Age, will remember those kitchens with a special blend of nostalgia: a collective memory of sights and smells and sounds.

The sounds came in through the windows and the back door: a sleepy symphony of farmhouse life. Hens clucking in the yard, pigs snuffling and grunting in their pens, the cows clopping along like high-heeled ladies, full udders swinging as they came in to be milked, the distant complaint of sheep, the drone of machinery across the paddocks at seedtime or harvest, one of the boys chopping wood to feed the kitchen stove.

The old wood-burning stove, bright with nickel and enamel and well recessed under a high mantelpiece, was the high spot of the kitchen. It glowed away like the warm heart of the house and gave the kitchen a special kind of snugness. There was nothing like a wood stove on frosty mornings, and it was a kind of multi-purpose facility that dried wet socks, kept a siphon of hot water steaming, welcomed the homecomer, and gave a unique savour to the meals it cooked. Sometimes a newborn lamb or a clutch of chicks lay in a box by the stove, gaining strength in its benevolent warmth.

Everyone gravitated towards the stove. It was one of the principal sights of the kitchen, like the dresser laden with everything from show trophies to assorted crockery, and the big old table that seemed like one of the family, and Mum's creaking basket chair into which she sank to rest her feet while she shelled a pot of peas. None of them were beautiful pieces of furniture. They'd never have won design awards. But they were homely, familiar, rich with long and comforting associations.

And then there were the smells. The marvellous smells of country cooking, as different from the smells of packaged foods as a paddock of deep, rich, loamy soil, ripe with fertility, is different from a parking lot. The smell of a batch of newbaked bread, that seemed to set all the juices in your body flowing. Bacon and eggs on a frosty morning. Apricots being bottled. Of a great roast sizzling in the oven, surrounded by potatoes and carrots and onions. The green smell of fresh salad. Tomatoes frying. The sharp pungency of onions and spices and vinegar boiling for pickles. The garden smell of fresh vegetables, heaped on the table ready to be chopped or sliced or peeled. The earth smell of potatoes dug freshly from the soil. Jam boiling. The sumptuous steam that escaped when the knife made its first cut through the crisp golden crust of a meat pie.

The food in a country kitchen seemed to have its own special dimension of textures and fragrances. It was natural, fresh, and free from processing. The cunning packages were provided by nature. Who has ever improved upon the packaging of an egg, or a pod full of peas, or a walnut?

Life was not easy for a country housewife. She'd never heard of most of today's labour-saving devices and maybe she was lucky if she even had a refrigerator. But there were compensations. Like a pan of fresh milk, with the cream clotted so thickly on its surface that it was as stiff as cardboard. Eggs so large that they make the battery-produced variety look like marbles. Fresh-killed meat, and fresh-picked fruit, and vegetables straight from the garden. Probably she had to draw her water from the rainwater tank, but it was clean, clear, free from chlorine and any other chemicals. Often she was miles from the nearest store, but she had her own pantry stowed with jams, pickles, and preserves.

The country housewife was a craftswoman who took a particular pride in her cooking. There was the regular daily fare that stoked the energies of people working long hours in the open air, and Sunday dinner that was always a high spot of the week, and then there were the great occasions like church suppers when every housewife turned up with her own speciality. Cakes heavy with cream and fruit, tarts glowing with homemade jam, sausage rolls that were savoury morsels in jackets of featherlight pastry, crisp biscuits, high sponges as soft as a cloud, scones so delectable with their loads of jam and cream that it seemed you could eat them forever. The housewife's reward was clean plates and beaming faces. Cooking and eating were not chores to be fitted in, but integral parts of a life of hard but satisfying work. The kitchen was as much a part of this life as the grain rippling in the paddocks and the sheep grazing in the pastures.

Obviously it is not possible for everyone to be a country housewife, but at least it is possible to partake in some ways of the pleasures of country cooking. The key is simplicity. Good natural ingredients, prepared with that touch of tender loving care which makes all the difference. You can cook country style just as well (and, let's admit it, maybe even better) on your gas or electric stove as grandmother did on her wood stove, and it's a lot easier. All that you need is her belief that good cooking is worthwhile for its own sake: a satisfying craft that's open to everyone. The recipes in this book will help you to find that satisfaction.

Good Nourishing SOUPS

The many kinds and variations of soup make it one of the most versatile types of dish at the cook's disposal. A soup that is brimming with vegetables, meat, or fish, can form the main course of a simple meal, especially when accompanied with plenty of fresh bread or rolls. Soup also serves to stimulate the appetite and in this guise it can be used to introduce a meal of several courses; it should then be light—a consommé or broth—and served in modest quantity. Between the extremes of broth and stew lie many other versions—cream soups, thickened soups, purées, and clear soups supplemented with some of the more substantial garnishes listed below.

The main ingredient of most good soups is stock, which is also basic to many sauces and gravies. Stock is the liquid produced by the long, slow simmering of meat or fish, bones, and vegetables. It is cheap, nourishing, and easy to make. Stock may be cooked in a stock-pot or in a large saucepan with a tight-fitting lid. It is usually based on the proportions of 1 pint (625 millilitres) of liquid for each pound (500 grams) of solid ingredients. First stock is made from uncooked meat, bones, and vegetables; second stock is made from the same ingredients, which have already been used, with the original quantity of fresh cold water added, brought to the boil and then simmered for several hours to extract the gelatine from the bones. Stock should never be boiled, but gently simmered. Scum rises to the top of the simmering stock and should be skimmed off; if the stock is left to cool overnight before use the fat can then easily be removed. If the stock is to be used at once, a piece of tissue paper drawn across the surface will absorb any remaining fat.

Brown stock is made from beef or mutton, white stock from poultry or veal. Fish stock is made from fish bones, heads, and trimmings. Vegetable stock is made by simmering vegetables, including peelings, trimmings, and outer leaves; this produces a very delicately flavoured liquid, which is generally used only for meatless vegetables soups. Strongly flavoured ingredients such as pork, smoked or corned meat, and turnips should not be used in stock, as they overwhelm the other ingredients.

Accompaniments and Garnishes for Soups

Sippets—cubes of dry toast.
Croûtons—cubes of crisp-fried bread (see page 18).
Melba toast—wafer-thin slices of bread, with the crusts removed, toasted then sliced through and toasted again or dried in the oven until crisp and curled.
Spaghetti or macaroni—added to clear soups about 15 minutes before the end of cooking time.
Cheese straws (see page 84).
Small dumplings (see page 42).
Bacon, crisp-fried or grilled·and crumbled.
Hard-boiled egg-white or egg-yolk, chopped or sieved.
Grated hard cheese—with most vegetable soups, especially potato, leek, and onion soups.
Toasted blanched almonds, slivered or chopped—for cream soups, especially chicken.
Fried onion rings.
Cucumber, diced or sliced thinly.
Chopped fresh herbs.
Lightly fried mushrooms.
Boiled rice.
Cooked vegetables cut in matchsticks—for clear soups.

BONE STOCK

- 2 lb (1 kg) mutton, beef, or veal bones
- 2 qt (2·5 litres) cold water
- 1 onion, thickly sliced
- 2 small carrots, thickly sliced
- 1 thick slice of turnip or parsnip
- 1 tsp salt
- 2 cloves
- 8 peppercorns
- 1 sprig of parsley

Wash and roughly chop the bones, trimming off fat; place in a pan with the cold water. Bring slowly to the boil, then boil quickly until scum forms on top. Skim off scum, cover closely, and simmer gently for about 4 hours. Add the vegetables and other ingredients. Simmer for another 2 hours, until the bones are clean. Strain into a large bowl. Store in a cool place.

WHITE STOCK

- 2 lb (1 kg) knuckle of veal, or veal, fowl, or mutton bones
- 2 qt (2·5 litres) cold water
- 1 onion, thickly sliced
- 1 carrot, thickly sliced
- 2 stalks of celery, roughly diced
- 6 peppercorns
- 1 bay-leaf
- salt

Put the meat and bones in a pan, cover with the cold water, and leave to stand for 1 hour. Bring slowly to the boil and skim. Cover tightly and simmer for 2½ hours, skimming when necessary. Add the vegetables, which have been gently fried, without browning, in hot fat, and other ingredients. Simmer until the bones are clean. Strain into a bowl and store in a cool place.

SECOND WHITE STOCK

Follow the instructions for white stock (see above), using the same bones and meat. All other ingredients must be fresh.

BROWN STOCK

- 8 oz (250 g) bones
- 2 lb (1 kg) shin beef
- 2 qt (2·5 litres) cold water
- 1 carrot, thickly sliced
- 1 stalk of celery, roughly diced
- 1 thick slice of turnip
- 1 sprig of parsley
- ½ tsp salt
- 6 peppercorns
- 1 bay-leaf

Put the meat and bones in a pan, cover with the cold water, and leave to stand for 1 hour. Bring slowly to the boil, add salt, and skim immediately. Cover and simmer for 2 to 3 hours. Add the vegetables, which have been sautéed in hot fat, and the other ingredients. Simmer until the bones are clean. Strain into a bowl and store in a cool place.

If stock is tasteless and watery, boil it uncovered until it is reduced and concentrated.

SECOND BROWN STOCK

Follow the instructions for brown stock (see above), using the same bones and meat. All other ingredients must be fresh. Any cooked or uncooked bones or meat scraps can be added.

FISH STOCK

- 1 lb (500 g) fish bones and trimmings
- 1 blade of mace
- 1 qt (1·25 litres) cold water
- 6 peppercorns
- 2 thin pieces of lemon rind
- salt
- 1 sprig of parsley
- 1 stalk of celery, roughly chopped
- 1 onion, sliced (optional)

Place all the ingredients in a saucepan; bring slowly to the boil. Cover tightly, and simmer for 1½ to 2 hours. Strain and use as directed.

BROWN ONION SOUP

- 2 lb (1 kg) sliced onions
- 2 oz (60 g) butter
- 2 oz (60 g) plain flour
- 2 qt (2·5 litres) stock
- salt and pepper
- 1 tsp sugar

Fry the onions slowly in the butter until they are soft and golden. Stir in the flour and cook for a few minutes until brown. Add the stock, seasoning, and sugar. Bring to the boil, stirring, then simmer for about 1½ hours. Check the seasoning.

Serve with croûtons (see page 18).

CARROT SOUP

- 1 oz (30 g) butter
- 1 large onion, chopped
- 2 stalks of celery, chopped
- 3 large carrots, grated
- salt and pepper
- a pinch of sugar
- 1½ pt (940 ml) stock
- 1 tsp cornflour

Fry the onion in the butter until soft and light golden. Add the celery, carrots, seasoning, sugar, and stock. Bring to the boil and simmer for about 1½ hours. Remove any fat on the surface and rub the soup through a sieve. Return to the saucepan and stir in the cornflour, which has been blended with a little water. Heat through for a few minutes.

Serve with sippets (see page 10).

POTATO SOUP

- 1 oz (30 g) butter
- 1 lb (500 g) potatoes, sliced
- 1 onion, sliced
- 1 stalk of celery, chopped
- 1½ pt (940 ml) stock
- ¼ pt (150 ml) milk
- salt and pepper

Melt the butter and sauté the vegetables for about 10 minutes, making sure that they do not colour. Add the stock and cook until the vegetables are soft, about half an hour. Rub through a sieve and return to the saucepan with the milk. Bring to the boil, check the seasoning, and serve.

PUMPKIN SOUP

1½ lb (750 g) pumpkin, peeled and chopped
2 onions, chopped
1 stalk of celery, chopped
1½ pt (940 ml) water or stock
½ pt (315 ml) milk
1 oz (30 g) butter
2 tbsps cream (optional)
chopped parsley

Simmer the pumpkin, onions, and celery in the stock or water. When cooked, press the vegetables through a sieve into a saucepan. Add the milk and butter, and bring to the boil again. Stir in the cream and serve at once, sprinkled with parsley.

TOMATO SOUP

6 tomatoes, roughly chopped
1 small onion, roughly chopped
1 dsp sugar
1 tsp salt
a scrap of bacon
1 sprig of parsley
2-inch (5 cm) piece of lemon rind
2½ cups water
cornflour
a knob of butter

Put the tomatoes in a saucepan with the onion, sugar, salt, bacon, parsley, lemon rind, and water. Cover and simmer for 1½ hours. Press the mixture through a sieve, then return to the saucepan to heat through. Thicken with cornflour blended with a little cold water, and add the butter; simmer for a few minutes longer, to cook the flour.

TOMATO CREAM SOUP

2 lb (1 kg) tomatoes
2 oz (60 g) butter
approx. 1½ pt (940 ml) milk
salt and pepper
1 tbsp plain flour

Stew the tomatoes for 10 to 15 minutes in the butter. Rub through a sieve, then return to the saucepan. Stir in the milk, season to taste, and heat through. Thicken with the flour blended with a little water, and cook for a few minutes longer before serving.

MUSHROOM CREAM SOUP

8 oz (250 g) mushrooms, peeled and chopped
1 small onion, finely chopped
½ pt (315 ml) stock
1 tbsp butter
1 tbsp plain flour
¾ pt (475 ml) milk
salt and pepper
1 egg-yolk
1 tbsp cream

Simmer the mushrooms with the onion and stock in a covered saucepan until tender. Rub through a sieve. Melt the butter in a saucepan, stir in the flour, and cook gently for a minute or so. Gradually add the milk, stirring constantly until thickened. Add the mushroom purée, and seasoning, and simmer gently for 5 to 10 minutes. Remove from the heat and stir in the egg-yolk, which has been blended with the cream. Return to the heat briefly but do not allow to boil.

Avoid using starchy vegetables for stock, as they tend to produce a sour taste.

PEA SOUP

8 oz (250 g) split peas
2 qt (2·5 litres) stock
bacon bones
1 carrot, roughly chopped
1 turnip, roughly chopped
1 onion, roughly chopped
2 stalks of celery, roughly chopped
salt and pepper
dried mint

Soak the peas in water overnight. Next day, drain and put in a large saucepan with the stock and bacon bones. Bring to the boil then add the vegetables and simmer until they are tender, about 1½ to 2 hours. Remove the bones and rub the soup through a sieve. Return to the saucepan, and thicken, if necessary, with a tablespoon of flour blended with a little water. Heat through, check seasoning, and add mint to taste.

Serve with sippets (see page 10).

BEAN SOUP

1 cup dried beans
1 large onion, roughly chopped
1 qt (1·25 litres) stock
1 piece streaky salt pork
2 glasses claret
1 tsp allspice
salt and pepper
a knob of butter
1 egg-yolk

Soak the beans in water for 12 hours, then boil in water for half an hour. Add the onion, stock, and pork and simmer until tender. Rub through a fine sieve, then reheat with the claret. Season with allspice, salt, and pepper; just before serving, stir in the butter and egg-yolk, making sure not to boil.

MULLIGATAWNY

1 onion, sliced
1 oz (30 g) butter
1 carrot, sliced
1 turnip, sliced
2 stalks of celery, sliced
1 apple, sliced
1 tbsp plain flour
1 dsp curry powder
1 dsp lemon juice
1 qt (1·25 litres) stock
2 oz (60 g) rice, cooked

Brown the onion in the butter with the carrot, turnip, celery, and apple. Stir in the flour and curry powder and cook for a minute or so. Add the lemon juice and hot stock and simmer gently for 2 hours. Rub through a sieve then return to the saucepan with the rice to heat through.

COTTAGE SOUP

4 medium potatoes, sliced
1½ pt (940 ml) boiling water
1½ tsps salt
1 cup grated Cheddar cheese
1 cup cooked peas
1 small tin asparagus tips
1½ tbsps chopped chives
1 oz (30 g) butter
pepper

Cook the potatoes in boiling salted water until tender. Strain, but reserve the liquid. Press the potatoes through a sieve, stir in the cooking liquid, and return to the saucepan. Add the cheese, and stir until smooth. Add the peas, asparagus, chives, butter, and pepper to taste. Heat through, and serve.

BROWN VEGETABLE SOUP

2 carrots, roughly chopped
2 onions, roughly chopped
2 turnips, roughly chopped
2 stalks of celery, roughly chopped
2 oz (60 g) butter
1 oz (30 g) plain flour
3 tomatoes, roughly chopped
2 qt (2·5 litres) stock
1 tbsp Worcestershire sauce
salt and pepper

Fry the vegetables (except for the tomatoes) in the butter until brown. Stir in the flour and cook for a few minutes until brown. Stir in the tomatoes and stock and bring to the boil. Simmer until the vegetables are tender, about 1½ hours. Rub through a sieve. Return to the saucepan with the Worcestershire sauce, season to taste, and heat through.

Serve with croûtons (see page 18).

WINTER SOUP

6 large tomatoes, peeled and sliced
3 large onions, chopped
1 potato, grated
1 cooking apple, grated
2 qt (2·5 litres) water
salt
cayenne pepper
1 pt (625 ml) milk
6 oz (185 g) grated cheese
2 tbsps plain flour

Simmer the tomatoes, onions, potato, and apple in the water for 1 hour. Strain, and reserve the water. Press the vegetables through a sieve, then return them to the saucepan with the reserved cooking liquid. Season with salt and cayenne pepper and heat through. Meanwhile heat the milk until just below boiling-point. Pour a little milk over the cheese, stirring until it has melted. Stir the cheese into the soup, then add the flour, which has been blended with a little cold water. Stir the rest of the hot milk into the soup immediately before serving, but do not allow the soup to boil.

SALMON SOUP

1 small tin salmon
1 qt (1·25 litres) milk
2 oz (60 g) butter
2 tbsps plain flour
salt and pepper
1 tsp lemon juice
chopped parsley

Drain the salmon, remove the bones and skin, and rub through a sieve. Reserve ½ cup of the milk, and heat the rest to boiling-point. Meanwhile, melt the butter, and blend in the flour and salt and pepper; cook gently for a few minutes, then stir in the reserved cold milk. Stir well, then gradually add the hot milk, stirring constantly. Add the salmon, and cook until smooth and thick, stirring all the time. Allow to cool slightly then add the lemon juice. Sprinkle with parsley, and serve immediately.

Serve with sippets (see page 10).

If soup is too salty, add a cut potato and simmer to allow it to absorb the saltiness; remove the potato before serving the soup.

If soup is lumpy, beat it vigorously with a whisk then, if necessary, press through a sieve and reheat.

ALMOND SOUP

2 oz (60 g) ground blanched almonds
1 stalk of celery, chopped
1 onion, sliced
½ pt (315 ml) white stock
1½ pt (940 ml) milk
1 oz (30 g) butter
1 oz (30 g) plain flour
salt and pepper
a pinch of mace
1 tbsp cream

Heat the almonds, celery, and onion with the stock and milk until boiling-point is reached. Cover and simmer for an hour or so. Blend the flour into the butter and add piece by piece to the soup, stirring until it thickens. Season to taste, add the mace, and stir in the cream, making sure that the soup does not boil.

CREAM OF CHEESE SOUP

1 whole onion, peeled
1¼ pt (780 ml) milk
¾ pt (475 ml) white stock
1 sprig of parsley
1 small bay-leaf
1½ oz (45 g) butter
1 tbsp plain flour
4 oz (125 g) finely grated matured cheese
1 egg-yolk, beaten
salt and pepper
cayenne pepper

Put the onion in a saucepan with the milk and stock. Add the parsley and bay-leaf and bring slowly to the boil. Remove from the heat and leave to infuse until the milk is well flavoured. Strain and leave to cool. Melt the butter in a saucepan, add the flour, and cook gently for 2 or 3 minutes. Gradually stir in the milk and stock and bring to the boil, stirring constantly. Simmer for a few minutes then remove the saucepan from the heat and allow the soup to cool. Stir in the cheese and egg-yolk. Add salt, pepper, and cayenne pepper to taste, and heat through again for a few minutes, stirring all the time—do not allow to boil.

OXTAIL SOUP

1 oxtail
2 oz (60 g) butter
3 pt (1·8 litres) stock or water
2 onions, roughly chopped
1 turnip, roughly chopped
1 stalk of celery, roughly chopped
1 carrot, roughly chopped
a pinch of herbs
salt and pepper
1 tbsp plain flour

Wash and joint the tail. Fry in the butter until brown. Add the stock and bring to the boil. Add the vegetables, herbs, and seasoning, and cook for 3 to 4 hours. Strain off the stock and leave to stand overnight. Remove the meat from the bones and chop. Remove the fat and bring the stock to the boil with the meat. Stir in the flour, which has been blended with water, and cook for a few minutes longer.

If soup curdles (as may happen if it is heated too much after the addition of egg-yolks or cream), beat it vigorously with a whisk.

If some of the ingredients get slightly burnt, remove them, and mask the taste with a little curry powder.

SCOTCH BROTH

1 oz (30 g) pearl barley	1 turnip, chopped
1 lb (500 g) neck of mutton	salt and pepper
1 carrot, chopped	1 dsp chopped parsley
1 onion, chopped	

Soak the pearl barley in water overnight. Next day, put in a large saucepan with the meat, which has been cut into chops, salt, and water to cover. Bring slowly to the boil, skim off scum, and add the vegetables. Simmer for 1½ hours. Remove the chops, cut the meat from the bones, and chop. Skim fat from the soup, return the meat to the saucepan to heat through; check seasoning and add the parsley.

CHICKEN BROTH

1 small boiling fowl or carcass	salt and pepper
3 pt (1·8 litres) water	a pinch of mace
1 whole onion, peeled	1 tbsp chopped parsley

Joint and chop the fowl. Place in a saucepan with the water, onion, seasoning, and mace. Bring slowly to the boil, skimming off scum that rises to the surface. Cover and simmer for 3 to 4 hours. Strain and leave to get cold. Remove fat and reheat; check seasoning and stir in the parsley before serving.

GAME BROTH

carcass of any game	1 sprig of parsley
1 carrot, roughly chopped	pearl barley
1 onion, roughly chopped	salt and pepper
1 stalk of celery, roughly chopped	

Break up the carcass, and place in a pan, adding enough cold water to cover. Bring slowly to the boil. Add the vegetables and parsley, cover, and simmer gently for 2 or 3 hours. Strain the broth, and measure it. Allowing ½ ounce (15 grams) for every pint (625 millilitres) of broth, add pearl barley to a saucepan of cold water; bring to the boil, and strain. Heat the broth again, add the barley, and simmer until tender. Season to taste, and serve.

For rich brown stock, add a well-fried onion or the skins of brown onions.

To clarify soup, stir in a lightly beaten egg-white and a crushed egg-shell half an hour before the end of cooking time; stir until boiling and then simmer gently. Strain through muslin or a fine-mesh sieve before serving.

Tempting
SAVOURY
DISHES

The first recipes in this chapter are devoted to small, tasty foods that would serve equally well as appetisers before dinner or as party savouries. When choosing a first course, it is important to take into account the balance of the meal as a whole and to see that the principal ingredients of the first and main courses are neither too similar, nor too heavy. The appetisers are followed by a selection of pasta, cheese, and egg dishes for supper, lunch, or hearty snacks. Finally there is a collection of hints and suggested fillings for sandwiches of several types, offering something for every occasion. Many other savoury recipes can be found in the chapter 'Mouth-watering Pastries and Pies'.

Making Breadcrumbs

Fresh Breadcrumbs: Remove the crusts from one- or two-day-old white bread and grate or crumble finely.

Dried Breadcrumbs: Arrange pieces of bread on oven trays and dry out in a slow oven until crisp; for browned crumbs, raise the oven temperature. Crush the dried bread with a rolling pin and store the crumbs in an airtight container.

Buttered Breadcrumbs: Toss 1 cup of fresh breadcrumbs in 1 dessertspoon of melted butter. These are especially suitable for savoury dishes that are to be browned in the oven or under the griller.

DEVILLED ALMONDS

8 oz (250 g) almonds
1 tbsp butter
salt
cayenne pepper

Pour boiling water over the almonds, leave to soak for a few minutes, then slip off the skins. Dry the almonds and put in a small baking tin with the butter. Cook in a moderate oven, turning frequently, until they are an even gold colour. Drain on absorbent paper and sprinkle generously with salt and a little cayenne. Store in an airtight tin.

PIGS IN BLANKETS

12 oysters
juice of 1 lemon
cayenne pepper
6 bacon rashers, halved

Sprinkle the lemon juice over the oysters and sprinkle with cayenne. Roll a piece of bacon around each oyster and fasten with a toothpick. Arrange tightly in a small ovenproof dish and heat through until the bacon is crisp.

CELERY STICKS

stalks of firm white celery
4 oz (125 g) cream cheese
4 tbsps cream
1 tbsp butter
salt and pepper
chopped chives
mustard
paprika pepper
chopped toasted almonds

Cut the celery into 3-inch (7·5-centimetre) lengths. Blend the cream cheese with the cream and butter; season to taste with chives, mustard, and salt and pepper. Fill the celery sticks with the cheese mixture. Sprinkle paprika over half the sticks and garnish the rest with almonds.

ANCHOVY-STUFFED EGGS

6 hard-boiled eggs
1 dsp anchovy essence
salt and pepper
butter
sprigs of parsley

Halve the eggs lengthwise and remove the yolks. Mash the yolks with the anchovy essence, salt and pepper, and butter to bind. Pile into the whites and garnish with sprigs of parsley.

HAM AND RICE BALLS

4 oz (125 g) finely minced ham
4 oz (125 g) cold boiled rice
cayenne pepper
a pinch of mace
1 egg
1 egg, beaten
dried breadcrumbs
fat or oil

Mix together the ham and rice; season with cayenne and mace and bind with the egg. Form into tiny balls and dip in the beaten egg and then in breadcrumbs. Deep-fry in fat or oil until golden. Drain and serve at once.

Garnish with fried parsley (see page 52).

SCOTCH EGGS

6 hard-boiled eggs, shelled
6 oz (185 g) sausage-meat
beaten egg
dried breadcrumbs
fat or oil
sprigs of parsley

Enclose the eggs in sausage-meat. Coat with egg and breadcrumbs. Deep-fry in fat or oil until golden. Drain on absorbent paper. Serve cold, cut in halves and garnished with sprigs of parsley.

POTATO BISCUITS

6 oz (185 g) plain flour
1 dsp salt
a pinch of cayenne pepper
4 oz (125 g) butter
12 oz (375 g) grated cheese
6 oz (185 g) mashed potatoes

Sift the flour, salt, and cayenne into a mixing bowl. Rub in the butter, then mix in the cheese and potatoes to form a stiff dough. Roll out thinly, cut into shapes, and bake in a moderate oven for about 15 minutes. Store in an airtight tin.

SALMON IN BOATS

Filling

4 tbsps butter
4 tbsps plain flour
2 cups hot milk
¾ tsp salt
a dash of pepper
1 tsp Worcestershire sauce
2 tbsps green pepper strips
2 tbsps red pepper strips
½ cup cooked or tinned mushrooms
2 cups tinned salmon
sprigs of parsley

Boats

6 x 2-inch (5 cm)-thick slices of day-old bread
melted butter
grated cheese

Filling: Melt the butter, stir in the flour, and cook gently for 2 or 3 minutes. Remove from heat and stir in the hot milk. Return to heat and, stirring constantly, bring to the boil; season. Pour boiling water over the pepper strips; drain. Add to the sauce the peppers, mushrooms, and flaked salmon; heat thoroughly. Pour into the hot boats and serve garnished with parsley.

Boats: Remove crusts from the bread and cut off the corners so that each slice is boat-shaped. With a sharp-pointed knife, hollow out the centre of each 'boat', leaving the sides and bottom ½ inch (1 centimetre) thick. Brush the outside with melted butter. Sprinkle with grated cheese and bake in a hot oven until lightly brown.

ANCHOVY SAVOURIES

2 hard-boiled eggs
1 tin anchovy fillets
cayenne pepper
lightly toasted bread
butter
sprigs of parsley

Mash the eggs with the oil from the anchovies and season with a little cayenne. Cut the toast into wide fingers, butter, and spread the egg mixture on top. Put half an anchovy fillet on each toast finger and garnish with a sprig of parsley. Heat through in the oven.

DEVILLED SARDINES

1 tsp chutney
1 tsp prepared mustard
1 dsp oil
½ tsp Worcestershire sauce
1 tin sardines
fingers of fried bread

Mix the chutney with the mustard, oil, and sauce. Skin the sardines and coat them with the mixture. Lay a sardine on each finger of crisp-fried bread and heat through in the oven. Drain and serve very hot.

CHEESE SAVOURIES

1 tbsp tomato sauce
1 tbsp finely chopped gherkin
4 oz (125 g) grated cheese
1 egg-white, stiffly beaten
18 fingers of bread

Blend the sauce with the gherkin and cheese; fold in the egg-white. Spread on the bread fingers and bake in a moderate oven for about 10 minutes until golden.

FRIED CHEESE

8 oz (250 g) cheese
batter
salt
cayenne pepper
fat or oil

Cut the cheese into small squares or rounds. Dip into the batter, which has been well seasoned with salt and cayenne. Deep-fry in fat or oil until golden. Drain and serve at once.

CROUTONS

slices of white bread with the crusts removed
butter

Cut the bread into a variety of shapes using biscuit cutters. Fry in plenty of butter until golden and crisp. Drain on absorbent paper and store in airtight tins. Use hot or cold as required.

CHEESE-TOPPED CROUTONS

2 oz (60 g) grated cheese
2 tbsps chutney
prepared mustard
cayenne pepper
croûtons (see above)

Blend the cheese with the chutney and a little mustard and cayenne. Spread on the croûtons and heat through in the oven. Serve at once.

TOMATO-TOPPED CROUTONS

2 medium tomatoes, sliced
butter
grated cheese
capers
round croûtons

Fry the tomato slices briefly in the butter. Put one slice on each croûton, sprinkle with cheese, and garnish with capers. Heat through in the oven. Serve at once.

Cheese

Cheese deteriorates quickly when exposed to the air and becomes hard and dry. If, on the other hand, it is kept tightly covered, it is likely to become mouldy. It should always be stored in a cool place and loosely covered or refrigerated in a covered container. Different varieties of cheese should be wrapped separately. Hard dry types of cheese to be used in cooked dishes can be grated and stored in a jar.

CHEESE AND POTATO CAKES

4 oz (125 g) grated cheese
½ cup mashed potatoes
1 tsp Worcestershire sauce
finely chopped parsley or chives
salt and pepper
2 eggs, beaten
plain flour
dried breadcrumbs
fat or oil
sprigs of parsley

Mix the cheese with the potatoes, Worcestershire sauce, herbs, and seasoning; bind with some of the beaten egg. Form into small patties and coat with flour. Dip in egg and coat with breadcrumbs. Fry for a few minutes on each side until golden. Drain and serve at once, garnished with sprigs of parsley.

POTATO CHEESE PUFFS

Filling
¼ cup grated Cheddar cheese
2 tbsps finely chopped tomatoes
1 tsp salt
a pinch of cayenne pepper
fat or oil
1 tomato, sliced
1 onion, sliced

Pastry
5 potatoes
1 dsp finely chopped parsley
½ cup milk
¾ cup plain flour
1 tsp baking powder

Filling: Mix together the cheese, chopped tomatoes, salt, and cayenne. Put 1 dessertspoon of this mixture on each pastry square.

Fold over, pressing the edges together tightly. Deep-fry in fat or oil until golden. Drain and serve at once.

Pastry: Boil the potatoes then mash with the parsley and milk. Sift the flour and baking powder into the potatoes; stir well. Roll the mixture out to ¼-inch (5-millimetre) thickness on a well-floured board. Cut into squares.

CHEESE PATTIES

6 oz (185 g) cheese	2 oz (60 g) butter
1 tbsp finely chopped ham	1 egg, beaten
3 tbsps fresh breadcrumbs	dried breadcrumbs
1 dsp mustard	fat or oil

Mix the cheese, ham, fresh breadcrumbs, mustard, and butter, beating until smooth. Form into small cakes and dip in egg and breadcrumbs. Deep-fry in fat or oil until golden. Drain and serve.

CHEESELETTES

3 eggs	3 tbsps finely chopped parsley
2 oz (60 g) self-raising flour	salt and pepper
4 oz (125 g) grated cheese	oil or butter
1 tbsp finely chopped onion	

Beat the eggs in a mixing bowl. Blend in the flour, cheese, onion, parsley, and seasoning. Heat oil or butter in a frying pan and drop in spoonfuls of the mixture. Fry on all sides until crisp and golden. Drain well and serve at once.

CHEESE PUDDING

3 oz (90 g) fresh breadcrumbs	2 eggs, separated
1 pt (625 ml) milk	salt and pepper
4 oz (125 g) grated cheese	

Put the breadcrumbs in a mixing bowl. Bring the milk to the boil and pour over the crumbs; leave to stand for a few minutes. Stir in the cheese, egg-yolks, and seasoning. Fold in the egg-whites, which have been stiffly beaten. Pour into a greased ovenproof dish and cook in a moderate oven until set.

CHEESE DISH

1 cup fresh breadcrumbs	1 oz (30 g) butter
1 cup milk	salt
1 cup grated cheese	cayenne pepper
1 small onion, finely chopped	2 eggs, separated

Place the breadcrumbs in an ovenproof dish. Boil the milk and pour over the breadcrumbs. Add cheese, onion, butter, salt, and cayenne. Beat the egg-yolks, and add to the other ingredients. Whip the egg-whites until stiff, and fold into the mixture. Bake in a moderate oven for 20 minutes.

MACARONI CHEESE

4 oz (125 g) macaroni	prepared mustard
breadcrumbs	¼–½ cup milk
cayenne pepper	1 oz (30 g) butter
salt	4 oz (125 g) grated cheese

Cook the macaroni in boiling salted water for about 20 minutes.

Drain and put a layer of macaroni in a greased ovenproof dish. Sprinkle over some breadcrumbs, a little cayenne and salt, mustard, milk, and a few tiny knobs of butter; sprinkle over some of the cheese. Continue layering thus until all the ingredients are used, ending with cheese and breadcrumbs. Bake in a hot oven for about 20 minutes.

HAM AND MACARONI

4 oz (125 g) macaroni	1 tsp mustard
1 dsp butter	12 oz (375 g) finely chopped
1 dsp plain flour	ham
¾ pt (475 ml) milk	fresh brown breadcrumbs
1 egg, well beaten	extra butter
½ tsp pepper	

Cook the macaroni in boiling salted water until tender; drain and transfer to an ovenproof dish. Melt the butter in a small saucepan, blend in the flour, and cook gently for 2 or 3 minutes. Gradually add the milk and heat, stirring constantly, until boiling-point is reached. Remove from the heat and beat in the egg and seasonings. Stir in the ham and pour the sauce over the macaroni. Sprinkle generously with breadcrumbs, dot with butter, and heat through in a moderately hot oven until golden.

TOMATO MACARONI CHEESE

1 cup macaroni	1 tsp salt
2 oz (60 g) butter	a good pinch of pepper
1 green pepper, sliced	8 oz (250 g) grated Cheddar
1 medium onion, chopped	cheese
2 tbsps plain flour	2 medium tomatoes, peeled
1¾ cups milk	and sliced

Cook the macaroni in 3 pints (1·8 litres) of boiling salted water until tender; rinse and drain. Fry the green pepper and onion in the butter until tender. Add the flour, and cook for a few minutes. Stir in the milk gradually, and bring to the boil. Add the salt, pepper, and 6 ounces (185 grams) of the cheese; stir until the cheese has melted. Spoon half the macaroni into a casserole, arrange half the tomato slices on top, then pour over half the cheese sauce. Repeat layers, and sprinkle the remaining cheese on top. Bake in a moderate oven for 25 to 30 minutes.

DEVILLED SPAGHETTI

8 oz (250 g) spaghetti	3–4 slices of cooked bacon,
1½ oz (45 g) butter	finely chopped
1 tbsp finely chopped onion	1 tsp Worcestershire sauce
1 tbsp finely chopped green	1 tsp dry mustard
pepper	salt and pepper
3 tbsps plain flour	¾ cup grated cheese
1 pt (625 ml) milk	

Cook the spaghetti in boiling salted water until tender; drain. Melt the butter in a saucepan; add the onion and green pepper and cook lightly without browning. Add the flour, and cook gently for 2 or 3 minutes. Gradually add the milk, stirring until the sauce thickens and boils. Mix in the bacon, Worcestershire sauce, mustard, and salt and pepper to taste. Add the spaghetti and turn into a greased ovenproof dish. Sprinkle over the cheese and bake in a moderate oven until browned, about 20 minutes.

BANANA HAM ROLLS

6 bananas
juice of 1 large lemon
6 slices of ham
2 oz (60 g) butter
3 tbsps plain flour

2 cups milk
½ tsp salt
a pinch of cayenne pepper
1 cup grated cheese

Peel the bananas, roll in lemon juice, and wrap each in a slice of ham. Secure with toothpicks, and arrange in a greased ovenproof dish. Melt the butter in a saucepan and stir in the flour. Cook gently for 2 or 3 minutes, but do not allow the flour to brown. Gradually stir in the milk, and keep stirring until the mixture thickens. Add the salt, cayenne, and cheese. Stir until the cheese melts. Pour the sauce over the rolls. Bake in a moderate oven for 15 to 20 minutes.

SAVOURY HOT-POT

Place a layer of thinly sliced bacon in an ovenproof dish, cover with a layer of sliced onions, and then a layer of sliced potatoes. Repeat the layers until the dish is full; cover, and cook in a slow oven for approximately 3 hours.

WELSH RAREBIT

2 oz (60 g) butter
¼ pt (150 ml) beer
4 oz (125 g) grated cheese

salt
cayenne pepper
1 dsp prepared mustard

Melt the butter in the beer then add the remaining ingredients and stir until the cheese is melted.
Serve at once on buttered toast.

RAISIN RICE

1 lb (500 g) long-grain rice
2 medium onions, finely chopped
2 oz (60 g) butter
salt

cayenne pepper
1 cup raisins
2 oz (60 g) desiccated coconut
2 cups chicken stock
1 cup cashew nuts

Wash the rice, and cook in boiling salted water for 13 minutes; drain. Melt the butter, add the onions, and sauté for 2 or 3 minutes without browning. Season well with salt and cayenne. Place in an ovenproof dish and add the rice, raisins, coconut, and chicken stock. Mix without mashing, and allow to stand overnight. Next day, cover, and cook in a moderate oven for about half an hour. Fluff the rice with a fork, and just before serving add the cashew nuts.
Serve with curry or fried or baked chicken.

STUFFED BACON ROLLS

4 sausages
½ tsp chopped sage
1 tbsp minced onion

8 bacon rashers
1 lb (500 g) apples, peeled and cored

Skin the sausages, and mix the meat with the sage and onion. Remove rind from bacon, and spread some of the sausage mixture on each rasher. Roll up, fastening with toothpicks. Arrange in an ovenproof dish, and cook for 25 minutes in a moderate oven. Meanwhile, cut the apples into rings. When the rolls are cooked, strain the bacon fat into a frying pan, and fry the apple rings until tender. Serve the apples and bacon rolls hot.

Eggs

Eggs should be stored, pointed end down, in a cool place away from strong-flavoured foods, as their porous shells quickly absorb smells. If eggs are kept in the refrigerator, they should be brought to room-temperature before being cooked. A fresh egg dropped into a bowl of salted water will sink to the bottom; an egg several days old will drift about; a stale egg will float. The freshest eggs should be used for boiling, coddling, and poaching; older eggs are more suitable for hard-boiling, as they are more easily peeled. Most egg dishes should be cooked lightly and gently; eggs that are overcooked or cooked at too high a temperature will be tough. Remove hard-boiled eggs from the cooking water as soon as they are ready or they will continue cooking.

ASPARAGUS SOUFFLE OMELETTE

4 eggs, separated
salt and pepper

1 tin asparagus tips
1 oz (30 g) butter

Beat the egg-yolks in a mixing bowl. Season well; chop 2 tablespoons of the asparagus tips and add to the egg-yolks. Fold in the egg-whites, which have been stiffly beaten. Heat the butter in a frying pan. Pour in the egg mixture and cook over fairly strong heat until set and golden underneath. Put the pan under the griller to brown the top. Cut in half and fold each half on to a heated plate. Serve garnished with some of the remaining tinned asparagus tips.

TOMATO OMELETTE

2 small onions, finely chopped
4 large tomatoes, peeled and chopped
2 oz (60 g) butter

6 eggs
½ cup milk
salt and pepper

Fry the onions gently with the tomatoes and seasoning in 1 ounce (30 grams) of the butter. Beat the eggs with the milk and seasoning. Melt the remaining ounce (30 grams) of butter in an omelette pan, pour in the egg mixture, and cook quickly until set underneath, tilting the pan and lifting the set parts of the omelette so that the liquid egg can run under. Pour in the tomato filling, fold the omelette over, and turn out on to a heated plate.

BAKED EGGS ON SPINACH

1 bunch of spinach, cooked
  and chopped
6 eggs
salt

cayenne pepper
3 oz (90 g) grated cheese
butter

Divide the spinach between six greased, small ovenproof dishes. Carefully break an egg into each dish. Season, sprinkle with cheese, and dot with butter. Bake in a moderate oven until the eggs are set.

Serve with croûtons (see page 18) or toast.

EGG SAVOURY

2 tbsps butter
1 dsp tomato sauce
1 dsp Worcestershire sauce

1 tsp anchovy sauce
1 tsp mustard
6 hard-boiled eggs, sliced

Gently heat the butter, sauces, and mustard in a saucepan. Add the eggs and heat through.

Serve on buttered toast.

Sandwiches

Use thinly sliced fresh bread and cover it completely with well-softened butter, to form a barrier that will prevent a moist filling from making the bread soggy. Remove the crusts for dainty sandwiches for afternoon tea or parties. Season fillings generously and contrast textures; for example, add something crisp, such as nuts or chopped celery or sweet peppers, to a cream cheese or egg filling. Half a pound (250 grams) of thinly sliced cheese or meat will fill approximately eight sandwiches. Sandwiches may be made the night before they are needed, wrapped and packed closely, and stored in the refrigerator.

SANDWICH FILLINGS

*   Chopped prunes, chopped walnuts, and mayonnaise
*   Chopped dates and cream cheese
*   Finely chopped pineapple, cream cheese, and nuts
*   Crumbled crisp-fried bacon, egg, and mayonnaise
*   Sultanas and chopped almonds
*   Sardines mashed with chopped hard-boiled egg and tomato sauce
*   Chopped hard-boiled eggs and mayonnaise
*   Chopped celery, grated cheese, and cream
*   Cream cheese, finely chopped gherkins, and chopped peeled tomato
*   Mashed bananas and crumbled grilled bacon
*   Grated cheese, crumbled crisp-cooked bacon, chutney, and salad dressing
*   Chopped hard-boiled eggs, chopped pickle, and mayonnaise
*   Mashed sardines, vinegar, mustard, and cayenne pepper
*   Cream cheese, chopped nuts, grated onion, Worcestershire sauce, and mayonnaise

*   Minced chicken or ham, pickle, and mayonnaise
*   Sliced cold roast beef and horseradish sauce
*   Minced tongue and pickle
*   Chopped celery, chopped apple, nuts, and a little salad cream
*   Grated cheese with chutney or watercress
*   Cream cheese with chopped gherkin and mayonnaise
*   Cream cheese with sliced cucumber and mayonnaise
*   Cream cheese with chopped pineapple and a little mayonnaise
*   Minced dates with nuts and honey or mayonnaise
*   Hard-boiled egg with anchovy fillets and mayonnaise
*   Grated cheese with cold scrambled egg
*   Salmon, mayonnaise, and thinly sliced cucumber
*   Scrambled egg with chopped peeled tomato
*   Lemon butter and curry paste, topped with cold minced meat
*   Minced chicken mixed with cooked mixed vegetables and mayonnaise
*   Potted meat mixed with mint butter

FISH PASTE

6 red herrings
4 oz (125 g) butter
2 tbsps cream

½ tsp cayenne pepper
clarified butter (see page 30)

Mince or sieve the fish. Mix the fish with the butter, cream, and cayenne in a saucepan and cook for a few minutes. Transfer to small pots and cover with clarified butter.

CHEESE SPREAD

3 lb (1·5 kg) grated Cheddar
  cheese
8 oz (250 g) butter

¾ cup sherry
salt and pepper

Place the cheese and butter in a saucepan. Cook over a moderate heat, stirring constantly until melted. If the mixture separates, remove from the heat, and beat well. Beat in the sherry and salt and pepper to taste. Pour into small pots and allow to cool and set.

MOCK CHICKEN

1 large tomato, peeled and
  chopped
1 small onion, finely chopped
1 dsp butter

½ tsp herbs
3 oz (90 g) grated cheese
1 egg, beaten

Simmer all ingredients, except for the egg, in a saucepan for 10 minutes. Add the egg and heat gently until the mixture thickens—do not allow to boil. Remove from heat and stir until thick. Cool, transfer to a jar, and keep refrigerated.

POTTED MEAT

1 lb (500 g) finely chopped steak
4 oz (125 g) butter
2 tbsps anchovy sauce
1 tsp salt
cayenne pepper
grated nutmeg
clarified butter (see page 30)

Simmer the steak with the butter, anchovy sauce, salt, cayenne, and nutmeg for several hours. Press into small pots and cover with a little clarified butter.

CHEESE FILLING

8 oz (250 g) finely grated cheese
2 tbsps cream
1 tbsp butter
1 tsp prepared mustard
salt
cayenne pepper

Put the cheese, cream, butter, and mustard in the top of a double saucepan and season to taste with salt and cayenne. Cook, stirring, for about 15 minutes. Store in small jars.

TOMATO FILLING

1 oz (30 g) butter
1 large tomato, peeled and chopped
1 oz (30 g) grated cheese
1 tsp grated onion
salt and pepper
$\frac{1}{4}$ cup fresh breadcrumbs

Melt the butter, add the remaining ingredients, and cook for about 5 minutes. Cool then pour into a jar to store.

ASPARAGUS ROLLS

very thin slices of fresh bread
butter
tinned asparagus tips, drained

Remove the crusts from the bread. Stand the bread on a damp tea-towel and spread with softened butter. Put two asparagus tips on each slice and roll up, securing with toothpicks. Arrange on a plate, cover securely, and chill. Remove toothpicks and serve.

PIN-WHEEL SANDWICHES

very thin slices of fresh bread
butter
cream cheese
salmon
fish or meat paste

Remove the crusts from the bread. Stand the bread on a damp tea-towel and spread with softened butter. Spread with a selection of fillings and spreads. Roll up each slice and secure with toothpicks. Put on a plate, cover securely, and chill. Remove toothpicks, cut each roll into thin slices, and serve.

CLUB SANDWICHES

freshly toasted slices of bread
butter
lettuce leaves
sliced or chopped cheese, sausage, cold cooked meat or egg, pineapple rings, tomato slices, onion rings
mustard, sauce, pickles, or mayonnaise

Use three slices of toast for each sandwich. Butter the first slice, cover with a lettuce leaf, and fill as you wish, top with the second slice and butter it; add the second filling and top with the third slice of toast, buttered side down. Garnish with sliced olives, gherkins, parsley, or shredded lettuce.

CHICKEN CLUB SANDWICH

Butter the first slice of toast and spread with mayonnaise. Cover with a lettuce leaf and slices of cooked chicken. Add the second slice of toast; butter and cover with crisp-cooked bacon and another lettuce leaf. Put the third slice of toast on top and add a slice of tomato, spread with mayonnaise. Garnish with shredded lettuce and sliced olives.

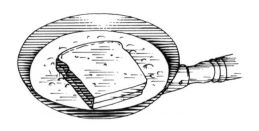

FRIED SANDWICHES

slices of bread
butter
slices of cheese, meat, or eggs
sauce, mustard, or pickles
1 egg
milk

Butter the bread and fill as you wish. Cut the sandwiches in half. Soak the sandwiches briefly in the egg beaten with milk. Fry on both sides in sizzling butter until golden. Drain and serve at once.

Delicious FISH

Fish is a valuable high-protein food that should always be eaten fresh, within a day of purchase. Indications of freshness are firm flesh, bright-looking scales and eyes, red gills, and the absence of a strong 'fishy' smell. Avoid buying fish with sunken eyes and dry or flabby flesh. Shellfish should be heavy for its size and with a firm shell.

Fish should not be left in its wrapping paper. It should be kept loosely covered on a plate or in a covered container in the refrigerator. All fish should be washed under cold water and dried thoroughly before cooking. Fillets should be handled carefully to avoid breaking the flesh.

White-fleshed fish are very low in fat and calories while oily fish have a high fat content, are rich in vitamins A and D, and tend to have darker flesh.

Cleaning Fish

Wash the fish and scrape off the scales with a sharp knife, working from the tail to the head. Fish to be cooked whole should have the head, fins, and intestines removed. For round fish, slit along the stomach from the gills to the tail and remove the intestines; wash well and rub with salt to remove the black skin. For flat fish, make a cut under the gills and remove the entrails. Small fish can be cleaned without having the stomach cut; make a cut at the back of the head and pull the head away from the fish—the intestines will come away at the same time.

Skinning Fish

For small whole fish, remove the fins, cutting from the tail towards the head. Cut a thin strip of skin along the spine. Make a cut through the skin below the head and loosen the skin. Dip your fingers in salt and hold the fish by the head. Carefully pull the skin away from the fish. For fillets, put them skin side down and make a cut through the skin at the tail end. Dip your fingers in salt, hold the tail firmly, and gently peel the skin from the fish with a sharp knife. The dark skin of flat whole fish is removed in the same way as for fillets, after the fins have been cut off. The skin and bones of fish can be used for making stock.

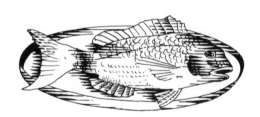

Cooking Times for Fish

Method	Type of Fish	Cooking Time
Boiling, Poaching	whole fish, fillets, steaks	10–15 minutes per pound (500 g)
Steaming	thin fillets or slices	10–15 minutes, depending on size
Baking	whole white fish, fillets, steaks	10–20 minutes for fillets, 20 minutes for steaks, 25–30 minutes for small fish, 45 minutes–1 hour for large fish
Grilling	small whole fish, fillets, cutlets	4–20 minutes, depending on size
Shallow Frying	small whole fish, fillets, cutlets	6–15 minutes, depending on size
Deep-frying	small whole fish, coated fillets, small shellfish	5–10 minutes

Cooking Times for Boiling Shellfish

Lobster	20–40 minutes
Crayfish	15–20 minutes
Crabs	15–20 minutes
Prawns	10–15 minutes
Mussels	5–6 minutes

Types of Fish

Oily: Salmon, mullet, trout, mackerel, herrings, butterfish, whitebait, trevally, moki, kahawai, kingfish.

White: Whiting, sole, garfish, snapper, flounder, flathead, bream, Murray cod, tuna, terakihi, John Dory, groper, hapuka.

Shellfish: Lobster, crayfish, crab, prawns, mussels, scallops, oysters, abalone (paua), tuatuas, toheroas.

MARINATED FISH

1½ lb (750 g) cod or other white fish
salt and pepper
1 medium carrot, sliced
1 onion, sliced
1 bay-leaf
3 tbsps salad oil

juice of ½ lemon, or a little white wine or cider
1 tbsp butter
4 potatoes, cooked and mashed
2 tbsps dried breadcrumbs
1 tsp chopped parsley
1 dsp butter, melted

Make cuts in the skin of the fish on both sides, and season with salt and pepper. Put into a deep dish with the carrot, onion, bay-leaf, oil, and lemon juice. Leave for 1 or 2 hours, turning from time to time. Remove fish from the marinade, and transfer to an ovenproof dish. Strain the liquid over the fish, and add a few knobs of butter. Bake, basting often, for 15 to 20 minutes in a hot oven. Pipe the mashed potato around the edge of the dish; sprinkle with the breadcrumbs. Bake for another 15 minutes, or until the fish is cooked. Remove from the oven, sprinkle with parsley, and pour over the melted butter.

SOUSED FISH

2 lb (1 kg) fish
1 onion, sliced
4 cloves
1 tsp peppercorns

fresh herbs
1 tsp salt
1 tsp sugar
¾ pt (475 ml) vinegar

Clean and trim the fish. Arrange in a casserole. Put the sliced onion on top and sprinkle over the herbs and seasoning. Pour over the vinegar and cover. Bake in a slow oven for 1½ hours. Leave in the dish to get cold then transfer the fish to a serving plate. Strain the liquid and use to accompany the fish.

Serve with boiled potatoes and green salad.

GRILLED SOLE

2 whole sole
1 oz (30 g) butter, melted
salt and pepper

lemon wedges
sprigs of parsley

Skin and wash the fish. Arrange on a greased grilling pan and brush with melted butter. Season with salt and pepper and grill for about 6 minutes on each side, brushing with more of the butter. Transfer to heated plates and serve garnished with lemon wedges and sprigs of parsley.

TROUT WITH ALMONDS

4 trout
plain flour
salt and pepper
6 oz (185 g) butter

4 oz (125 g) slivered blanched almonds
juice of ½ lemon
sprigs of parsley

Clean the whole fish, leaving the heads on. Coat with seasoned flour. Fry the fish in 4 ounces (125 grams) of the butter for about 6 minutes on each side, until golden and cooked through. Drain and remove to a heated serving dish and keep hot. Add the remaining butter to the pan and, when melted, add the almonds; fry until golden. Add a squeeze of lemon juice and pour over the fish. Serve at once, garnished with sprigs of parsley.

WHITING WITH OLIVE SAUCE

4 whiting fillets
salt and pepper
juice of 1 lemon
Sauce
1 tbsp butter
1 dsp plain flour
½ pt (315 ml) milk

8 stuffed olives
1 tbsp butter

4 stuffed olives, chopped
salt and pepper

Skin, rinse, and dry the fillets. Sprinkle with salt, pepper, and lemon juice. Place an olive on each, and roll up. Put the fish rolls in a buttered shallow ovenproof dish. Dot with butter and cover with buttered paper. Cook in a moderate oven until tender. Arrange on a heated serving dish, garnish with the remaining olives, halved, and keep hot while you prepare the sauce. Pour the sauce over the fish and serve.
Sauce: Melt the butter, add a little of the cooking liquid from the fish, and stir in the flour. Cook for a few minutes. Add the milk and stir constantly until it boils. Simmer gently for a few minutes. Add the olives, and salt and pepper.

SHALLOW-FRIED FISH

fish fillets or cutlets
milk
plain flour

salt and pepper
butter

Wash and dry the fish; dip first in milk then in seasoned flour. Fry gently in hot butter for about 3 minutes on each side, longer for thick fish and cutlets. Drain on absorbent paper and serve very hot, on heated plates. If you prefer, coat the fish with flour, egg, and breadcrumbs, or batter before frying.

DEEP-FRIED FISH

fish fillets

fat or oil

Wash and dry the fish then coat completely with batter or flour, egg, and breadcrumbs. Heat the fat or oil until a piece of bread will turn golden in less than a minute when dropped into it. Lower the fish into the fat and cook for 4 to 7 minutes, depending on the thickness of the fish. Drain on absorbent paper and serve very hot, on heated plates.

STEAMED FISH

fish fillets
butter
salt and pepper

lemon juice
sprigs of parsley

Wash, dry, and season the fillets, skinning them if you prefer. Arrange the fish, cutting them into smaller pieces if necessary, on a generously buttered plate; cover with greased paper and a saucepan lid. Put the plate on a saucepan of boiling water and cook until the fish turns white all through. Serve with the cooking juices poured over and a squeeze of lemon juice. Garnish with sprigs of parsley.

Serve with mashed potatoes and buttered spinach.

BAKED WHITE FISH

onions
chopped parsley
1 bay-leaf
white fish fillets

salt and pepper
butter
1/4 pt (150 ml) water

The quantities needed for this recipe will vary according to the number of people to be served. Grease a casserole. Put in a layer of chopped onion and parsley with the bay-leaf. Cover with fish and season. Sprinkle over a little more chopped onion and parsley, add a few knobs of butter, and pour on the water. Bake for 20 minutes in a moderately hot oven.

Serve with cucumber sauce (see page 60).

BAKED COD STEAKS

4 cod steaks
8 oz (250 g) peeled and
chopped tomatoes
1 oz (30 g) grated cheese
1 small onion, finely chopped

a little chopped parsley
salt and pepper
fresh breadcrumbs
butter

Arrange the fish in a greased, shallow ovenproof dish. Mix the tomatoes with the cheese, onion, parsley, and seasoning; spread over the fish. Cover with breadcrumbs and dot with butter. Bake in a moderate oven for about 20 minutes.

FISH FILLETS IN ORANGE JUICE

8 fish fillets
salt and pepper

juice of 3 oranges

Wash and dry the fish. Season with salt and pepper, then roll up with the skin outwards. Arrange the rolls in a pie-dish, and strain the orange juice over. Cover with greased greaseproof paper and bake for 15 to 20 minutes.

PAPRIKA FISH

4 oz (125 g) butter
2 large onions, sliced
8 snapper or jewfish steaks
1 cup cream or evaporated
milk

1 dsp paprika pepper
1/4 tsp salt
1/4 tsp pepper

Melt the butter in a roasting tin; sauté the onions in butter until golden. Put the fish on top of the onions. Add the lightly beaten cream, paprika, salt, and pepper. Bake in a moderate oven, basting frequently, until the fish is tender.

SCALLOPED SMOKED FISH

1 1/2 lb (750 g) smoked fish
2 cups milk
2 oz (60 g) butter
2 tbsps plain flour
1 tsp Worcestershire sauce
2 hard-boiled eggs, chopped
2 tbsps chopped green pepper

salt and pepper
cayenne pepper
breadcrumbs
6 black olives, sliced
(optional)
a few lemon wedges
sprigs of parsley

Divide the fish into serving sized pieces. Place in a frying pan, and cover with cold water. Bring to the boil and drain, then cover with more cold water, and add 1/2 cup of the milk. Cook gently until the fish is tender. Strain and reserve 1/2 cup of liquid. Flake the fish into a bowl, removing bones and skin. Melt the butter in a small saucepan; blend in the flour and cook for 2 or 3 minutes without browning. Gradually add the remaining milk, the reserved fish liquid, and the sauce, stirring all the time, and bring to the boil, still stirring. Add the eggs, green pepper, and seasonings to taste. Pour the sauce over the fish, mix well, and spoon into an ovenproof dish. Sprinkle with breadcrumbs and decorate with sliced olives. Heat through in a moderate oven. Before serving, garnish with lemon wedges and sprigs of parsley.

SMOKED HADDOCK PANCAKES

Pancakes
1 cup plain flour
a pinch of salt
1 egg
Filling
1 cup flaked smoked haddock
1/4 cup chopped parsley

1/2 pt (315 ml) milk
1/4 cup chopped parsley
butter

1/4 pt (150 ml) white binding
sauce (see page 60)

Pancakes: Sift the flour and salt into a mixing bowl. Make a well in the centre and break the egg into it; gradually draw the flour into the egg, then add the milk, a little at a time, beating well all the time. Leave to stand for at least an hour. Blend the parsley with 2 tablespoons of butter and season; chill to firm. Prepare the filling. Melt some butter in a frying pan and add one-quarter of the batter. As the pancake sets, spread one-quarter of the filling over the top to heat through. When cooked, roll the pancake around the filling and transfer to a plate over simmering water; cover. Make another three pancakes in the same way. Before serving, top each pancake with a dessertspoon of the chilled parsley butter.
Filling: Mix the fish with the parsley and bind with the white sauce.

SMOKED HADDOCK AND EGGS

1 large cup flaked smoked
haddock
1/2 pt (315 ml) white binding
sauce (see page 60)
1 gherkin, chopped, or a few
capers

3-4 eggs
salt and pepper
grated cheese

Mix the fish with the white sauce, season with salt and pepper, and heat carefully. Add the chopped gherkin or capers. Turn the mixture into a buttered ovenproof dish and make hollows for the eggs. Break an egg into each hollow. Sprinkle with salt and pepper and grated cheese. Cook in a moderately hot oven until the eggs are set and the cheese is golden.

FISH IN POTATO SHELLS

4 large baked potatoes
butter
milk
salt
2 cups flaked fish
¼ cup mayonnaise (see page 62)

1 tbsp chopped parsley
a dash of paprika pepper
¾ cup white binding sauce (see page 60)
8 slices of cheese

Bake the potatoes in their skins for about an hour, or until soft. Cut in half lengthwise. Scoop out the centres, taking care not to break the skins, and mash with butter, milk, and salt. In another bowl mix the fish with the mayonnaise, parsley, and paprika; bind with the white sauce. Put a spoonful of fish mixture in each potato shell, then cover with a layer of mashed potato and a slice of cheese. Return to a hot oven until the potatoes are heated through and the cheese is melted and golden.

FISH FRITTERS

2 eggs
4 tbsps flaked cooked fish
1 dsp parsley

salt and pepper
1 dsp water
fat or oil

Beat the eggs in a mixing bowl; add the fish, parsley, salt, pepper, and water. Beat well. Heat the fat in a frying pan; cook tablespoons of the mixture on each side until brown.

Serve with watercress and tomato salad.

FISH PATTIES AND SAUCE

2 cups cooked fish
1½ cups mashed potatoes
1 tsp grated onion
1 tsp grated lemon rind
1 tsp lemon juice
1 tsp dry mustard

salt and pepper
2 eggs, beaten
a little milk
dried breadcrumbs
butter

Sauce

1 dsp plain flour
½ tsp curry powder
1 dsp tomato paste or purée

1 tbsp lemon juice
½ cup water
salt and pepper

Combine the fish with the potato, onion, lemon rind and juice, mustard, salt, and pepper. Bind with some of the beaten egg. Shape into flat cakes and dip first in the remaining beaten egg (adding a little milk if necessary) then in breadcrumbs. Fry in hot butter until golden. Serve with the hot sauce.
Sauce: Blend the flour and curry powder to a paste with a little cold water. Heat the remaining ingredients in a saucepan until boiling-point is reached. Remove from the heat and pour over the blended mixture, stirring all the time. Return to the saucepan and heat, stirring until the sauce thickens; simmer for 2 or 3 minutes.

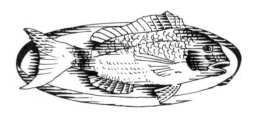

FISH CUTLETS WITH WALNUTS

2 oz (60 g) butter
2 oz (60 g) plain flour
½ pt (315 ml) milk
4 oz (125 g) chopped walnuts

12 oz (375 g) minced cooked fish
salt and pepper
1 egg, beaten

Melt the butter in a saucepan; blend in the flour, and cook for 2 or 3 minutes without browning. Pour in the milk, and stir constantly until the sauce is boiling and thickened. Simmer for 2 or 3 minutes. Remove the pan from the heat and add one-third of the walnuts. Add the fish, mix well, and season to taste with salt and pepper. Leave the mixture to become quite cold. Divide into ten portions and roll out on a floured board. Form into cutlet shapes with a knife. Dip the cutlets first in the egg and then in the remaining chopped nuts. Bake for 15 minutes in a hot oven.

Serve with caper sauce (see page 61).

FISH CUSTARDS

approx. 8 oz. (250 g) cooked fish
2 eggs

½ pt (315 ml) milk
anchovy essence

Skin and bone the fish, then pound it. Two-thirds fill small moulds or custard cups with the fish. Beat the eggs, mix in the milk, and flavour with anchovy essence; pour into the moulds, and leave to soak in. Tie buttered paper over each mould and steam for 10 minutes.

Serve hot with white sauce (see page 60) or cold with mayonnaise (see page 62).

FISH SOUFFLE

2 oz (60 g) butter
¼ pt (150 ml) milk
1 cup mashed potatoes

1 cup flaked, cooked fish
2 eggs, separated
salt and pepper

Bring the butter and milk to the boil; remove from the heat and beat the potatoes in vigorously. Stir in the fish, egg-yolks, and seasoning, combining thoroughly. Beat the egg-whites until stiff, then fold carefully into the mixture. Pour into a greased ovenproof dish and bake in a moderate oven for 25 to 30 minutes until risen and golden—do not open the oven for the first 20 minutes. Serve immediately.

FISH JELLY

1½ tbsps gelatine
¼ pt (150 ml) cold water
¾ pt (475 ml) boiling water
1 hard-boiled egg, sliced
1 cup flaked salmon or other cooked fish

2 tbsps lemon juice
salt and pepper
sprigs of parsley
radishes
extra hard-boiled eggs

Soften the gelatine in the cold water then dissolve it in the boiling water. Pour some of the liquid into a mould that has been rinsed with cold water. When it has set, arrange the sliced egg on top. Mix the salmon with the lemon juice, salt and pepper, and the remaining liquid; pour into the mould and leave to set. To serve, turn out on a bed of shredded lettuce and garnish with sprigs of parsley, sliced radishes, and sliced hard-boiled eggs.

KEDGEREE

2–3 oz (60–90 g) butter
4 oz (125 g) rice, cooked and
  drained
8 oz (250 g) cooked fish
salt and pepper
a pinch of nutmeg
1 hard-boiled egg, chopped
chopped parsley
cayenne pepper

Melt the butter in a pan. Add the rice and the fish. Mix thoroughly and season with salt, pepper, and nutmeg. Heat the mixture through, then pile it on a hot dish. Sprinkle with chopped hard-boiled egg and parsley. Sprinkle with cayenne.

SALMON LOAF

1 lb (500 g) tinned salmon
½ cup cold water
1 tbsp gelatine
¼ cup boiling water
½ tsp salt
1 tbsp lemon juice
1 tbsp vinegar
1 dsp grated onion
1 tbsp sugar
⅓ cup sliced stuffed green olives
¼ cup chopped celery
1 small cup mayonnaise
crisp lettuce leaves

Remove the bones and flake the salmon. Soften the gelatine in the cold water; add the boiling water, and dissolve. Mix in the salt, lemon juice, vinegar, grated onion, and sugar. Cool until slightly thickened. Stir in the salmon, olives, celery, and mayonnaise. Pour into a loaf-tin. Chill until firm. Turn out on a bed of lettuce leaves to serve.

SALMON NEWBURG

½ cup rice
1 tbsp butter
1 tbsp plain flour
2 cups milk
2 eggs, separated
2 tbsps grated cheese
2 tbsps sweet sherry
  (optional)
1 lb (500 g) tinned salmon
salt and pepper
fresh breadcrumbs
a little extra butter

Cook the rice in boiling water for 12 minutes; drain. Put the rice in a greased ovenproof dish. Melt the butter in a small saucepan; blend in the flour and cook for 2 or 3 minutes without browning. Gradually add the milk, and stir constantly until thick and boiling. Remove from the heat, add the beaten egg-yolks, then cook gently for a little longer. Add the cheese and sherry, then the salmon. Fold in the stiffly beaten egg-whites. Pour on to the rice. Top with breadcrumbs, and dot with butter. Heat through in a moderately hot oven for about 20 minutes.

CURRIED SALMON CASSEROLE

1 tbsp butter
2 tbsps plain flour
1 dsp curry powder
1 cup milk
1½ cups chicken soup
1 medium tin salmon
chopped parsley
1 dsp lemon juice
2 cups cooked rice
fresh breadcrumbs
extra butter

Melt the butter; stir in the flour and curry powder. Cook for 1 minute. Add the milk, stirring constantly, and heat until thickened and boiling, still stirring. Add the chicken soup, salmon, parsley, and lemon juice. Arrange alternating layers of salmon and rice in a greased ovenproof dish. Top with breadcrumbs and dot with butter. Bake in a moderately hot oven for 20 minutes.

SALMON BAKE

1 large tin salmon
1 dsp butter
1 dsp plain flour
approx. ¾ cup milk
1 tsp lemon juice
1 tsp grated lemon rind
salt and pepper
1 dsp chopped parsley
8 oz (250 g) potatoes, boiled
  and mashed
1 onion, finely chopped
breadcrumbs
extra butter

Drain the salmon and reserve the liquid. Remove the skin and bones from the fish and mash. Melt the butter, add the flour, and cook gently for 2 minutes without browning. Gradually add the milk and salmon liquid and stir until the sauce boils and thickens. Simmer for 3 minutes and then stir in the salmon, lemon juice, rind, salt and pepper, and parsley. Pour into a greased ovenproof dish. Mix the onion into the mashed potatoes and spread over the salmon. Roughen the top with a fork, sprinkle with breadcrumbs, and dot with a few knobs of butter. Heat through in a moderately hot oven until the potato topping is golden.

Serve with a green vegetable or salad.

SALMON PIE

4 oz (125 g) butter
8 oz (250 g) crushed cheese
  biscuits
2 eggs
8 oz (250 g) tinned salmon,
  mashed
½ cup fried onions
½ cup fried chopped celery
¼ pt (150 ml) evaporated milk
cayenne pepper
½ cup grated cheese
1 dsp chopped parsley
salt

Melt the butter. Stir in the biscuit crumbs, then press into a greased pie-dish. Cook in a moderate oven for 8 minutes. Leave to cool. Beat the eggs in a mixing bowl and add all the remaining ingredients. Pour on to the biscuit base. Cook in a moderate oven for half an hour, or until set.

Serve hot or cold with tartare sauce (see page 61).

OYSTERS NATURAL

fresh oysters
salt
cayenne pepper
lemon juice
lemon wedges

Chill the oysters. Shortly before serving, wash the oyster shells, open, and remove the beards. Arrange on serving plates and sprinkle with salt, cayenne, and lemon juice. Garnish with lemon wedges.

Serve with buttered brown bread.

POTTED PRAWNS

1 lb (500 g) peeled prawns
cayenne pepper
salt
a pinch of powdered cloves or
  mixed spice
clarified butter (see page 30)

Season the prawns well, adding just a little of the powdered cloves or spice. Press them into pots and pour a little of the clarified butter over them; cook for a few minutes in a moderate oven. Leave to get cold, then fill the pots with clarified butter. Keep refrigerated.

CLARIFIED BUTTER

8 oz (250 g) butter

Melt the butter in a saucepan over gentle heat. When it is foaming but not darkened, pour it into a bowl. Skim and leave to cool. Scrape away the sediment that has collected on the bottom.

CURRIED PRAWNS

1 *onion, finely chopped*	$\frac{3}{4}$ *pt (475 ml) stock*
2 *tbsps butter*	1 *tsp curry paste*
1 *tbsp curry powder*	1 *dsp chutney*
1 *tbsp cornflour*	1 *tbsp desiccated coconut*
1 *small apple, peeled and finely*	1 *lb (500 g) peeled prawns*
chopped	2 *tbsps cream*
a pinch of sugar	1 *tbsp lemon juice*
salt	

Fry the onion gently in the butter until transparent but not browned. Stir in the curry powder and cornflour and cook for 2 or 3 minutes. Stir in the apple, sugar, and salt; then add the stock, curry paste, chutney, and coconut. Cook gently for an hour then add the prawns; continue cooking for 10 minutes. Stir in the cream and the lemon juice just before serving.

Serve on a bed of boiled rice.

FRIED SCALLOPS

12 *scallops*	3 *tbsps butter*
salt and pepper	1 *tbsp oil*
1$\frac{1}{2}$ *tbsps lemon juice*	*lemon wedges*
4 *tbsps plain flour*	

Wash the scallops, cut in half, and dry. Sprinkle with salt, pepper, and lemon juice, then coat in flour. Heat the butter and oil until sizzling then fry the scallops for about 4 minutes on each side. Transfer to heated plates and garnish with lemon.

DRESSED CRAB

1 *cooked crab*	*cayenne pepper*
2 *tbsps vinegar*	*crisp lettuce leaves*
2 *tbsps oil*	*lemon wedges*
salt	*sprigs of parsley*
dry mustard	

Combine the crab flesh with the vinegar, oil, and seasonings. Transfer to a chilled serving plate lined with lettuce and garnish with lemon wedges and sprigs of parsley.

SCALLOPED CRAB

1 *cooked crab*	*cayenne pepper*
$\frac{1}{2}$ *pt (315 ml) white coating*	*breadcrumbs*
sauce (see page 60)	*butter*
1 *tbsp lemon juice*	
salt	

Remove the flesh from the crab and mix it with the sauce and lemon juice, seasoning to taste with salt and cayenne. Pour into buttered small ovenproof dishes or scallop shells and sprinkle with breadcrumbs; dot with a little butter. Cook in a moderately hot oven until brown.

CRAYFISH WITH MUSHROOM AND TOMATO SAUCE

1 *large cooked crayfish*	1 *cup peeled, chopped tomatoes*
1 *pt (625 ml) white binding*	1 *cup cream*
sauce (see page 60)	1 *cup grated cheese*
1 *cup white wine*	
1 *cup mushrooms fried in butter*	

Split the crayfish in half lengthwise and remove the intestinal vein. Mix the white sauce with the wine, mushrooms, tomatoes, cream, and cheese. Pour the sauce over the crayfish halves and heat through in a moderately hot oven until the sauce is golden and bubbling.

LOBSTER THERMIDOR

2 *cooked lobsters*	*salt and pepper*
$\frac{1}{2}$ *pt (315 ml) white coating*	6 *oz (185 g) grated cheese*
sauce (see page 60)	*butter*
3 *tbsps cream*	
1 *tsp dry mustard*	

Halve the lobsters lengthwise and remove the intestinal vein. Remove the meat and chop it. Stir the cream and mustard into the white sauce and heat through—do not boil. Season generously. Add the lobster meat and return the mixture to the shells. Sprinkle with cheese, dot with butter, and brown under the griller.

BROILED LOBSTER

small cooked lobsters	*salt*
butter	*sprigs of parsley*
cayenne pepper	

Split the lobsters in half lengthwise and remove the intestinal vein. Spread softened butter over the halves and sprinkle with cayenne and salt. Grill until heated through and golden on top. Serve garnished with sprigs of parsley.

Serve with green salad.

Traditional
POULTRY
and GAME

Chicken that is to be roasted, grilled, or fried should be young, with firm flesh, soft feet, plump breast, flexible breastbone, and heavy in proportion to its size. An older bird, weighing up to 7 pounds (3·5 kilograms), is suitable for stewing or other long, slow cooking methods. The same general principle applies to game—young birds should be roasted and older ones braised or casseroled. Poultry should be plucked and hung by the feet in a cool, airy place for 2 or 3 hours between killing and cooking; game birds generally need to be hung, unplucked, for several days, until a tail feather can be easily pulled. Young turkeys have smooth legs and plump white flesh; young ducks and geese have smooth legs and soft, pliable feet; rabbits and hares have stiff, whitish flesh, while young game birds can be recognised by soft feathers, smooth, pliable legs, and plump breast.

The strong smell and distinctive flavour of game is much improved by marinating before cooking. Its characteristic dry meat will be moistened by a covering of bacon while roasting, combined with frequent basting.

Plucking

Feathers are most easily removed when the bird has just been killed. Otherwise, plunge the bird into boiling water before plucking. Taking firm hold of the bird, pluck several feathers at a time, pulling towards the head. The wing feathers have to be removed one at a time. Remove any down or remaining hairs by singeing with a lighted taper or holding the bird over a gas flame.

Drawing

Cut a small slit in the leg, just above the claw, and pull out the exposed sinews, one at a time, with a skewer. Cut the neck skin 2 or 3 inches from the body and cut off the head and neck; cut off the feet. Make a slit in the skin a little way down the back, put your fingers inside, and loosen the gullet and windpipe. Cut around the vent, carefully to avoid puncturing the entrails, and make a hole large enough to put your fingers in. Take hold of the gizzard, which is large and hard; draw out the entrails, including the windpipe and gullet, taking care not to break the gall bladder. Wipe the inside of the bird with a damp cloth. Cut the gall bladder from the liver and throw it away. Cut through the gizzard and remove the crop. Wash the liver, gizzard, and heart (the giblets).

Jointing

Bend the wing back and away from the body to find the joint; cut through, taking a slice of breast meat with the wing. Repeat for the other wing. Cut through the skin where the leg joins the body and bend the leg away from the body to find the joint; cut through, taking bone ends only if you wish. If the bird is large, cut the leg into two pieces—thigh and drumstick. Repeat for the other leg. Cut through the rib-bones along each side of the body, to separate the breast from the back. Cut through the middle of the breastbone to divide the breast in half. Chop the back across in two pieces.

Pumpkin soup (page 12)

Anchovy-stuffed eggs (page 17), devilled almonds (page 17), and pigs in blankets (page 17)

Cheeselettes (page 19)

Baked eggs on spinach (page 21)

Potted meat (page 22)

Trout with almonds (page 26)

Lobster thermidor (page 30)

Chicken with prawns (page 34) and boiled rice

Trussing

If the bird is to be stuffed, this should have been done before beginning the procedure of trussing. Put the bird on its breast. Fold the neck skin under and cross the wingtips over to secure it. Turn the bird on to its back and push the legs into the side. Cut a slit in the skin above the vent and push the tail, or parson's nose, through this. Thread a trussing needle with fine string. Push the needle through the second joint of the right wing, right through the body, to catch the wing on the opposite side. Pass the needle through the first joint of the left wing and through the wingtips, neck skin, and the right wing; tie the string to secure. Insert the needle in the gristle at the right of the tail and pass it over the right and then the left leg, through the gristle at the left of the tail, and then behind the tail; tie firmly.

Carving

Position the bird with the neck end towards you and secure it with the carving fork through the back. Prise the leg outwards with the knife, exposing the joint, and cut through; if the bird is large, divide the thigh from the drumstick. Cut through the outer layer of the breast, where it meets the wishbone, and ease the wing joint away from the bird, cutting through the gristle; if the bird is large, cut the wing in half. Repeat this procedure for the other side of the bird. Cut the breast in slices, with the fork inserted across the highest point of the breastbone, carving across the grain.

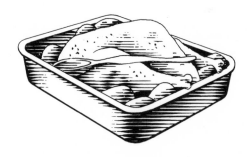

ROAST CHICKEN

4-lb (2 kg) roasting chicken   salt and pepper
3 oz (90 g) butter or fat   a few bacon rashers (optional)

Wash and dry the chicken, then put it in a roasting tin. Put half the butter in the body cavity (or you may prefer to use an onion or a cut lemon). Melt the rest of the butter and pour it over the chicken; sprinkle with salt and pepper. Lay the bacon rashers over the breast to prevent the chicken from drying out too much. Bake in the centre of a moderately hot oven, allowing 20 minutes per pound (500 grams), plus 20 minutes. Cover with greased paper if the bird browns too quickly. Baste from time to time.

Serve with roast potatoes, a green vegetable, bacon rolls, gravy, and bread sauce (see page 61).

CHICKEN IN MILK

Simmer a roasting chicken in ½ pint (315 millilitres) of milk for 20 minutes. Drain, reserving the liquid to use for a sauce. Cook in the same way as for roast chicken.

CHICKEN WITH PRAWNS

3 lb (1·5 kg) chicken pieces   ½ tsp pepper
½ cup oil   1 dsp lemon juice
1 large onion, chopped   ½ tsp thyme
1 clove of garlic, crushed   ½ cup chopped celery
1 tbsp plain flour   ½ cup chopped shallots
3 cups chicken stock   1 red and 1 green pepper,
2 tomatoes, peeled and chopped   chopped
1½ tsps salt   1 lb (500 g) peeled prawns

Heat the oil in a large pan and cook the chicken, turning occasionally until lightly browned (about 10 minutes). Remove the chicken pieces from the pan and set aside. Add the onion and garlic and sauté until transparent. Add the flour to the pan and cook, stirring, for 2 minutes. Stir in the stock and tomatoes, mixing well. Add the chicken pieces, salt, pepper, lemon juice, and thyme. Cook, covered, over low heat for 35 minutes, or until the chicken is tender. Add extra stock if necessary. Add the celery, shallots, and peppers. Simmer for 15 minutes, adding the prawns after 10 minutes.

Serve with boiled rice, tossed with chopped parsley.

CHICKEN WITH ALMONDS

3 oz (90 g) butter   1 bay-leaf
1 tbsp finely chopped onion   3 cups diced cooked chicken
¼ pt (150 ml) white wine   ¼ cup seeded raisins
½ pt (315 ml) chicken stock   ½ cup chopped blanched almonds
½ pt (315 ml) white coating   ¼ cup sherry
  sauce (see page 60)   2 egg-yolks, lightly beaten
1 tsp salt   ¼ pt (150 ml) cream

Sauté the onion in the butter until golden. Add the wine, stock, white sauce, salt, and bay-leaf. Add the diced chicken, raisins, and almonds; heat thoroughly. Mix together the sherry, egg-yolks, and cream; add to the chicken. Cook for 2 minutes longer, stirring constantly, but do not allow to boil, or the sauce will curdle.

CHICKEN CORONET

4 oz (125 g) mushrooms   ¼ pt (150 ml) strong stock
1 spring chicken   2 tbsps white wine
2 oz (60 g) butter   1½ tsps finely chopped parsley
1 medium onion, finely chopped   salt and pepper
2 small slices of lean ham or 2   1 tbsp grated Gruyère cheese
  small lean bacon rashers, diced

Slice all but two of the mushrooms. Divide the chicken into equal halves, cutting through the breast. Cook gently in the butter for 12 to 15 minutes, until barely cooked, with still the merest fraction of pink around the leg joints. Transfer the chicken to a buttered ovenproof dish, and keep warm. Fry the onion in the fat remaining in the pan until tender but not brown. Add the sliced mushrooms and the ham. Cook lightly, then transfer the mixture to the ovenproof dish, arranging it under the chicken. Put one whole mushroom on each chicken half. Add the stock to the cooking juices and stir thoroughly. Stir in the wine, parsley, and salt and pepper. Pour the sauce over the chicken and sprinkle with the cheese. Cook in a slow oven for 8 to 10 minutes, until the surface becomes glazed. Serve immediately.

Serve with fried potato straws.

FRIED CHICKEN

6 chicken pieces   4 oz (125 g) butter
milk   1½ tbsps oil
3 tbsps plain flour   1 tbsp lemon juice
salt and pepper   1 tbsp finely chopped parsley

Wash and dry the chicken pieces; dip them first in milk, then in the flour seasoned with salt and pepper. Fry the chicken in the hot butter and oil, turning until brown on all sides. Cover and cook slowly for 20 to 30 minutes, or until tender. Transfer to a hot serving dish and keep warm. Add the lemon juice and parsley to the cooking juices, heat through, and pour over the chicken before serving.

CHICKEN FRICASSEE

2½-lb (1·25 kg) boiling chicken,   ½ tsp salt
  jointed   2 oz (60 g) butter
4 oz (125 g) chopped bacon   2 oz (60 g) plain flour
½ pt (315 ml) milk   1 tbsp finely chopped parsley
1 large onion   lemon wedges
2 cloves   4 bacon rashers, rolled and
a generous pinch of mixed herbs   grilled

Put the chicken pieces in a saucepan with the bacon, milk, and enough water to cover. Add the onion studded with the cloves, the mixed herbs, and the salt. Bring to the boil, then lower the heat, cover, and simmer gently for about 1 hour, or until the chicken is tender. Strain the chicken, reserving 1 pint (625 millilitres) of the liquid. Remove the chicken meat from the bones, chop it, and keep hot. Melt the butter in a pan, stir in the flour, and cook gently for 2 or 3 minutes without browning. Gradually blend in the stock, stirring constantly, and cook until thickened and boiling. Simmer for 2 minutes, then pour over the chicken. Garnish with the parsley, lemon wedges, and the hot bacon rolls.

CHICKEN CROQUETTES

left-over cooked chicken
chopped fresh herbs
salt and pepper
½ cup fresh breadcrumbs
2 eggs

plain flour
milk
dried breadcrumbs
butter

Mince the chicken flesh and mix with the herbs, salt and pepper, and the fresh breadcrumbs. Bind with one of the eggs. Form into small cakes and dip in flour, then in the other egg beaten with milk. Coat with dried breadcrumbs and fry in butter until golden on both sides.

QUICK CHICKEN CURRY

1 large steamed chicken
2 large onions, chopped
1 green pepper, chopped
2 oz (60 g) butter
1 dsp curry powder

3 tbsps plain flour
1 tsp salt
½ tsp pepper
1 tsp sugar
3 cups chicken stock

Remove the skin and bones from the chicken, and chop into small pieces. Sauté the onions and green pepper in the butter for 5 minutes. Add the curry powder, flour, salt, and pepper; fry for 2 minutes. Add the sugar and stock, then stir until thickened. Add the chicken, and simmer for 10 minutes.

ROAST TURKEY

Stuff the turkey from the neck with veal forcemeat (see below), then sew it up or secure it with skewers. Truss it with the wings folded over the body and the legs tied together. Put the turkey in a roasting tin with 2 ounces (60 grams) of butter and brush with melted butter; cover the breast with slices of bacon if you like, to keep the bird moist. Cover with greased paper and bake in a hot oven for 10 minutes then reduce the temperature to moderate. Allow 3 hours for a turkey up to 10 pounds (5 kilograms), 3½ to 4 hours for a turkey between 10 and 14 pounds (5 and 7 kilograms), and 4½ to 5 hours for a bird between 14 and 20 pounds (7 and 10 kilograms). Baste from time to time and remove the paper 20 minutes before the end of cooking time, so that the breast will brown.

Serve with roast potatoes, a green vegetable, grilled bacon rolls, gravy, bread sauce (see page 61), and cranberry sauce.

VEAL FORCEMEAT

4 oz (125 g) veal
3 oz (90 g) bacon
1 onion, finely chopped and fried
  in butter
3 oz (90 g) fresh breadcrumbs

1 tsp finely chopped parsley
¼ tsp mixed herbs
salt and pepper
1 egg, beaten

Mince the veal and bacon finely then combine with the fried onion, breadcrumbs, herbs, and seasoning. Bind with the egg. A large turkey will require double quantity.

DEVILLED TURKEY LEGS

cooked turkey legs or drumsticks
melted butter
1 dsp prepared mustard
1 dsp chutney

a pinch of ground ginger
salt and pepper
a pinch of cayenne pepper

Score the flesh deeply with a sharp knife, then brush with melted butter. Blend together the mustard, chutney, ginger, salt and pepper, and cayenne. Spread this paste over the turkey pieces and into the cuts. Leave for at least 1 hour. Grill until crisp and golden, turning regularly.

ROAST DUCK

Wash and dry the duck. A young duckling does not need stuffing but an older bird should be filled at the tail end with sage and onion stuffing (see page 36). Sew up or secure with skewers and stand in a roasting tin. Sprinkle with salt and pepper and cook in the centre of a hot oven for 15 minutes. Reduce the temperature to moderate and continue cooking, allowing 20 minutes per pound (500 grams). Do not cover or baste.

Serve with roast potatoes, a green vegetable, gravy, and apple sauce (see page 62).

DUCK WITH CHERRIES

1 tin black cherries
1 tbsp cornflour
¼ pt (150 g) stock

salt and pepper
watercress

Follow the recipe for roast duck. About 10 minutes before the end of cooking time, remove the duck from the roasting tin and pour off the fat. Return the duck to the pan with the cherries and their syrup and continue cooking until the bird is tender, basting occasionally. Remove the duck to a heated serving plate and keep warm. Blend the cornflour with the stock and put in a saucepan with the cherry liquid strained from the roasting tin. Heat gently, stirring all the time, until thickened and boiling. Add the cherries; adjust the seasoning, and simmer for 2 minutes. Pour the sauce over the duck and garnish with watercress.

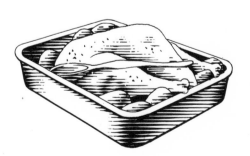

DUCK WITH ORANGE SAUCE

1 tbsp plain flour
grated rind and juice of 2 oranges
2 tbsps red wine
2 tbsps redcurrant jelly

2 tbsps dry sherry
salt and pepper
1 extra orange, peeled and sliced
watercress

Follow the recipe for roast duck. Transfer the cooked bird to a heated serving plate and keep hot. Pour off all but 1 tablespoon of fat from the roasting tin. Stir in the flour and cook over gentle heat for 2 minutes without browning. Add the orange rind and juice, the wine, the redcurrant jelly, and the sherry. Heat, stirring all the time, until the sauce thickens and boils. Adjust the seasoning and simmer for 2 minutes longer. Pour the sauce over the duck and garnish with the orange slices and watercress.

ROAST GOOSE

Stuff the prepared goose at the tail end with sage and onion stuffing (see below). Put the bird on a rack in a roasting tin and sprinkle with salt. Cover the breast with greased paper. Cook in a moderate oven, allowing 20 minutes per pound (500 grams) plus an extra 20 minutes, and basting frequently. Remove the paper for the last 20 minutes.

Serve with gravy and apple sauce (see page 62).

SAGE AND ONION STUFFING

2 large onions, finely chopped
4 oz (125 g) fresh
  breadcrumbs

1 dsp dried sage
salt and pepper
1 oz (30 g) butter, melted

Simmer the onions in boiling water until tender; drain well. Combine the onions with the breadcrumbs, sage, and salt and pepper. Bind with the melted butter, and milk if necessary.

JUGGED HARE

1 hare (or 2 rabbits)
2 oz (60 g) butter
2 carrots, sliced
2 onions, sliced
1 stalk of celery, sliced
1½ pt (940 ml) stock
1 bay-leaf

1 blade of mace
6 peppercorns
2 cloves
2 tbsps plain flour
¼ pt (150 ml) port
1 tbsp redcurrant jelly

Joint the hare and fry the pieces in the hot butter until brown. Transfer to a casserole and add the vegetables and stock. Tie the bay-leaf, mace, peppercorns, and cloves in a muslin bag and add to the casserole. Cover and cook in the middle of the oven for 3 to 4 hours, or until the hare is tender. Transfer the joints to a heated serving dish and keep warm. Strain the cooking liquid and transfer to another pan. Blend the flour to a paste with the port and the redcurrant jelly; add to the liquid and heat, stirring constantly, until thickened and boiling. Simmer for 2 minutes longer.

Serve with forcemeat balls (see below) and redcurrant jelly (see page 137).

FORCEMEAT BALLS

4 oz (125 g) fresh white
  breadcrumbs
2 oz (60 g) finely shredded suet
1 tsp finely chopped parsley
½ tsp mixed herbs

½ tsp finely grated lemon rind
salt and pepper
1 egg, beaten
2 oz (60 g) butter

Mix the breadcrumbs with the suet, herbs, lemon peel, and salt and pepper. Bind with the egg, and a little milk if necessary. Form into about twelve balls and fry in the butter until golden.

STUFFED BAKED RABBIT

1 rabbit
veal forcemeat (see page 35)
a few bacon rashers
dripping

1 dsp plain flour
½ pt (315 ml) stock or water
6 bacon rashers, rolled and
  grilled

Prepare the rabbit, washing and drying thoroughly. Put the liver, heart, and kidneys in a saucepan of cold water and bring to the boil. Strain and chop finely; mix with the veal forcemeat. Stuff the rabbit, sew up, and truss. Tie a few bacon rashers over the back of the rabbit and cover with greaseproof paper. Cook in a roasting tin with a little dripping for 1 to 1½ hours, basting regularly. Remove the bacon and the paper 15 minutes before the end of cooking time. Transfer the rabbit to a heated serving dish, remove the string and skewers, and keep hot. Drain all but 1 tablespoon of fat from the roasting tin and blend in the flour. Cook for 2 or 3 minutes then gradually stir in the stock or water. Bring to the boil and simmer for several minutes. Pour the gravy round the rabbit and garnish with bacon rolls.

Serve with bread sauce (see page 61) and redcurrant jelly (see page 137).

RABBIT CASSEROLE

6 rabbit joints
1 large onion, finely chopped
8 oz (250 g) bacon rashers,
  chopped
3 large carrots, sliced
1½ pt (940 ml) milk

salt and pepper
grated nutmeg
1 tbsp cornflour
a little extra milk
1 tbsp chopped parsley

Wash and dry the rabbit pieces. Arrange in a casserole and cover with the prepared onion, bacon, and carrot. Pour the milk over and season well with salt, pepper, and nutmeg. Cover and cook in a slow to moderate oven for 2 hours, or until the rabbit is tender. Transfer the rabbit and vegetables to a heated serving dish and keep hot. Blend the cornflour to a smooth paste with a little milk and stir into the cooking juices in the casserole. Bring to the boil, stirring all the time, then simmer for 2 or 3 minutes. Pour the sauce over the rabbit and sprinkle with the parsley.

Hearty Sustaining MEAT

The meat from younger animals is generally much more tender than that from older animals and tends, therefore, to be most in demand and most expensive. Such prime cuts are suited to quick methods of cooking—frying or grilling—while the less tender cuts need slow, careful cooking to yield their best. Older animals have a good flavour, however, and are at least as nutritious as younger animals, so the extra time and care involved in their preparation is worthwhile. The most frequently used muscles of animals have the greatest concentration of connective tissue, gristle, and so on, causing the meat to be tough—for example, the muscles of the leg can be assumed to have worked harder than those of the rump—and to require either slow cooking in liquid, or mincing.

After purchase, meat may be left in the wrapping paper for a few hours or transferred to a dish and loosely covered with paper. It should be kept in the coldest part of the refrigerator and not covered in such a way that the air cannot circulate freely around it. Minced meat and offal should be used within one day of purchase; chops and steaks can be kept for three to four days; and large joints will keep for up to a week. Cooked meat should be allowed to cool before being covered and stored in the refrigerator.

Guide to Choosing Meat

Veal: Pinkish, fine-grained flesh; a little soft creamy fat.
Beef: Firm, bright red, fine-grained flesh; fine, pale yellow fat.
Lamb: Pinkish red, fine-grained flesh; firm white fat.
Mutton: Firm, dark red, medium-grained flesh; hard white fat.
Pork: Firm, light pink, fine-grained flesh; firm white fat.

Cooking Methods

Roasting: Before roasting, meat should be removed from the refrigerator and brought to room-temperature. It should then be wiped, weighed, and the cooking time worked out. Cook in a pre-heated oven according to the times and instructions given under the appropriate recipe. In general, the juiciness of meat is most effectively retained by an initial cooking time at a high temperature. Tougher cuts of meat, however, are improved by longer cooking at a low temperature. A lean joint should be dotted with fat before roasting; a fatty joint should be cooked on a rack. For a self-basting roast, cook the joint in a covered roasting tin; remove the lid for the final half-hour, to allow the meat to brown.
Pot-roasting: This is an easy way of cooking a cheap joint of meat and transforming it into a moist, tender dish. A large, heavy pot with a lid is needed. The meat is browned, then cooked slowly either on the stove or in the oven with vegetables, seasonings, and a little liquid.
Braising: This is an excellent way of cooking cheap cuts of meat in order to extract the maximum amount of flavour from them. A heavy pot with a lid is needed. The meat, a large cut or chopped pieces, is cooked gently on a bed of sautéed vegetables with a couple of inches of water and assorted herbs and seasonings.
Grilling: Wipe the meat and sprinkle it with pepper; nick the fat at intervals to prevent it from curling when cooking. Pre-heat the griller and the grilling rack to the strongest heat—if it is not extremely hot the meat will stick and tear when turned. The meat should be seared for 1 or 2 minutes on each side and then the heat lowered to moderate. The meat may be salted when cooked; if salt is added before cooking, it will draw the juices from the meat. Grilled meat should be served as soon as it is cooked.

Frying: Rissoles, fritters, and meats dipped in batter may be deep-fried but meat is more usually shallow-fried in butter, oil, or a mixture of both. Meat to be braised, pot-roasted, or stewed is often given a preliminary browning in hot fat before the slow cooking process is started. Fried meat should be turned only once. The pan-juices may be used to make a delicious quick sauce or gravy.

Boiling: Plunge the meat into a large pan of rapidly boiling salted water, perhaps with a few root vegetables and seasonings. Bring to the boil then lower the heat, cover, and simmer gently until the meat is tender. Scum should be skimmed from the surface from time to time and the boiling water topped up as necessary. Salted meat should first be covered with cold unsalted water, brought slowly to the boil, and then drained; proceed then as for unsalted meat.

Stewing: For brown stews the meat, and sometimes the vegetables, are browned in hot fat, then covered with water and slowly simmered with the other ingredients until tender. For white stews, the meat may be blanched before the long cooking process and thickened with blended flour near the end of cooking time. Stews may be cooked on top of the stove or in the oven.

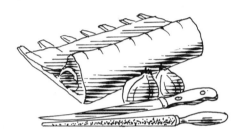

Cooking Methods for Basic Cuts of Meat

VEAL
Roasting: Leg, loin, shoulder, topside, silverside, rump.
Grilling, Frying: Fillet, loin, best end of neck, round, rump, topside, silverside.
Pot-roasting, Braising: Best end of neck, loin, breast, round, topside, silverside, rump.
Boiling, Stewing: Breast, neck, scrag, shoulder, knuckle, shank.

BEEF
Roasting: Topside, rump, round, sirloin, standing ribs, wing rib, rolled ribs, silverside, blade roast.
Grilling, Frying: Rump, sirloin, fillet, Scotch fillet, silverside, blade, oyster blade, T-bone, porterhouse.
Pot-roasting, Braising: Aitch-bone, middle rump, ribs, shoulder, chuck, brisket, blade, oyster blade, skirt, topside, round, flank.
Stewing, Boiling, Pies: Leg, shin, flank, skirt, chuck, brisket, gravy beef, silverside.

LAMB
Roasting: Leg, loin, chump, best end of neck, rolled breast, shoulder, rib.
Grilling, Frying: Best end of neck, loin, leg, rib, or chump chops.
Pot-roasting, Braising: Middle neck, scrag, breast, forequarter or shoulder chops.
Stewing, Boiling: Leg of mutton, neck, scrag, breast, loin of mutton chops, shank.

PORK
Roasting: Leg, loin, shoulder.
Grilling, Frying: Loin or chump chops.
Pot-roasting, Braising: Spareribs, best end of neck, chump chops, bladebone.
Stewing, Boiling: Leg, spareribs, best end of neck, bladebone, belly, hand and spring, neck, trotters, head, chuck.

ROAST VEAL

Trim and wipe the joint, then weigh it. Season generously and put in a roasting tin, which has been greased with 1 ounce (30 grams) of butter or fat. Spread another ounce (30 grams) of butter or fat on top of the meat and cover with bacon rashers if you wish. Bake in the centre of a moderate oven, allowing 30 minutes per pound (500 grams) plus an extra 30 minutes, and basting frequently. Add some rolled bacon rashers to the pan 15 minutes before the end of cooking time. Remove the meat to a heated serving plate with the bacon rolls and keep hot while you make the gravy; garnish with parsley. Pour off all but 1 tablespoon of the fat from the roasting tin and stir in 1 tablespoon of plain flour; cook for 2 or 3 minutes. Gradually stir in $\frac{1}{2}$ pint (315 millilitres) of stock or vegetable cooking liquid and continue stirring until the gravy thickens and boils. Season and simmer for 2 minutes longer. Pour the gravy into a sauceboat.

Serve with roast potatoes and a green vegetable.

STUFFED BREAST OF VEAL

3–4-lb (1·5–2 kg) breast of veal	2 tbsps butter
salt and pepper	sprigs of parsley
lemon juice	bacon rashers, rolled
veal forcemeat (see page 35)	1 tbsp plain flour

Remove all bones from the veal; wipe the meat with a damp cloth, trim carefully, and season with salt, pepper, and a little lemon juice. Flatten the meat with the skin side underneath and spread the stuffing over it. Roll up and sew securely with fine string; alternatively, secure with toothpicks. Sprinkle with salt and pepper, and roast in a buttered tin in a moderately slow oven for $1\frac{1}{2}$ hours, or until tender; spread some of the butter on top of the meat, lift on to a hot dish, remove the string, and keep hot; garnish with sprigs of parsley and grilled bacon rolls before serving. Pour off all but 1 tablespoon of fat from the roasting tin and stir in the flour. Cook the flour for 1 or 2 minutes, then gradually stir in $\frac{1}{2}$ pint (315 millilitres) of stock or vegetable cooking liquid. Stir until the gravy thickens and boils; season with salt and pepper and simmer for 2 minutes longer. Serve in a sauceboat.

Serve with roast potatoes and a green vegetable.

KEEPSAKE CASSEROLE

butter	1 bay-leaf (optional)
1–2 onions, thinly sliced	a little lemon juice
4 oz (125 g) mushrooms	pepper
$1\frac{1}{2}$ lb (750 g) veal	1 cup sour cream
plain flour	buttered dried breadcrumbs
1 tsp paprika pepper	
salt	
2 cups chicken stock	
1 cup chopped parsley	

Cook the onions and mushrooms in butter until tender; transfer to a casserole. Brown the veal in the frying pan; transfer the veal to the casserole. Stir the flour, paprika, and salt into the frying pan. Slowly add the chicken stock, stirring constantly until the sauce thickens. Add the parsley, bay-leaf, lemon juice, and pepper. Pour the mixture into the casserole and cook in a slow oven for about 1 hour. When the veal is tender, remove the bay-leaf. Stir in the sour cream and sprinkle with buttered breadcrumbs. Increase the temperature to moderate and return the casserole to the oven to brown.

Serve with rice or noodles.

VEAL CASSEROLE

1 lb (500 g) veal	1 stalk of celery, chopped
2 oz (60 g) bacon	2 thin slices of lemon rind
1 oz (30 g) butter	salt and pepper
1 onion, sliced	a pinch of nutmeg
1 carrot, sliced	1 cup water or stock
1 tbsp plain flour	

Wipe the veal and cut it and the bacon into small pieces. Melt the butter in a casserole and add the bacon, then the onion and carrot. Cook for a few minutes without browning. Add the flour and cook until light brown. Add the veal, celery, lemon rind, seasoning, nutmeg, and then the water or stock. Stir and bring to the boil. Cook in a moderate oven for $1\frac{1}{2}$ to 2 hours.

VEAL CUTLETS

6 veal cutlets	$1\frac{1}{2}$ cups fresh white breadcrumbs
lemon juice	3 tbsps butter
salt and pepper	1 tbsp oil
plain flour	sprigs of parsley
1–2 eggs, beaten	lemon wedges

Trim and flatten the cutlets. Sprinkle them with lemon juice and salt and pepper. Allow to stand for about half an hour then coat the cutlets in flour and dip them in beaten egg. Finally, coat them with breadcrumbs, pressing them on firmly. Refrigerate for half an hour. Fry in the hot butter and oil for 4 or 5 minutes, turning them when they are golden underneath and cooking on the other side for 4 or 5 minutes until they are browned. Drain and serve garnished with sprigs of parsley and lemon wedges.

Serve with mashed potatoes, grilled or fried tomatoes, boiled carrots, and a green vegetable or salad.

ROAST BEEF

Wipe and weigh the meat; tie it in a neat shape if necessary. Put the meat in a roasting tin with the thickest layer of fat uppermost. Melt 2 ounces (60 grams) of butter or fat and brush some over the meat; pour the rest into the pan. Cook uncovered in the middle of a hot oven for about 20 minutes, reducing the temperature to moderately hot for the rest of the cooking time. Allow 20 minutes per pound (500 grams) plus an extra 20 minutes for meat on the bone; and 25 minutes per pound (500 grams) plus an extra 25 minutes for rolled meat. Baste from time to time with the cooking juices. Remove string or skewers before carving.

Serve with roast potatoes, a green vegetable, Yorkshire pudding (see below), horseradish cream (see page 62), and gravy.

YORKSHIRE PUDDING

4 oz (125 g) plain flour	$\frac{1}{2}$ pt (315 ml) milk
a pinch of salt	1 dsp melted butter
1 egg	2 oz (60 g) dripping

Sift the flour and salt into a mixing bowl. Make a well in the centre of the dry ingredients and break the egg into it and pour in half the milk and the butter. Gradually draw the flour from the sides of the bowl into the liquid. Beat thoroughly to make a smooth batter then add the rest of the milk. Heat the dripping in a roasting tin in a hot oven until it splutters. Pour in the batter and cook for 30 to 40 minutes, until puffed and golden.

POT-ROASTED BEEF

4 lb (2 kg) topside or round of   4 carrots, sliced
   beef   4 stalks of celery, chopped
salt and pepper   2 ripe tomatoes, peeled and
plain flour   chopped
4 oz (125 g) butter   ½ pt (315 ml) stock or water
1 tbsp oil   ¼ pt (150 ml) red wine
2 onions, sliced

Season the meat with salt and pepper and dredge in flour. Brown on all sides in the hot butter and oil in a heavy-based pan or casserole. Remove the meat and sauté the onions, carrots, and celery until golden. Return the meat to the pan, laying it on the bed of vegetables. Add the tomatoes and liquid, season well, and bring to the boil. Reduce the heat, cover, and simmer gently for about 3 hours, or until tender, turning from time to time.

BRAISED BEEF

4 lb (2 kg) topside or round of   2 stalks of celery, sliced
   beef   rind of 3 bacon rashers
salt and pepper   a few sprigs of parsley
1 tbsp fat   4 peppercorns
4 onions, sliced   1 bay-leaf
4 carrots, sliced   stock or water
1 turnip, sliced

Season the meat generously then brown on all sides in the hot fat in a heavy-based saucepan. Remove the meat and brown the vegetables and bacon rind in the fat until golden; pour off the fat. Add the parsley, peppercorns, and bay-leaf and enough stock or water to cover the vegetables; bring to the boil. Return the meat to the pan and cover tightly. Cook gently, allowing 25 minutes per pound (500 grams) of meat plus an extra 25 minutes; baste from time to time. Serve the meat sliced and surrounded with the vegetables; serve with gravy made from the cooking liquid.

BEEF STEW

1½ lb (750 g) stewing steak   8 small carrots, peeled
2 tbsps plain flour   2 stalks of celery, sliced
salt and pepper   ¾ pt (475 ml) stock or water
2 tbsps butter   1–2 tbsps finely chopped parsley
8 small onions, peeled

Cut the meat into cubes, then coat them in the flour, which has been well seasoned with salt and pepper. Fry the meat in the hot butter until brown on all sides; remove the meat from the pan. Add the vegetables and fry in the remaining butter until light golden. Return the meat to the pan and pour in the stock, stirring. Bring slowly to the boil. Cover and simmer gently for about 2 hours, or until the meat is tender, stirring from time to time. Sprinkle with parsley before serving.

STEWED BEEF

2 lb (1 kg) stewing beef   water
salt and pepper   1 sprig of thyme
dripping   1 sprig of parsley
1 onion, sliced   1–2 bay-leaves
1 carrot, sliced   2–3 tomatoes, thickly sliced
1 small turnip, sliced   ½ head of celery
1 clove of garlic, crushed   3–4 potatoes, thickly sliced
a pinch of sugar   extra chopped parsley
2 tbsps plain flour

Cut the meat in small pieces, season, and fry in hot dripping in a frying pan. When lightly brown, transfer to a saucepan. Lightly fry the onion, carrot, turnip, and garlic in the frying pan. Sprinkle the sugar over, cook for a few minutes, then transfer to the saucepan. Add the flour to the frying pan, brown lightly, then stir in enough water to make a sauce to cover the meat. Add the thyme, parsley, and bay-leaves tied in muslin. Pour the sauce over the meat and vegetables. Cover with a tight-fitting lid. Bring to the boil, then simmer over a low heat for 1½ hours. Remove the herbs. Add the tomatoes, celery, potatoes, and extra chopped parsley. Baste the vegetables with the gravy, bring to the boil, and cook slowly for half an hour to an hour, until the meat is tender.

BEEF WITH ALMONDS

2 onions, sliced   1 sprig of parsley
1 clove of garlic, chopped   ½ pt (315 ml) water
2 oz (60 g) dripping   3 tbsps rice
1 lb (500 g) stewing steak,   a few raisins or sultanas
   chopped   5 almonds, roughly chopped
salt and pepper   1 tbsp paprika pepper

Using a deep frying pan with a lid, fry the onions and garlic in the dripping. Add the meat and fry until lightly brown. Season with salt and pepper; add the parsley and enough water to cook the meat. Cover with greased paper then put the lid on top. Bring to the boil. Simmer gently until tender; if the beef is tough this may take 2½ hours. Add the rice, sultanas, almonds, and paprika. Add water if there is not enough liquid to cover the rice. Simmer gently until the rice has absorbed the liquid, about 15 to 20 minutes.

BEEF OLIVES

1½-lb (750 g) piece of topside   1 oz (30 g) butter
plain flour   2 onions, thinly sliced
salt and pepper   ½ pt (315 ml) stock or water
Stuffing
2 oz (60 g) finely chopped suet   ½ tsp finely grated lemon rind
2 oz (60 g) chopped ham or   salt and pepper
   bacon   1 egg, beaten
4 oz (125 g) fresh breadcrumbs
1 dsp finely chopped parsley
¼ tsp mixed herbs

Slice the meat thinly, trimming off all the fat, into pieces about 2½ by 3 inches (6 by 8 centimetres). Spread a little of the stuffing over each piece, roll up, and secure with string. Coat the rolls in flour seasoned with salt and pepper. Brown lightly in the hot butter in a casserole or heavy saucepan. Remove the meat and fry the onions until light golden. Stir in 1 tablespoon of plain flour and cook gently for 1 or 2 minutes. Gradually add the stock or water and stir all the time until it thickens and boils. Season and return the meat to the pan. Cover and simmer gently on top of the stove or in a moderate oven for 1½ hours, or until tender. Transfer the rolls to a heated serving dish and remove the string. Pour the cooking liquid over.

Stuffing: Combine the suet in a mixing bowl with the ham, breadcrumbs, parsley, herbs, lemon rind, and salt and pepper. Bind with the egg.

Serve with mashed potatoes, boiled diced carrots, and a green vegetable.

HOT-POT

1½ lb (750 g) blade or chuck steak
plain flour
salt and pepper
4 onions, thinly sliced

1½ lb (750 g) potatoes, sliced
¾ pt (475 ml) stock
1 tbsp butter
1 tbsp finely chopped parsley

Trim the meat and cut it into 1-inch (2·5-centimetre) cubes. Toss the meat in flour seasoned with salt and pepper. Arrange a layer of sliced onion in the bottom of a casserole, then a layer of meat; cover with a layer of potatoes. Continue in the same way, seasoning between layers; finish with a layer of overlapping potatoes. Pour in the stock, season well, and dot with butter. Cover and cook in a moderate oven for about 2 hours. Remove the lid about 20 minutes before the end of cooking time to allow the potatoes to brown. Sprinkle with the parsley before serving.

Serve with a green vegetable.

SAVOURY STEAK

2 lb (1 kg) topside or rump steak
1 onion, finely chopped
1 tsp brown sugar
1 tsp salt
¼ tsp pepper
a pinch of cayenne pepper

1 tsp herbs
1 tsp chopped capers
2 tbsps tomato sauce
1 dsp Worcestershire sauce
2 tbsps vinegar
1 gherkin, sliced

Trim the steak and cut into pieces. Arrange in a shallow ovenproof dish. Sprinkle the onion over the steak. Mix the sugar with the salt, pepper, cayenne, herbs, and capers; blend in the sauces and vinegar and pour over the steak. Leave the steak to soak for 2 hours then cover and cook in a moderate oven for an hour, or until the steak is tender. Garnish with the sliced gherkin.

FRUITY CURRY

1½–2 lb (750 g–1 kg) topside steak
2 tbsps butter
2 onions, finely chopped
1 apple, finely chopped
1 banana, thickly sliced
2 tomatoes, peeled and chopped
1 dsp curry powder

2 tbsps plain flour
½ pt (315 ml) water
salt and pepper
1 cup pineapple pieces
½ cup desiccated coconut
2 tbsps sultanas
a good squeeze of lemon juice

Cut the meat into small cubes. Melt the butter and sauté the onions, apple, banana, tomatoes, and curry powder for about 10 minutes. Add the meat and brown well. Add the flour and cook for a further 2 minutes. Add the water and salt and pepper. Bring to the boil and simmer for 1½ hours. Add the pineapple pieces, coconut, sultanas, and lemon juice. Simmer for a further 20 to 30 minutes.

Serve with boiled rice.

DRY CURRY

1 oz (30 g) butter
1 onion, diced
1 apple, diced
1 tomato, diced
1 dsp curry powder
1 lb (500 g) topside steak, cut into cubes

1 tbsp sultanas
1 tsp sugar
1 tbsp desiccated coconut
1 banana, sliced
1 dsp lemon juice
salt

Heat the butter and fry the apple, onion, and tomato in a saucepan or a deep frying pan. Cook without burning for 10 minutes. Stir in the curry powder and cook for a few minutes. Add all the remaining ingredients and simmer gently for 1 hour.

Serve with boiled rice.

STEAK NELSON

1½ lb (750 g) topside steak
1 tbsp seasoned flour
1 oz (30 g) butter
1 onion, chopped
8 oz (250 g) tinned mushrooms

¼ cup cream
1¼ cups stock
salt and pepper
4 potatoes, diced

Cut the meat into small pieces and toss in the seasoned flour. Fry in the hot butter until brown. Remove the steak and sauté the onion in the pan until transparent. Add the steak, mushrooms, cream, and stock. Season with salt and pepper. Transfer to a buttered ovenproof dish and bake for 1½ hours in a moderate oven. Add the potatoes and cook for half an hour longer.

GRILLED STEAK

4–6-oz (125–185 g) pieces of fillet or rump steak
1 oz (30 g) butter, melted

pepper
salt

Pre-heat the griller and the grilling rack. Brush the steaks with butter, season with pepper, and grill for 1 minute. Turn the steaks, brush with more butter, and grill for 1 minute on the other side. Grill for about 3 minutes longer on each side for medium rare steak; 5 minutes on each side for medium-cooked steak; and 7 minutes on each side for well-done steak. The exact cooking times will vary according to the thickness of the steaks and the heat of the griller. When cooked, sprinkle with salt and transfer to heated plates. Top with a knob of flavoured butter if you wish (see page 62).

Serve with grilled tomatoes and mushrooms, mashed or fried potatoes, and a green vegetable.

BOILED CORNED BEEF

3–4 lb (1·5–2 kg) corned silverside or brisket
1 dsp sugar

10 peppercorns
5 cloves
1 tbsp vinegar

Wipe and weigh the meat. Put it in a deep saucepan and pour in enough cold water to cover. Bring slowly to the boil, then pour off the water. Cover the meat with boiling water and add the sugar, peppercorns, cloves, and vinegar. Cover and simmer, allowing 40 minutes per pound (500 grams). Top up with boiling water as needed. If the beef is to be served cold, allow it to cool in the cooking liquid.

Serve hot with boiled carrots, onions, and potatoes, dumplings (see below), and parsley sauce (see page 60) or mustard sauce (see page 60).

DUMPLINGS

4 oz (125 g) self-raising flour
a pinch of salt
1 tbsp butter
1 egg
¼ pt (150 ml) milk
2 tbsps finely chopped parsley
(optional)

Sift the flour and salt into a mixing bowl. Rub in the butter with the fingertips. Mix to a soft dough with the egg and milk, which have first been beaten with the parsley. Drop spoonfuls into the boiling cooking liquid; cover and simmer for 15 minutes.

BEEF HAM

1 aitch-bone piece of corned
silverside
½ cup brown sugar
1 tsp mixed spice
fat

Rub the meat with the sugar and spice. Leave overnight, or longer if possible. Turn occasionally, rubbing in the sugar and spice. When ready, cut into wafer-thin slices and fry quickly in hot fat. Alternatively, bake in a casserole and serve covered with gravy.
Serve with fried eggs.

ROAST LAMB WITH MINTED STUFFING

1 loin of lamb, boned
1 onion, finely chopped
1 oz (30 g) butter
2½ cups fresh breadcrumbs
2 stalks of celery, chopped
1 small carrot, grated
1 tsp grated lemon rind
½ tsp mixed herbs
1½ tbsps finely chopped mint
dripping or oil

Get your butcher to bone the loin of lamb for you. Make the stuffing: sauté the onion in the butter until tender; combine with the breadcrumbs, celery, carrot, lemon rind, herbs, and mint, mixing well. Roll the loin of lamb out flat and spread the stuffing over. Roll up, and tie or skewer so that the filling is held securely. Put in a roasting tin with a little dripping. Bake in a moderate oven, allowing 25 minutes per pound (500 grams).

LAMB CUTLETS AND MINT BUTTER

lamb cutlets
lemon juice
seasoned flour
1 egg, beaten
fresh breadcrumbs
thyme
butter

Mint Butter
several sprigs of mint
1 tbsp butter
½ tsp prepared mustard
juice of 1 lemon
1 tsp sugar

Take as many cutlets as required and dip them first in lemon juice and then in seasoned flour. Coat the cutlets in the egg and then cover with the breadcrumbs, which have been seasoned with thyme. Fry in butter until golden. Top each cutlet with a knob of mint butter before serving.
Mint Butter: Pour boiling water over a few sprigs of mint, then drain and chop finely. Cream the butter with the mint, mustard, and lemon juice. Add the sugar. Chill until firm.
Serve with mashed potatoes.

GRILLED LAMB CHOPS

Pre-heat the griller and grilling rack. Trim surplus fat from the chops. Grill the chops for 1 minute, then turn and grill for 1 minute on the other side. Continue grilling and turning frequently for about 10 minutes longer; the exact time will depend upon the thickness of the chops and the heat of the griller. Serve at once on heated plates, topping the chops with a savoury butter (see page 62) if you wish.
Serve with grilled tomatoes, boiled or mashed potatoes, and a green vegetable.

SAVOURY CHOPS

6–8 lamb chops
2 tbsps plain flour
1 tbsp sugar
¼ tsp ground ginger
¼ tsp dry mustard
¼ tsp curry powder
¼ tsp mixed spice
2 tbsps tomato sauce
2 tbsps vinegar
1 cup water, stock, or gravy
salt and pepper
chopped parsley

Trim fat from the chops and arrange them in a buttered casserole. Mix the other ingredients together, and pour over the chops. Leave to soak for 1 hour then bake for 2 hours in a slow oven.

TOMATO CASSEROLE

1½ lb (750 g) best end neck of
lamb chops
salt and pepper
butter
1 large onion, chopped
1 tbsp rice or barley
2 carrots, diced
2 parsnips, diced
1 small tin tomato soup
4–5 large potatoes, peeled and
halved

Trim the chops and sprinkle with salt and pepper. Brown on both sides in butter in a deep casserole. Add the onion and rice and enough water to cover. Cover and simmer gently for 1½ hours. Add the carrots and parsnips, and continue to simmer for half an hour. Stir the tomato soup into the casserole, arrange the potatoes on top, and continue to cook until the potatoes are soft. This dish can be made a day in advance and left to stand for the fat to rise. The final stages, including the addition of the tomato soup and potatoes, should be left until the casserole is reheated before serving.

MUTTON CHOPS WITH GRAPES

6 lean mutton chops
1 onion, sliced
2 tbsps vinegar
2 tbsps oil
½ tsp pepper
1 tsp salt
a pinch of herbs
1 lb (500 g) white grapes
1 tbsp butter
redcurrant jelly (see page 137)

Neatly remove the bone from the chops; flatten the meat. Form into rounds, securing with toothpicks and string or skewers. Lay the chops in a shallow dish and arrange the onion on top. Sprinkle over the vinegar, oil, pepper, salt, and herbs. Cover and leave to stand for 1 hour, turning the meat at least twice during this time. Remove the stems from the grapes, then wash, drain, and lightly dry them on a tea-towel. Drain the chops, then grill them for 4 to 5 minutes on each side. Meanwhile fry the grapes lightly in the butter for 5 minutes. Arrange the chops on a hot dish and garnish with the grapes and redcurrant jelly.

DEVILLED BREAST OF MUTTON

3-lb (1·5 kg) breast of mutton | ½ tsp mustard
4 tbsps sugar | 2 tbsps Worcestershire sauce
2 tbsps vinegar | 2 tbsps tomato sauce

Cut the mutton into serving-sized pieces. Simmer it slowly in enough boiling water to cover. When tender, drain and leave to cool. Mix the sugar with the vinegar, mustard, and tomato and Worcestershire sauces; pour over the meat. Leave to marinate overnight, turning the meat occasionally. Drain the meat and reserve the marinade to use as a sauce. Grill the meat carefully and heat the marinade in a small pan; pour the sauce over the meat before serving.

BOILED MUTTON

½ leg of mutton or hogget | 4 turnips, diced
4· carrots, sliced | salt and pepper
4 onions, sliced

Wipe the meat then put it in a large saucepan and cover with cold water. Bring slowly to the boil then remove scum from the top. Add the vegetables and seasoning. Cover, lower the heat, and simmer gently, allowing 25 minutes per pound (500 grams), plus an extra 25 minutes. Transfer the meat to a heated serving dish, surround with the vegetables, and keep hot. Make caper sauce (see page 61), using the hot cooking liquid instead of milk.

Serve with boiled potatoes.

IRISH STEW

2 lb (1 kg) best end neck of lamb chops | salt and pepper
2 lb (1 kg) potatoes, thinly sliced | approx. ¾ pt (475 ml) stock or water
8 oz (250 g) onions, thinly sliced | 2 tbsps finely chopped parsley

Trim the chops. Arrange the chops in layers in a saucepan, alternating them with layers of potatoes and onions, and seasoning generously; finish with a layer of potatoes. Add just enough stock or water to cover the ingredients. Bring to the boil then cover and lower the heat. Simmer gently for 2 to 3 hours, until tender. Alternatively, the stew may be cooked in a casserole in a moderate oven. Serve sprinkled with the parsley.

CASSEROLE CHOPS

1½ lb (750 g) mutton chops | ½ tsp curry powder
1 onion, sliced | ½ tsp dry mustard
2 tbsps plain flour | ½ tsp ground ginger
1¾ cups water |
2 tbsps tomato sauce |
1 tbsp brown sugar |
½ tsp mixed spice |

Trim the fat from the chops, and arrange them in a lightly greased ovenproof dish. Layer the onion over the chops. Blend the water into the flour in a mixing bowl, then stir in the remaining ingredients; pour over the chops. Allow to stand for 1 hour, then cover, and bake in a moderate oven for 1½ hours, or until the chops are tender.

FRICASSEE OF LAMB

2 lb (1 kg) neck of lamb chops | 2 lb (1 kg) peas, shelled
2 onions, finely sliced | ½ pt (315 ml) milk
3 sprigs of mint | salt and pepper
1 sprig of thyme | 1 tbsp cornflour

Chop the meat, trimming off fat. Put in a saucepan with enough water to cover and bring to the boil. Lower the heat and simmer gently for half an hour. Remove scum and add the onions, mint, and thyme; simmer for another half-hour. Add the peas and continue cooking until they are tender. Add the milk and bring to boiling-point. Blend the cornflour with a little water and stir into the pan until the liquid thickens; simmer for a few minutes longer.

Serve with new potatoes boiled in their jackets.

LAMB-CAKE

½ cup bread cubes | 3 tbsps dry red wine
milk | 3 tbsps cream
1 lb (500 g) minced raw lamb |
1 clove of garlic, crushed |
salt and pepper |
1 egg |
2 bacon rashers |

Soak the bread in milk for at least half an hour, then mix with the meat and garlic; season with salt and pepper. Bind with the egg. Pack into a loaf-tin and spread bacon rashers over the top. Bake in a moderate oven for 20 minutes. Pour over the wine and the cream, and return to the oven for 10 minutes longer. Turn out and serve.

ROAST PORK

Score the rind of a joint of pork at intervals, or get the butcher to do this. Secure the pork in a neat shape with string or skewers. Fill a boned joint with sage and onion stuffing (see page 36). Rub salt into the rind and stand the joint on a rack in a roasting tin. Cook in a pre-heated hot oven for half an hour, then reduce the temperature to moderate and continue cooking, allowing 30 minutes per pound (500 grams) plus an extra 30 minutes for loin of pork, and 45 minutes per pound (500 grams) plus an extra 45 minutes for leg of pork. Transfer the pork to a heated dish, remove the string or skewers, and keep hot. Pour off all but 1 tablespoon of fat from the roasting tin, stir in 1 tablespoon of plain flour, and cook for 2 or 3 minutes until brown. Gradually add ½ pint (315 millilitres) of stock or vegetable cooking liquid and stir until the gravy boils and thickens. Season and simmer for 2 or 3 minutes.

Serve with roast potatoes, apple sauce (see page 62) or cranberry sauce, and a green vegetable.

FRUIT-STUFFED PORK

2 cups dried apricots
juice and grated rind of 1 lemon
juice and grated rind of 1 orange
4 cups fresh breadcrumbs
½ cup walnuts
salt and pepper
4 oz (125 g) butter
1 loin of pork, boned

Soak the apricots, then stew them; drain and leave to cool. Chop the apricots and mix with the grated rind and juices. Stir in the breadcrumbs, walnuts, salt, pepper, and butter. Work all together and spread thickly over the pork. Roll up the meat and skewer well. Cook in a hot oven, allowing 35 minutes per pound (500 grams). Baste well while cooking.
Serve with mashed potatoes and other vegetables.

FRIED PORK CHOPS

8 large pork chops
butter
oil
2 cooking apples, peeled, cored, and thickly sliced

Coat the chops with flour, egg, and breadcrumbs if you wish and refrigerate for half an hour before cooking. Fry the chops in a little butter and oil until golden on each side and cooked through, about 20 minutes altogether. Fry the apple slices for a few minutes on each side while the chops are cooking. Drain the chops on paper and serve with the apple slices.
Serve with mashed potatoes and a green vegetable.

PORK CHOPS WITH APPLE AND PRUNES

2 oz (60 g) prunes, soaked and stoned
2 oz (60 g) rice, cooked
1 oz (30 g) fresh white breadcrumbs
1 green cooking apple, peeled, cored, and roughly chopped
juice and finely grated rind of ½ lemon
salt and pepper
1 egg
6 pork chops

Combine the prunes with the rice, breadcrumbs, apple, lemon rind and juice, and seasoning; bind with the egg. Trim the chops and divide the apple and prune mixture between them, spreading evenly over the top. Arrange the chops in one layer in a greased ovenproof dish and cover with greased greaseproof paper. Bake in a moderately hot oven for 1 hour, or until tender.
Serve with mashed potatoes and a green vegetable.

PORK PATTIES

8 oz (250 g) minced cooked pork
4 oz (125 g) minced bacon
4 oz (125 g) fresh white breadcrumbs
½ tsp mixed dried herbs
1 egg
¼ pt (150 ml) milk
salt and pepper
½ pt (315 ml) mustard sauce (see page 60)

Mix the pork with the bacon, breadcrumbs, and herbs; bind with the egg, which has been beaten with the milk. Season. Divide the mixture into equal portions and shape into 1-inch (2·5 centimetre) thick rounds. Arrange the patties on an ovenproof dish, pour over the sauce, and heat through in a moderately hot oven for 20 minutes.

PICKLED PORK

1 oz (30 g) powdered saltpetre
1½ lb (750 g) salt
8 oz (250 g) brown sugar
1 tsp allspice
1 leg of pork

Mix together the saltpetre, salt, sugar, and allspice; rub the mixture into the leg of pork. Keep the pork in a covered container and turn it daily for a fortnight, rubbing in more salt. Wash with cold water and put in a large saucepan with enough water to cover. Slowly bring to the boil and remove scum from the surface. Lower the heat and simmer gently for 3 hours, or until tender. This method of pickling is best in cold weather; in hot weather, it is preferable to pickle the meat in a brine solution. Heat 1 gallon (5 litres) of water with 1½ pounds (750 grams) of salt, 1 ounce (30 grams) of saltpetre, and 4 ounces (125 grams) of brown sugar; boil for about 20 minutes then strain into a container large enough to take the leg of pork and allow to cool. Add the meat, cover, and leave to stand for a fortnight. Wash the meat and cook as described above.

BAKED HAM

Soak the ham in water for 24 hours. Next day, dry the ham then trim and weigh it. Make a paste, allowing about 1 pound (500 grams) of plain flour for every 5 pounds (2·5 kilograms) of ham; mix to a stiff paste with water and spread all over the ham. Place in a roasting tin with 3 or 4 tablespoons of butter and bake for about 4 hours in a moderate oven. Remove the crust and skin, then cover with dried breadcrumbs.

SPICED BAKED HAM WITH SAUCE

1 ham
1 onion, stuck with 4 cloves
2 stalks of celery
1 large carrot, sliced
a bunch of parsley
6 peppercorns
1 bay-leaf
8 oz (250 g) brown sugar
4 oz (125 g) coarse breadcrumbs
extra cloves
juice of 1 orange and 1 lemon, or a little cider

Sauce
2 oz (60 g) brown sugar
a pinch of salt
½ pt (315 ml) cider
2 tbsps sultanas
1 tbsp cornflour
6 cloves and a stick of cinnamon tied in muslin

Soak the ham overnight in water. Next day, transfer it to a large pan, cover with water, and slowly bring to the boil. Add the onion, celery, carrot, parsley, peppercorns, and bay-leaf. Simmer gently, allowing 30 minutes per pound (500 grams). Leave the ham in the cooking liquid to cool, then strip off the skin. Mix the brown sugar with the breadcrumbs, and moisten with a little of the cooking liquid. Spread thickly over the ham, pressing in well, and stick with cloves. Bake the ham for 20 to 30 minutes in a hot oven. Meanwhile, strain off ½ cup of the remaining ham stock and mix it with the lemon and orange juice; baste the ham with this mixture. Serve hot or cold.

Sauce: Combine all the ingredients in a saucepan, and cook for 10 minutes, stirring until the sugar has dissolved and the mixture is blended. Remove the bag of herbs and pour the sauce over the ham.

BOILED HAM

Soak the ham in cold water overnight. Next day, put it in a large saucepan with enough water to cover and a bunch of herbs. Bring to the boil then lower the heat and simmer gently, allowing 25 minutes per pound (500 grams) plus an extra 25 minutes. If the ham is to be served hot, skin it and cover with dried breadcrumbs. If it is to be served cold, leave it to cool in the cooking liquid.

BOBOTIE

½ pt (315 ml) milk	1 tsp curry powder
1½ cups bread cubes	a pinch of salt
1 cup minced meat	1 egg, well beaten
1 small onion, minced	

Boil the milk, and then pour over the bread. Cover, and leave to soak for about half an hour. Add the mince, onion, curry powder, salt, and egg. Mix well. Pour into a greased pie-dish, and bake in a moderate oven for 20 to 30 minutes, or until well risen and golden.

SHEPHERD'S PIE

1½ lb (750 g) potatoes	2 tbsps finely chopped parsley
2 tbsps butter	approx. ½ pt (315 ml) stock
3 tbsps milk	
salt and pepper	
1 large onion, finely chopped	
1 lb (500 g) finely minced cooked lamb or beef	

Boil the potatoes, then drain them and mash with 1 tablespoon of the butter, the milk, and salt and pepper. Fry the onion gently in the remaining tablespoon of butter until soft and transparent. Mix the minced meat with the fried onion, parsley, and seasoning; add enough stock to make a soft, moist mixture. Transfer to an ovenproof dish and cover with the mashed potatoes, marking them with a fork. Cook near the top of a moderately hot oven for about 25 minutes, until golden and heated through.

MEAT FRITTERS

4 oz (125 g) plain flour	3 oz (90 g) mashed cold cooked vegetables
1 egg	
½ pt (315 ml) milk mixed with 2 tbsps water	salt and pepper
2 large onions, halved	butter
3 oz (90 g) diced cold cooked meat	

Sift the flour into a mixing bowl; make a well in the centre and break in the egg. Gradually draw the flour into the egg, then slowly add the milk and water, continuing to beat the flour in from the sides of the bowl. Beat thoroughly, and allow to stand for an hour or more. Parboil the onions and cut them roughly. Mix the onions with the meat and vegetables. Add to the batter, season, and mix well. Heat butter in a frying pan. Drop in spoonfuls of the mixture, and flatten to cook thoroughly. Fry slowly, turning the fritters when golden.
Serve with vegetables and gravy.

DEVILLED KIDNEYS

4 kidneys	1 dsp tomato sauce
2 tbsps plain flour	½ pt (315 ml) water
salt and pepper	1 dsp prepared mustard
2 tbsps butter	1 tbsp finely chopped parsley
1 onion, finely chopped	a pinch of cayenne pepper
1 dsp Worcestershire sauce	

Wash, skin, and core the kidneys, then slice them. Dredge them in the flour seasoned with salt and pepper. Fry the onion in the butter until soft and golden. Add the kidneys and cook gently for 5 minutes, turning several times. Mix the sauces and water with the mustard, parsley, and cayenne; add to the pan and cook slowly, stirring all the time, until the sauce thickens and boils. Cover and simmer gently for 15 minutes.
Serve with buttered toast.

TASTY KIDNEYS

4 sheep's kidneys	½ cup diced celery
3 tbsps seasoned plain flour	1 cup milk
3 bacon rashers, chopped	8 oz (250 g) tomato purée
2 medium onions, finely chopped	salt and pepper
3 tbsps chopped green pepper	chopped parsley

Wash the kidneys, remove the skin, and cut in half; remove fat and tubes. Soak in water for about 5 minutes. Roughly dice the kidneys, and toss in the seasoned flour. Lightly fry the bacon and kidneys, adding a little extra fat if necessary; brown well. Add the onions, green pepper, and celery; cook until the onion is lightly browned. Add the milk, purée, and salt and pepper, mixing thoroughly. Cover and simmer for 30 to 40 minutes. Garnish with parsley.
Serve with fingers of toast.

SAVOURY BAKED LIVER

1 calf's liver	stock, gravy, or water
butter	plain flour
breadcrumbs	Worcestershire sauce
bacon rashers	

Forcemeat Stuffing

1 cup fresh breadcrumbs	salt and pepper
2 shallots, finely chopped	1 egg
1 tbsp chopped parsley	milk
1 tsp mixed herbs	

Wash, dry, and trim the liver. Cut in slices about ¼ inch (5 millimetres) thick. Grease a shallow roasting tin thickly with butter. Sprinkle breadcrumbs generously over, shaking the dish so that they stick to the butter. Arrange the slices of liver in a single layer in the dish. Spread a large tablespoon of the stuffing over each piece of liver then cover each with a bacon rasher. Pour a little stock, gravy, or water into the dish and bake slowly for 40 minutes to 1 hour. Transfer the meat to a heated serving dish and keep hot. Thicken the gravy with a little blended flour and add Worcestershire sauce to flavour if you like.
Forcemeat Stuffing: Combine the breadcrumbs with the shallots, parsley, herbs, and salt and pepper. Mix to a stiff paste with the egg, and a little milk.
Serve with mashed potatoes.

LAMB'S FRY AND BACON

1 *lamb's liver*
8 *oz (250 g) bacon rashers*
1 *dsp plain flour*
salt and pepper
a pinch of dried herbs

½ *pt (315 ml) water*
1 *dsp tomato sauce*
sprigs of parsley

Wipe the liver. Remove the rind from the bacon and cut the rashers in half. Slice the liver thinly. Mix the flour with the salt and pepper and dried herbs; dredge the slices of liver in the flour mixture. Fry the bacon on each side; remove from the pan and keep hot. Add a little butter to the bacon fat and fry the liver gently for 4 to 5 minutes on each side. Remove the liver. Pour off all but 1 tablespoon of the fat; stir in the remaining herbed flour mixture and cook for 2 or 3 minutes. Gradually stir in the water and sauce and continue stirring until the sauce thickens and boils. Return the liver to the pan and heat through for 5 minutes or so. Serve with the bacon and the sauce, garnished with parsley.

TRIPE AND ONIONS

1 *lb (500 g) tripe*
1 *pt (625 ml) milk*
3 *onions, chopped*
salt and pepper

1 *tbsp butter*
1 *tbsp plain flour*
chopped parsley

Cover the tripe with the milk, add the onions and salt and pepper, and bring to the boil. Cover, lower the heat, and simmer gently for about 2 hours, or until tender. Strain and measure 1 pint (625 millilitres) of the liquid. Melt the butter in a clean saucepan, stir in the flour, and cook for 2 or 3 minutes without browning. Gradually stir in the cooking liquid and continue stirring until the sauce thickens and boils. Add the tripe and onions, check the seasoning, and heat through. Serve garnished with parsley.

BOILED TONGUE

1 *ox-tongue*
2 *onions, sliced*
2 *carrots, sliced*
2 *stalks of celery, sliced*

5 *peppercorns*
a few sprigs of parsley
herbs

Trim and wash the tongue. Soak it in cold water overnight. Next day, put the tongue in a saucepan with enough water to cover. Bring slowly to the boil then drain. Cover with fresh cold water, add the remaining ingredients, and bring to the boil. Cover, lower the heat, and simmer for 3 or 4 hours, or until tender, skimming occasionally. Drain and leave to cool slightly. Skin the tongue and remove any bones or gristle. If you are going to serve the tongue hot, sprinkle it with browned breadcrumbs and serve with parsley sauce (see page 60). If it is to be served cold, put it in a suitably sized cake-tin, add a little of the cooking liquid, and weight with a heavy object; leave to set.

BRAWN

½ *pig's or calf's head*
1 *large onion, peeled*
1 *large carrot, peeled*
1 *small turnip, peeled*
a bunch of fresh herbs

12 *peppercorns*
salt and pepper
grated nutmeg
1 *hard-boiled egg, sliced*

Wash the head thoroughly, then soak it for at least an hour in

salted water. Remove the brains. Put the head in a large saucepan with the vegetables, herbs, and peppercorns. Pour in enough water to cover the head and heat gently to boiling-point. Remove scum from the surface, cover, and cook slowly for 2 to 3 hours, or until very tender. Remove the meat. Strain the cooking liquid, return it to the saucepan with the brains tied in a muslin bag, and boil until it has reduced by half. Cut the meat into small, neat pieces and season with salt, pepper, and nutmeg. Arrange the sliced egg over the bottom of a mould that has been rinsed with cold water. Layer the meat over the egg and pour some of the reduced liquid over. Cover and put a weight on top; leave until cold and set. Turn out before serving.

STEWED OXTAIL

1 *oxtail*
1 *tbsp butter*
1 *large onion, sliced*
1 *carrot, sliced*
1 *turnip, diced*
a bunch of herbs or ½ *tsp mixed dried herbs*
¾ *pt (475 ml) water*

salt and pepper
1 *tbsp plain flour*
2 *tbsps finely chopped parsley*

Wipe the oxtail then cut it into neat joints, trimming off the fat. Fry the onion in the butter until soft and golden. Add the oxtail, the carrot, and the turnip. Fry over fairly strong heat for a few minutes, stirring. Add the herbs, water, and salt and bring to the boil. Lower the heat, cover, and simmer for 3 or 4 hours, or until tender. Remove the herbs and leave to stand overnight. Next day, remove the fat from the surface and heat the stew to boiling-point. Blend the flour with a little water and add to the stew; stir until boiling and thickened. Simmer for a few minutes longer then check the seasoning. Sprinkle with the parsley before serving.

BRAINS IN BATTER

2 *sets sheep or calf brains*
fat or oil

1 *lemon, sliced*

Batter

1 *cup self-raising flour*
a pinch of salt
1 *egg, separated*

⅓ *cup water*
⅓ *cup milk*
1 *tsp melted butter*

Wash the brains and soak them for at least an hour in cold water. Remove as much skin and membrane as possible under cold running water. Put the brains in a saucepan of boiling salted water and simmer for 5 minutes. Drain them and leave to cool. Cut them into small pieces. Coat them with the batter and then deep-fry them in hot fat or oil until golden. Drain on absorbent paper and serve garnished with lemon slices.

Batter: Sift the flour and salt into a mixing bowl and form a well in the centre; put the egg-yolk in the well and gradually draw the flour in from the sides, using a wooden spoon. Gradually add the water, milk, and melted butter in the same way and beat thoroughly. Fold in the egg-white, which has been stiffly beaten.

A Harvest of VEGETABLES

The colour and texture of vegetables are important elements to consider when planning meals. A plain vegetable such as asparagus or sweetcorn served with melted butter makes an excellent first course, while many vegetable dishes are suitable for light meals in themselves (for example, cauliflower with cheese sauce, stuffed marrow, or spinach casserole).

Vegetables should be bought in season whenever possible—they are then at their peak, cheap, plentiful, and with good flavour. They should ideally be used soon after picking or purchase; otherwise they should be stored in a cool, airy place away from strong light. Green, leafy vegetables will deteriorate quickly and must be kept cool. Prepare all vegetables as close to cooking time as practicable.

For boiling, root vegetables should be prepared and put in a saucepan with cold salted water, brought to the boil, covered, and cooked slowly. Green vegetables should be prepared and cooked briskly in boiling salted water in an uncovered saucepan. Steaming is a valuable cooking method for most vegetables. Prepare the vegetables and put them in a steamer or drainer with 2 or 3 inches (5 or 8 centimetres) of water; they will take about twice as long as boiled vegetables and they must be watched carefully, so that the water does not boil away. Much of the nutritional value of vegetables is in the skin, or just below the surface, so it is worthwhile to cook them unpeeled, even if you peel them when they are done; or at least peel or scrape them very thinly. Vegetables should never be overcooked and it will be necessary to test them, as the cooking times vary considerably, according to the age and size of the vegetable.

Serve vegetables as soon as they are cooked. Fried vegetables particularly should be drained well and served at once; do not cover them after cooking or they will become soggy. Boiled vegetables should be drained as soon as they are ready and the liquid kept for sauces, stews, or soup. Plain boiled or steamed vegetables are generally much improved if they are generously seasoned and tossed in butter before serving; most vegetables lack fat and the butter makes up the balance. A white sauce or cheese sauce offers variety to the standard vegetables such as onions, carrots, cauliflower, and marrow.

Dried vegetables, or pulses, need preliminary soaking before being cooked. Dried or split peas and haricot or butter beans need to be soaked overnight, then drained and heated to boiling-point in fresh water in a covered saucepan. They will have to be simmered for between half an hour and an hour. They can then be served hot with butter or a sauce, used in other dishes, or cooled for a salad. Lentils may be soaked for as little as 2 hours and then heated in the same way as other dried vegetables. For extra flavour, add herbs or a bacon bone or rinds to the cooking water.

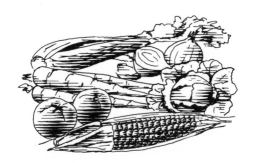

Cooking Times for Boiling Vegetables

Asparagus	15–20 minutes	Onions, small	30–45 minutes
Broad Beans	15–20 minutes	Onions, large	1–2 hours
French Beans	10–15 minutes	Parsnips	30–45 minutes
Beetroot	1–2 hours	Peas	10–20 minutes
Brussels Sprouts	8–15 minutes	Potatoes, new	15–20 minutes
Cabbage (shredded)	8–10 minutes	Potatoes, old	20–30 minutes
Carrots, new	15–20 minutes	Pumpkin	30 minutes
Carrots, old	20–30 minutes	Spinach	10–15 minutes
Cauliflower	15–20 minutes	Sweetcorn	5–12 minutes
Celery	20–30 minutes	Turnips	20–45 minutes
Leeks	10–15 minutes	Vegetable Marrow	20–30 minutes

Note: The minimum times are appropriate for new or finely cut vegetables, the maximum for old or whole vegetables.

ASPARAGUS

Scrape the asparagus, wash, and tie into bundles. Stand in a saucepan with enough boiling salted water to come halfway up the bundles; add a teaspoon of lemon juice and cook for about 20 minutes. Put a slice of toast in a heated vegetable dish; lift the asparagus on to this and pour melted butter over before serving.

FRENCH BEANS

1 lb (500 g) beans	pepper
1 oz (30 g) butter	

Top, tail, and string the beans. Slice diagonally and cook, uncovered, in boiling salted water for 15 minutes. Drain in a colander. Melt the butter in the saucepan, return the beans, season with pepper, and cover; toss over low heat for a minute or so before serving.

BOILED BEETROOT

Wash the beetroot carefully and trim without peeling. Cook in boiling salted water for 1 to 2 hours, until tender when pierced with a skewer. Drain and peel.

BRUSSELS SPROUTS

Remove any discoloured leaves and ends of stalks. Cut a cross in the stalks and soak the sprouts in salted water for half an hour. Cook in a little boiling salted water until tender. Drain in a colander. Return to the saucepan and toss with seasoning and a knob of butter.

SHARP CABBAGE

4 cups thinly shredded cabbage	¼ pt (150 ml) water
4 bacon rashers, chopped	⅛ pt (75 ml) vinegar
1½ tbsps plain flour	1 small onion, grated
1½ tbsps brown sugar	

Cook the cabbage in boiling salted water till tender. Cook the bacon in a small frying pan gently until fat flows, then quickly until the bacon is crisp; remove bacon. Stir the flour into the bacon fat, adding a little more fat if there is not enough to blend smoothly with the flour. Stir in the sugar, water, and vinegar, which have been heated together to simmering-point. Add the onion and cook, stirring all the time, till the sauce thickens. Stir in the cabbage and bacon and heat through.

BOILED CABBAGE

Wash the cabbage; remove the outer leaves, trim the stalk, and cut a cross in it. Soak in salted water for half an hour. Cook in boiling salted water for 20 minutes. Drain in a colander. Cut into wedges or chop. Return to the pan and toss briefly in butter. Sprinkle with pepper and serve.

CARROT PANCAKES

1 cup hot cooked carrots	¼ pt (150 ml) milk
1 tbsp butter	1 egg, beaten
4 oz (125 g) plain flour	extra butter
1 tsp baking powder	bacon rashers (optional)
½ tsp salt	

Mash the carrots with the butter. Sift the flour, baking powder, and salt into a mixing bowl. Beat to a smooth batter with the milk and the egg. Add the hot carrot pulp, beat until smooth, and cook spoonfuls on each side in sizzling butter. Serve with crisp-cooked bacon rashers.

GLAZED CARROTS

1 cup water	pepper
4 large carrots, sliced or diced	1 tsp sugar
1 oz (30 g) butter	

Heat the water to boiling-point in a small saucepan. Add the carrots, butter, pepper, and sugar. Simmer gently until the carrots are tender and the liquid has been absorbed.

CAULIFLOWER CHEESE

1 cauliflower	salt and pepper
milk	2 oz (60 g) grated cheese
1 oz (30 g) butter	paprika pepper
1 oz (30 g) plain flour	

Boil the cauliflower, uncovered, in milk until the stalks are tender when tried with a fork. Drain and reserve the milk. Put the cauliflower on an ovenproof plate. Melt the butter in a small saucepan, stir in the flour, and cook gently for 2 or 3 minutes. Gradually add the reserved milk, made up to ½ pint (315 millilitres) if necessary, and stir constantly until the sauce thickens and boils. Season well and stir in the cheese. Pour the sauce over the cauliflower, sprinkle with paprika, and heat through in the oven.

CAULIFLOWER AND TOMATOES

1 large cauliflower	2 tbsps butter
1 lb (500 g) medium tomatoes, thickly sliced	approx. ½ cup hot milk
	salt and pepper
2 tbsps seasoned plain flour	finely chopped parsley

Cook the cauliflower until tender in boiling water. Transfer to a heated serving dish and keep hot. Coat the tomato slices thoroughly with seasoned flour. Melt the butter in a frying pan. When hot, add the tomatoes, and cook on both sides. Arrange the tomato slices around the cauliflower. Stir the cooking juices left from the tomatoes; when smooth, gradually stir in enough milk to make a thin sauce. Add seasoning and parsley. Pour the sauce over the cauliflower.

Serve with fish.

CAULIFLOWER SOUFFLE

1 large cauliflower, parboiled	2 eggs, separated
3–4 tomatoes, sliced	2 oz (60 g) grated cheese
2 oz (60 g) butter	salt and pepper
2½ tbsps plain flour	fresh breadcrumbs
½ pt (315 ml) milk	finely chopped parsley

Break the cauliflower into sprigs. Layer the cauliflower and tomatoes in a well-greased ovenproof dish. Melt the butter; stir in the flour and cook gently for 2 or 3 minutes. Gradually add the milk, and stir constantly until the sauce thickens and reaches boiling-point. Remove from the heat and stir in the egg-yolks, cheese, and seasoning. Fold in the stiffly beaten egg-whites. Pour the sauce over the vegetables and sprinkle with breadcrumbs. Bake in a moderate oven for 20 to 30 minutes. Serve sprinkled with parsley.

CORN AND TOMATO SCALLOP

2 cups sweetcorn kernels
2 cups peeled and chopped
  tomatoes
½ cup finely chopped onion
1 dsp Worcestershire sauce
1 cup fresh breadcrumbs

2 tbsps cream
2 eggs, beaten
salt and pepper
buttered breadcrumbs mixed
  with grated cheese

Mix the corn with the tomatoes and onion. Add the sauce, breadcrumbs, cream, eggs, and salt and pepper. Transfer to a greased ovenproof dish. Sprinkle with a thick layer of buttered crumbs and cheese. Bake in a moderate oven for about 40 minutes.

CUCUMBER WITH TOMATO

1 large cucumber
2 oz (60 g) butter
salt and pepper
8 oz (250 g) sliced tomatoes

1 shallot, sliced
¼ pt (150 ml) water
plain flour

Peel the cucumber and cut into slices about ¼ inch (5 millimetres) thick. Melt 1 ounce (30 grams) of the butter in a saucepan. Add the cucumber, season with salt and pepper, and simmer gently for about 15 minutes. Carefully arrange on a heated ovenproof dish and keep hot in the oven. Cook the tomatoes and the shallot in the rest of the butter, adding the water and salt and pepper. When cooked, press though a sieve. Return to the saucepan, and thicken with a little flour blended with water. Simmer for a few minutes, then pour over the cucumber. Serve hot.

STUFFED MARROW

1 medium-sized vegetable
  marrow
12 oz (375 g) minced cooked
  meat
4 oz (125 g) fresh
  breadcrumbs
1 onion, chopped and fried
2 oz (60 g) chopped
  mushrooms

1 tsp finely chopped parsley
a pinch of dried herbs
salt and pepper
1 egg, beaten
a little stock
2 tbsps butter

Cut the marrow in quarters; remove seeds. Parboil in boiling salted water for about 10 minutes; drain. Mix together the meat, breadcrumbs, onion, mushrooms, parsley, and herbs; season and bind with the egg and stock. Put two portions of the marrow in the bottom of an ovenproof dish with the butter. Pack the stuffing on top, pressing down, and cover with the other portions of the marrow. Cover and cook in a moderate oven for about 1 hour, basting from time to time.

STEWED MUSHROOMS

1 lb (500 g) mushrooms
1 cup water
1 tbsp lemon juice

1 dsp butter
salt and pepper

Wash and trim the mushrooms, peeling or cutting if you wish. Bring the water to the boil in a small saucepan with the lemon juice, butter, and seasoning. Add the mushrooms and cook gently for 5 to 10 minutes. Drain and serve.

BAKED MUSHROOMS

8 oz (250 g) mushrooms
2 oz (60 g) grated cheese
salt

cayenne pepper
fresh breadcrumbs
butter

Wash and peel the mushrooms. Put in a greased ovenproof dish. Sprinkle over the cheese, salt, and cayenne pepper then cover with a thick layer of breadcrumbs. Dot with butter and bake in a moderate oven for 15 to 20 minutes.

CHEESED ONIONS

9 medium onions, peeled
1 tbsp butter
1 tbsp plain flour

¾ cup milk
salt and pepper
½ cup grated cheese

Cook the onions in boiling salted water until tender, then drain. Heat the butter then blend in the flour, and cook for 2 or 3 minutes; gradually add the milk, and cook slowly until thick, stirring constantly. Add seasoning and cheese, and stir until melted. Add onions, and heat through.

FRIED PARSLEY

Wash the parsley, remove stalks, and drain and dry thoroughly. Deep-fry for a few seconds until the fat has almost stopped bubbling. Drain and serve.

PARSNIP CHIPS

Take cold, boiled parsnips, which have been peeled either before or after boiling. Cut off the small ends and then cut the large ends in quarters, lengthwise. Dip in milk, roll in flour, then deep-fry in fat or oil until golden; drain on absorbent paper. Sprinkle with salt and serve hot.

DELICIOUS PEAS

peas
2 oz (60 g) butter
½ tsp salt

½ tsp sugar
1 sprig of mint

Shell as many peas as required, and put in a preserving jar with the butter, salt, sugar, and mint. Cover the jar closely and stand in a large saucepan of boiling water. Cook until the peas are tender. Remove mint and serve.

BUTTERED PEAS

2 lb (1 kg) peas
1 sprig of mint

a pinch of sugar
1 oz (30 g) butter

Shell the peas and cook, uncovered, in boiling salted water with the mint and sugar for 15 to 20 minutes, or until tender. Drain in a colander. Return to the saucepan with the butter; cover and toss for a minute or so before serving.

PEASE PUDDING

1½ lb (750 g) split peas
4 oz (125 g) butter
salt and pepper

3 egg-yolks
1 whole egg

Soak the peas for several hours; drain. Tie the peas loosely in a cloth and lower into a saucepan of cold water; bring to the boil and simmer for 2½ hours. When tender, drain, and rub through a sieve. Beat in the butter, salt and pepper, and eggs. Tie the mixture in a cloth again, and boil for another hour. Turn out on to a dish.

Serve hot with boiled leg of pork.

NEW POTATOES

1 lb (500 g) small new potatoes	1 dsp finely chopped parsley
1 oz (30 g) butter	pepper

Scrub the potatoes well and cook, unpeeled, in boiling salted water for about 15 minutes. Drain in a colander. Melt the butter in the saucepan with the parsley; return the potatoes to the pan, season with pepper, cover and heat through briefly, shaking the pan to coat the potatoes with the butter and parsley.

POTATO CHIPS

Wash and peel potatoes. Cut into chips. Dry in a tea-towel. Deep-fry in fat or oil until tender but still white. Remove from the fat and drain. Reheat the fat and replace the chips, cooking for a couple of minutes until they are puffed and golden. Drain on absorbent paper and sprinkle with salt before serving.

FARMHOUSE POTATOES

1 lb (500 g) potatoes	1 onion, sliced
2 slices of brown bread	pepper
butter	finely chopped parsley

Peel and quarter the potatoes. Cook in boiling salted water until almost tender. Drain and chop roughly. Meanwhile remove the crusts from the bread, cut into small squares and fry in butter until golden, using a large frying pan; remove and drain on absorbent paper. Add the onion to the pan and fry until tender. Add more butter and fry the potatoes until browned on all sides. Return the fried bread squares to the pan to heat through. Drain, transfer to a heated serving dish, season with pepper, sprinkle with parsley, and serve at once.

STUFFED POTATOES

6 large potatoes	1½ cups grated cheese
⅓ cup milk	chopped chives
2 oz (60 g) butter	salt and pepper

Wash the unpeeled potatoes. Dry, rub with oil, and prick in several places with a fork. Bake in a moderate oven for an hour, or until cooked through. Remove from the oven and slice off the tops. Scoop out the centres, making sure to keep the cases intact, and mash with the milk and butter. Beat in the cheese (reserving a few tablespoons) and chives and season generously. Return the filling to the potato cases, sprinkle with the remaining cheese, and return to the oven until the cheese is melted and golden.

CREAMED POTATOES

1 pt (625 ml) milk	1 onion, chopped
1 oz (30 g) butter	parsley
salt and pepper	
1 tsp cornflour	
a little extra milk	
6–7 large potatoes, diced	

Pour the milk into a frying pan, and add the butter and salt and pepper; bring to the boil. Blend the cornflour with a little cold milk and add to the pan, stirring all the time until thickened. Place the potatoes in the pan and add the onion and parsley. Cover, and simmer gently for 15 minutes. Serve in a hot dish.

STOVIES

1 lb (500 g) potatoes, sliced	water
1 large onion, sliced	
salt and pepper	
1 dsp dripping	

Layer the potatoes and onion in an ovenproof dish, seasoning as you go and ending with potatoes. Scatter over a few knobs of the dripping and add enough water to cover. Cook in a moderate oven until the water has been absorbed.

CHEESY POTATO CASSEROLE

1 lb (500 g) potatoes, sliced	½ cup milk
1 onion, finely chopped	½ cup grated cheese
salt and pepper	
butter	

Arrange the potatoes in a greased pie-dish. Sprinkle the onion and seasoning over and sprinkle with knobs of butter. Pour over the milk and top with the cheese. Bake in a moderate oven for at least 1 hour, until the milk is absorbed and the cheese forms a crust on top.

POTATO PIE

1½ lb (750 g) potatoes, diced	a little milk
1 oz (30 g) butter	parsley
2 onions, chopped	
3 oz (90 g) grated cheese	
4 eggs	
salt and pepper	

Parboil the potatoes. Melt the butter, and fry the onions gently. Put the potatoes, fried onion, and grated cheese in an ovenproof dish. Beat the eggs with salt and pepper and a little milk. Pour this mixture over the potatoes. Bake in a slow oven for 30 to 45 minutes. Serve garnished with parsley.

This dish may be varied, and made more substantial, by the addition of bacon or diced meat.

SPINACH CASSEROLE

1 large bunch of spinach	1 oz (30 g) butter
salt and pepper	1 oz (30 g) plain flour
nutmeg	¾ pt (475 ml) milk
cayenne pepper	8 oz (250 g) grated cheese
8 oz (250 g) bacon rashers, grilled and crumbled	extra grated cheese
	paprika pepper

Cook the spinach, uncovered, in a large saucepan of boiling salted water. Remove to a colander and leave under cold running water for a few minutes. Drain and squeeze as much moisture as possible from the leaves. Chop finely and season well with salt, pepper, nutmeg, and cayenne. Transfer to a greased shallow ovenproof dish. Scatter over the bacon. Melt the butter in a small saucepan; stir in the flour and cook for 2 or 3 minutes without browning. Remove from the heat and add the milk, which has been heated to boiling-point; beat vigorously with a wire whisk and return to the heat. Heat to boiling-point, stirring constantly. Beat in the cheese and season well with salt, pepper, and cayenne. Pour over the spinach. Sprinkle over some extra grated cheese and paprika. Heat through in a moderately hot oven until golden and bubbling.

BAKED TOMATOES

Choose small red tomatoes of equal size. Neatly cut out the stem and season. Put in a shallow ovenproof dish, stem end down, and cook for about 10 minutes in a moderately hot oven. Serve sprinkled with chopped fresh herbs.

PEELING TOMATOES

Put the ripe tomatoes in a bowl and cover with boiling water. Leave for a couple of minutes then drain. The skins should then slip off easily.

TOMATO PIE

4 tomatoes, sliced	fresh breadcrumbs
2 small onions, sliced	butter
salt and pepper	

Butter an ovenproof dish. Layer the tomatoes and onions in the dish, seasoning as you go. Cover with a thick layer of breadcrumbs and dot with butter. Cook in a moderate oven for about 45 minutes.

STUFFED TURNIPS

small turnips	1 tbsp diced ham
1 lb (500 g) cooked peas	1 dsp butter
salt and pepper	

Cook as many turnips as required in boiling salted water. Drain and scoop out the centres. Season the peas and combine with the ham and butter. Fill the turnips with the stuffing. If necessary, heat through in the oven for a few minutes.

VEGETABLE PIE

1 tbsp haricot beans	1 parsnip, sliced
2 oz (60 g) butter	1 tsp finely chopped parsley
1 head of celery, diced	salt and pepper
2 carrots, sliced	1 lb (500 g) potatoes, cooked
2 turnips, sliced	and mashed
1 large onion, sliced	

Soak the beans in cold water overnight. Next day, boil the beans until tender in the water in which they soaked. Melt the butter in a saucepan and add the vegetables, which have just been washed and still have some water on them. Cover closely, and cook gently until tender. Transfer the vegetables and their cooking juices to an ovenproof dish. Add the cooked beans, and mix in the parsley, and a generous amount of salt and pepper. Cover with the mashed potatoes, and bake in a moderate oven until brown.

SALADS

Fresh salads are excellent and healthful additions to meals at any time of the year, while hearty meat, fish, or egg salads constitute a meal in themselves. Salads look attractive if they are served in bowls or platters of contrasting colour, perhaps lined with crisp lettuce shredded or in leaves, and garnished with bright ingredients.

Salad greens should be separated, washed well, drained, and dried in a tea-towel. This is best done in advance so that the leaves can then be wrapped securely and put in the refrigerator to crisp. The dressing can also be prepared and chilled but must not be added until the last possible moment, or the salad will become soggy. The dressing should be well seasoned and there should be just enough to moisten the salad, without leaving a pool of surplus liquid in the bottom of the bowl.

Cooked vegetables can form the basis of first-rate salads in the winter or when a more filling salad is wanted; individual or mixed vegetables simply need the addition of one of the standard dressings and fresh or dried herbs as available. Cooked vegetables can be diced, sliced, or cut in straws; they should generally be allowed to cool before use and they must be thoroughly drained.

Garnishes for Salads

Celery curls—short strips of celery with fringe-like cuts, soaked in water for an hour or so and then drained.

Cucumber—sliced and unpeeled green cucumber, which has been scored with a fork.

Gherkins, sliced or chopped.

Hard-boiled eggs—slices, wedges, mashed yolks, or finely chopped whites.

Herbs—freshly chopped parsley, chives, dill, mint, tarragon, and so on.

Nuts, chopped.

Radish roses—make half a dozen deep cuts around one end of each radish, soak in cold water for an hour or so, and drain.

Spring onions, sliced or whole with a few inches of green left on and sliced down two or three times.

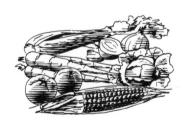

BEETROOT MOULD

2 large beetroot	½ cup vinegar
1 tbsp gelatine	salt and pepper
1¼ cups hot water	sugar

Slice enough beetroot to line a mould. Chop the rest and put in the mould. Sprinkle the gelatine over the hot water; dissolve. Add the vinegar, seasoning, and a little sugar. Leave until beginning to thicken, then pour over the beetroot and leave to set and chill.

Serve garnished with shredded lettuce and accompanied with mayonnaise (see page 62).

COMPLEXION SALAD

¼ cup cold water	1 dsp onion juice
1 tsp gelatine	¾ cup finely grated cabbage
¼ cup sugar	1 dsp chopped parsley or raw
1 tsp salt	spinach
1 cup hot water	¾ cup finely grated carrot
¼ cup vinegar	lettuce leaves or watercress
1 tbsp lemon juice	mayonnaise (see page 62)

Sprinkle the gelatine over the cold water in a bowl; leave to soak. Add the sugar, salt, and hot water and stir until the gelatine and sugar have dissolved. Add the vinegar, lemon juice, and onion juice. Chill. When the mixture begins to stiffen, add the remaining ingredients. Turn into a mould that has been rinsed with cold water; chill.

To serve, turn out on to a bed of lettuce leaves or watercress and garnish with mayonnaise.

ASPARAGUS MOULD

1 tin asparagus tips	juice of 1 lemon
1 tsp salt	pepper
2 thin white stalks of celery,	1½ tbsps gelatine
finely chopped	shredded lettuce

Drain the liquid from the asparagus into a saucepan and make up to 1½ pints (940 millilitres) with water. Add the salt, half the celery, the lemon juice, and pepper; bring to the boil and stir in the gelatine until dissolved. Arrange some of the asparagus tips in a mould with the remaining celery. Add the remaining asparagus to the liquid and pour into the mould. Leave to set and chill. Turn out and serve on a bed of shredded lettuce.

TOMATO AND CUCUMBER CREAM SALAD

4 tomatoes, sliced	salt
1 cucumber, peeled and sliced	cayenne pepper
1 tbsp cream	
juice of 1 lemon	
2 tbsps oil	

Arrange the tomatoes and cucumber in a glass dish. Put the cream in a small bowl; gradually beat in the lemon juice, and then the oil. Season with salt and cayenne and pour over the salad.

TOMATO SALAD

4–6 ripe red tomatoes	1 quantity French dressing.
1 small onion or 3 spring	(see page 63)
onions, chopped	1 tbsp chopped fresh parsley
salt and pepper	or chives

Slice the tomatoes or cut into small wedges. Put in a dish, and sprinkle over the onion and salt and pepper. Pour over the dressing and sprinkle with the herbs.

STUFFED TOMATOES

Peel large firm tomatoes (see page 54). Remove a thin slice from the top of each and scoop out the seeds and a little of the pulp. Sprinkle with salt, invert, and leave to stand for half an hour. Fill and leave to stand for half an hour in the refrigerator. Serve with lettuce.

Suggested Fillings

* Chopped chicken with shredded pineapple and mayonnaise
* Crabmeat mixed with equal parts of chopped celery and mayonnaise
* Cold cooked potato mixed with cold chopped carrots, green peas, chopped celery, and mayonnaise
* Equal parts of cold salmon and chopped cucumber mixed with mayonnaise
* Cold, grilled bacon mixed with sardines, tomatoes, and mayonnaise
* Caviare and cooked rice mixed with mayonnaise
* Cream cheese mixed with chopped gherkin, green pepper, stuffed olives, and mayonnaise

POTATO SALAD

2 lb (1 kg) boiled potatoes	salt and pepper
1 onion, finely chopped	1 cup mayonnaise or salad
chopped fresh mint, parsley,	dressing (see page 62)
and chives	

Dice the potatoes and put in a large mixing bowl with the onion and herbs. Cover and chill. Season well, pour in the mayonnaise, and toss thoroughly before serving.

HEARTY POTATO SALAD

2 lb (1 kg) boiled potatoes	chopped fresh dill and parsley
1 medium onion, chopped	1 quantity French dressing
2 hard-boiled eggs, chopped	(see page 63)
2 gherkins, chopped	salt and pepper

Chop the potatoes while still warm and mix with the onion, eggs, gherkins, and herbs in a large mixing bowl. Pour over the dressing, toss, and adjust the seasoning. Serve warm or chilled.

CARROT SALAD

2 cups cooked carrot straws or	chopped fresh parsley or chives
dice	
1 quantity well-seasoned	
French dressing (see page 63)	

Toss the carrots in the dressing, sprinkle with fresh herbs, and serve.

CELERY AND CHEESE SALAD

3 cups chopped celery
1½ cups diced cheese
salad dressing (see page 63)
salt and pepper

crisp lettuce leaves
2 tomatoes

Put the celery and cheese in a mixing bowl, pour over enough salad dressing to moisten, and toss; check the seasoning. Pile the salad on to lettuce leaves arranged on a platter. Garnish with small wedges of tomato.

PINEAPPLE CHEESE SALAD

cottage cheese
salt and pepper
chopped walnuts
crisp lettuce leaves
slices of pineapple

extra walnut halves

Season the cheese and stir in chopped walnuts. Form into small balls. Arrange lettuce on a platter and top with drained pineapple slices with a cheese ball in the centre of each. Garnish with walnut halves.

PINEAPPLE AND MANGO SALAD

1 sweet ripe pineapple,
    peeled, cored, and sliced

ripe mangoes, sliced
salad dressing (see page 63)

Place a layer of the pineapple slices in the bottom of a glass dish; add a layer of mangoes. Repeat the layers until the dish is full. Pour the dressing over the fruit half an hour before serving. Chill. Serve with cold meat.

PRUNE SALAD

4 tbsps cream cheese
1½ tbsps chopped celery
½ tsp chopped shallot or onion
24 large soft prunes, stoned
a few crisp lettuce leaves

a little shredded raw carrot
mayonnaise (see page 62) or
    French dressing (see page
    63)

Cream the cheese with the celery and onion. Fill the cavity of the prunes with the mixture. Arrange lettuce leaves on individual serving plates and place some stuffed prunes on each, decorating with a little carrot. Serve with mayonnaise or French dressing.

APPLE SALAD

red apples
⅓ cup chopped apple
⅓ cup chopped celery
⅓ cup peanuts
½ quantity French dressing
    (see page 63)

mayonnaise (see page 62)
shredded lettuce
sprigs of parsley
hard-boiled egg-yolk, chopped
grated lemon rind

Core the apples. Mix the chopped apple, celery, and peanuts with the dressing. Fill the apples with the mixture. Drop a teaspoon of mayonnaise on each apple before serving on shredded lettuce. Garnish with parsley, egg-yolk, and lemon rind.

ORANGE SALAD

2 large oranges, peeled and
    sliced
1 medium onion, thinly sliced
2 stalks of celery, chopped

1 quantity French dressing
    (see page 63)
chopped parsley

Arrange the oranges and onion in layers in a dish. Sprinkle over the celery. Chill. Pour over the dressing and garnish with parsley.

WALDORF SALAD

6 unpeeled red apples
juice of 1 lemon
1½ cups diced celery
½ cup chopped walnuts

¾ cup mayonnaise (see page
    62) or salad dressing (see
    page 63)
salt and pepper

Dice the apples and sprinkle with the lemon juice to prevent them from discolouring. Add the celery and walnuts and pour over the mayonnaise. Toss carefully and check the seasoning. Cream may be used instead of mayonnaise.

SALMON SALAD

2 hard-boiled egg-yolks
1 tsp mustard
1 tbsp oil
4 tbsps vinegar

4 tbsps cream
1 large tin salmon, drained
    and flaked
crisp lettuce leaves

Mash the egg-yolks and blend in the mustard, then the oil, vinegar, and cream. Fold the salmon in carefully and chill. Serve on a platter lined with lettuce leaves.
  Garnish with parsley, sliced radishes, and asparagus spears.

CHICKEN SALAD

2 tbsps chutney
½ pt (315 ml) salad dressing
    (see page 63)
salt and pepper
2 cups diced cooked chicken

1 cup diced celery
crisp lettuce leaves
2 tomatoes
sprigs of parsley

Mix the chutney into the dressing; season. Combine the chicken and celery, pour over the dressing, and toss. Arrange lettuce leaves on a platter and fill with the salad. Decorate with wedges of tomato and sprigs of parsley.

MEAT AND RICE SALAD

1 cup cold cooked rice
1 cup cold cooked meat or
    poultry
1 cup diced celery or cooked
    peas

1 tbsp chopped fresh herbs
½ cup mayonnaise (see page
    62)
salt and pepper

Mix together the rice, meat, celery, and herbs. Pour over the mayonnaise, season well, and toss.

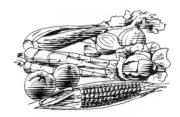

Superior
SAUCES and
DRESSINGS

The main purpose of a sauce is to improve the flavour and appearance of the accompanying food. It follows that the plainer the dish, the more important is the quality of the sauce. An interesting and nourishing sauce can transform vegetables, eggs, or pasta, for example, into a complete meal.

Sauces are usually thickened and there are two main ways of achieving this, both with the use of flour: the roux method, in which melted butter and flour are cooked together before liquid is added; and the blending method, which normally uses cornflour, mixed to a smooth paste and then combined with heated liquid—this method is common for sweet sauces and requires little, if any, fat. It is essential that the flour in a sauce should be thoroughly cooked and that the sauce should be smooth. The seasoning should be carefully checked at all stages.

The consistency of sauce made by either method can, of course, be varied by the amount of flour used: thin or pouring sauce, thick or coating sauce, and very thick binding sauce are the usual types. If a sauce is too thick, add more liquid; if it is too thin, reduce it over high heat. A lumpy sauce should be beaten hard and, if necessary, passed through a sieve.

The liquid in a sauce depends to some extent upon the food with which it is to be served. For a white sauce, the liquid should be milk or white stock; brown sauce and gravy are made with stock or vegetable cooking liquid; a sauce for fish is best made with fish stock or milk.

Sauce can be kept warm in a double saucepan or a water bath with a covering of buttered paper so that a skin does not form on top. Cold sauce should be reheated very gently to prevent lumps from forming.

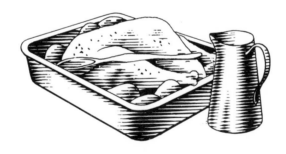

WHITE SAUCE—Roux Method

Pouring Sauce
½ pt (315 ml) milk   1 tbsp plain flour
1 tbsp butter   salt and pepper

Heat the milk to just below boiling-point. Melt the butter in a saucepan; stir in the flour and cook gently for 2 or 3 minutes without browning. Remove from the heat and add the hot milk, beating vigorously with a whisk. Return to the heat and bring to the boil, stirring constantly with a wooden spoon. When the sauce has thickened, cook for 1 or 2 minutes longer. Season to taste.

Coating Sauce
½ pt (315 ml) milk   2 tbsps plain flour
2 tbsps butter   salt and pepper

Make in the same way as for white pouring sauce (see above).

Binding Sauce
½ pt (315 ml) milk   3 tbsps plain flour
3 tbsps butter   salt and pepper

Make in the same way as for white pouring sauce (see above). Use for binding mixtures.

WHITE SAUCE—Blending Method

Pouring Sauce
1 tbsp cornflour   1 dsp butter
½ pt (315 ml) milk   salt and pepper

Blend the cornflour to a smooth paste with a little of the milk. Heat the remaining milk with the butter until boiling-point is reached; pour over the cornflour, beating all the time. Return to the pan and bring to the boil, stirring constantly. Cook for 1 or 2 minutes longer then season to taste.

Coating Sauce
2 tbsps cornflour   1 dsp butter
½ pt (315 ml) milk   salt and pepper

Make in the same way as for white pouring sauce (see above).

PARSLEY SAUCE

1–2 tbsps finely chopped   ½ pt (315 ml) white coating
parsley   sauce (see above)

Stir the parsley into the hot white sauce.
  Serve with vegetables, fish, or meat.

CHEESE SAUCE

2–4 tbsps grated cheese   a pinch of cayenne pepper
½ pt (315 ml) white coating
  sauce (see above)
a pinch of mustard

Stir the cheese into the hot white sauce and continue stirring until it has melted. Adjust the seasoning with mustard and cayenne.
  Serve with vegetables, pasta, eggs, or fish.

EGG SAUCE

1 hard-boiled egg, finely   ½ pt (315 ml) white coating
chopped   sauce (see this page)
1 tbsp finely chopped chives

Stir the egg and the chives into the hot white sauce and check the seasoning. Heat through gently.
  Serve with fish or poultry.

MUSTARD SAUCE

1 tbsp dry mustard   ½ pt (315 ml) white coating
1 tsp sugar   sauce (see this page)
1 tbsp vinegar

Blend the mustard and sugar with the vinegar. Stir into the hot white sauce and heat through.
  Serve with fish, ham, or bacon.

CURRY SAUCE

1 tbsp butter   ½ tsp curry paste
1 small onion, chopped   ½ pt (315 ml) milk
1 tbsp plain flour   salt
1 dsp curry powder   a squeeze of lemon juice

Melt the butter in a small pan, and fry the onion. Stir in the flour, curry powder, and curry paste. Cook for a few minutes. Add the milk gradually, stirring constantly, and then add salt. Cook gently in a covered pan until thick. When ready add lemon juice. Strain before serving.
  Serve with vegetables, eggs, fish, or meat.

ONION SAUCE

1 large white onion, boiled   ½ pt (315 ml) white coating
and chopped finely   sauce (see this page)

Stir the onion into the hot white sauce and check the seasoning. Heat through gently.
  Serve with lamb, tripe, or chicken.

MUSHROOM SAUCE

2–3 oz (60–90 g) sliced   ½ pt (315 ml) white coating
mushrooms fried in butter   sauce (see this page)

Stir the fried mushrooms into the hot white sauce and check the seasoning. Heat through.
  Serve with fish, meat, or poultry.

CUCUMBER SAUCE

2 oz (60 g) butter   a few drops of lemon juice
1 cucumber, peeled and sliced
½ pt (315 ml) white coating
  sauce (see this page)

Melt the butter in a pan and fry the cucumber slices until lightly browned. Add the cucumber to the hot white sauce and stir in the lemon juice.
  Serve with fish.

CAPER SAUCE

1 tbsp capers
1–2 tbsps juice from the capers

½ pt (315 ml) white coating sauce (see page 60)

Stir the capers and juice into the hot white sauce and make sure that it is generously seasoned.
 Serve with lamb or herrings.

ANCHOVY SAUCE

1 tsp anchovy essence
¼ tsp lemon juice

½ pt (315 ml) white coating sauce (see page 60)

Add the anchovy essence and lemon juice to the hot white sauce. Stir well.
 Serve with fish.

WINE SAUCE FOR FISH

¼ pt (150 ml) milk
¼ pt (150 ml) fish stock
1–2 tbsps butter
1–2 tbsps plain flour

salt and pepper
¼ pt (150 ml) dry white wine

Heat the milk and fish stock. Melt the butter in a saucepan; stir in the flour and cook for 2 or 3 minutes over a gentle heat. Remove from the heat and beat in the hot liquid; return to the heat and bring to the boil, stirring constantly. Season to taste and stir in the wine; heat through gently for 10 minutes.

SHRIMP SAUCE

2 oz (60 g) finely chopped shrimps
1 egg-yolk
a pinch of mustard
1 dsp lemon juice

a few drops of red food colouring (optional)
½ tsp anchovy essence
½ pt (315 ml) white coating sauce (see page 60)

Beat the shrimps, egg-yolk, mustard, lemon juice, colouring, and anchovy essence into the hot white sauce. Reheat gently.
 Serve with fish.

HOLLANDAISE SAUCE

2 tbsps hot water
1 tbsp lemon juice
3 egg-yolks
4 oz (125 g) diced softened butter

salt and pepper
a pinch of cayenne pepper

Beat the water, lemon juice, and egg-yolks in a double saucepan or a bowl over hot water; the water must not boil and the bowl must not touch the water. Stir constantly until the mixture thickens. Gradually add the butter, piece by piece, letting each piece melt and blend into the sauce before adding another. Do not allow the sauce to boil or it will curdle. When all the butter has been added and the sauce is thickened, season with salt, pepper, and cayenne.
 Serve hot or cold with vegetables, eggs, fish, or poultry.

MOCK HOLLANDAISE SAUCE

½ pt (315 ml) white coating sauce (see page 60)
1 egg-yolk
a few drops of vinegar

a few drops of lemon juice

Allow the white sauce to cool slightly, then mix a tablespoon of the sauce with the egg-yolk. Beat this mixture into the remaining white sauce. Reheat to boiling-point then add the vinegar and lemon juice.
 Serve with poultry or fish.

BREAD SAUCE

1 onion
2 cloves
½ pt (315 ml) milk
½ small bay-leaf
1 blade of mace
a few peppercorns
3 oz (90 g) fine fresh breadcrumbs

1 oz (30 g) butter
salt and pepper

Stick the cloves into the peeled onion and put it in a saucepan with the milk, bay-leaf, mace, and peppercorns. Heat gently to boiling-point. Cover and simmer for 15 minutes. Strain and combine with the breadcrumbs and butter. Season to taste and return to the pan to heat through.
 Serve with poultry.

TARTARE SAUCE

1 egg-yolk
2 tbsps cream
1 tbsp finely chopped parsley
1 dsp finely chopped gherkins
1 dsp finely chopped capers

½ pt (315 ml) white coating sauce (see page 60)

Beat the egg-yolk, cream, parsley, gherkins, and capers into the hot white sauce; check the seasoning. Heat through gently.
 Serve with fish.

TOMATO SAUCE

2 tbsps butter
1 small onion, sliced
1 small carrot, sliced
1 small clove of garlic, sliced

8 oz (250 g) sliced tomatoes
½ pt (315 ml) water
salt and pepper
1 tbsp plain flour

Melt 1 tablespoon of the butter in a frying pan, and fry the onion, carrot, and garlic lightly. Add the tomatoes and water. Season with salt and pepper. Cover and simmer for about 10 minutes. Strain through a sieve. Melt the remaining butter, blend in the flour, and cook gently for a few minutes. Add the strained tomato purée. Bring to the boil, stirring all the time. Adjust the seasoning and simmer for 2 or 3 minutes longer.
 Serve with vegetables, eggs, fish, or meat.

TOMATO GRAVY

1 tbsp butter   1 cup strained tomato pulp
1 dsp plain flour

Melt the butter; blend in the flour and cook, stirring well, until brown. Add the tomato pulp. Stir until the sauce boils and is smooth.
  Serve with meat.

BASIC BROWN SAUCE

2 tbsps butter   3 tbsps plain flour
1 small carrot, sliced $2\frac{1}{2}$ cups stock or water
1 onion, sliced   salt and pepper

Melt the butter and fry the vegetables until brown. Add the flour and cook slowly until it is a good brown colour. Remove from the heat and add the liquid gradually, mixing until smooth. Return to the heat and bring to the boil, stirring constantly. Simmer for a few minutes. Skim, strain, and reheat before using. Check the seasoning.
  Serve with vegetables, fish, meat, or poultry.

HORSERADISH CREAM

$\frac{1}{3}$ pt (200 ml) cream   1 tsp sugar
3 tbsps bottled horseradish, $\frac{1}{2}$ tsp salt
  drained $\frac{1}{2}$ tsp pepper
$\frac{1}{2}$ tsp dry mustard
1 tbsp vinegar

Beat the cream until stiff. Mix together all the remaining ingredients then fold them into the cream.
  Serve with roast beef, herrings, or smoked trout or eel.

APPLE SAUCE

1 lb (500 g) cooking apples,   2 tbsps water
  peeled, cored, and sliced   1 tbsp butter
1 tbsp sugar

Put the apples in a saucepan with the sugar and water and bring to the boil. Simmer gently until tender, about 10 minutes. Beat to a pulp and add the butter.
  Serve with duck, pork, or sausages.

MINT SAUCE

3 tbsps finely chopped mint   3 tbsps vinegar
3 tbsps boiling water
1 tbsp sugar
a pinch of salt

Pour the boiling water over the mint. Add the sugar and salt and leave to cool. Add the vinegar and mix well.
  Serve with lamb.

MUSTARD BUTTER

2 tbsps butter   1 tsp prepared mustard

Cream the butter then beat in the mustard. Chill until firm.
  Serve with meat or fish.

MAITRE D'HOTEL BUTTER

2 tbsps butter   juice of $\frac{1}{2}$ lemon
pepper
1 tbsp finely chopped parsley

Cream the butter then beat in the remaining ingredients. Chill until firm.
  Serve in pats on steaks or fish.

ANCHOVY BUTTER

2 tbsps butter   1 tsp lemon juice
1 tsp anchovy essence

Cream the butter then beat in the remaining ingredients. Chill until firm.
  Serve with steak or fish.

DEVILLED BUTTER

2 tbsps butter   1 tsp lemon juice
$\frac{1}{2}$ tsp prepared mustard   a pinch of cayenne pepper
1 tsp Worcestershire sauce

Cream the butter then beat in the remaining ingredients. Chill until firm.
  Serve with ham or bacon.

GARLIC BUTTER

2 cloves of garlic, finely   2 tbsps butter
  chopped

Cream the butter then beat in the garlic. Chill until firm.
  Serve with steak.

MAYONNAISE

2 egg-yolks $\frac{1}{2}$ pt (315 ml) oil
$\frac{1}{2}$ tsp prepared mustard   1–2 tbsps vinegar or lemon
$\frac{1}{2}$ tsp salt   juice
$\frac{1}{4}$ tsp pepper

Beat the egg-yolks with the mustard, salt, and pepper. Add half the oil, *drop by drop*, beating vigorously all the time. Add the remaining oil by dessertspoonfuls until it is all used and the sauce is thick and smooth. Gradually add the vinegar, mixing well. Adjust the seasoning as you wish. Keep refrigerated in a covered container.

HEALTH MAYONNAISE

1 egg   2 cups olive oil
1 tsp salt   2 tbsps lemon juice

Break the egg into a bowl and beat slowly for 30 seconds. Add the salt, and beat until light and fluffy. Add a teaspoon of the olive oil, and beat well. Add another teaspoon of oil, and beat again. Repeat this process until all the oil is used, by which time the mixture should be almost too thick to stir. Stir in the lemon juice, a teaspoon at a time.

UNCOOKED TARTARE SAUCE

½ pt (315 ml) mayonnaise (see page 62)
1 tbsp finely chopped gherkins
1 tbsp finely chopped capers
1 tbsp finely chopped parsley
1 dsp chopped tarragon or chives
2 tbsps lemon juice
salt and pepper

Mix all the ingredients together and chill before serving. Serve with fish.

FRENCH DRESSING

3 tbsps oil
1 tbsp vinegar or lemon juice
1 tsp dry mustard
1 tsp salt
freshly ground black pepper

Shake all the ingredients together in a screw-top jar. Chill before using.

QUICK SALAD DRESSING

1 tbsp dry mustard
1 dsp salt
1 tbsp plain flour
½ tsp pepper
2 tbsps sugar
1 tbsp oil or butter
1 egg
1 pt (625 ml) milk
½ pt (315 ml) vinegar

Blend the mustard with the salt, flour, pepper, sugar, and oil or butter. Beat the egg, add the milk, and stir gradually into the other ingredients. Add the vinegar gradually. Pour into a saucepan, and stir until boiling. Cook for 5 minutes, stirring all the time. Bottle when cold.

BOILED SALAD DRESSING

2 eggs
1 tsp dry mustard
salt and pepper
2 tbsps sugar
¼ pt (150 ml) milk
4 tbsps vinegar
1 tbsp butter

Beat the eggs with the mustard, salt and pepper, and sugar. Beat in the milk and then the vinegar. Melt the butter in a small saucepan and pour in the beaten mixture. Stir constantly over low heat until it thickens. Store in a covered container in the refrigerator.

UNCOOKED SALAD DRESSING

2 eggs
1 tsp salt
½ tsp pepper
1 tsp dry mustard
1 tin sweetened condensed milk
1 cup vinegar

Beat the eggs with the salt, pepper, and mustard. Beat in the milk gradually and then the vinegar, a little at a time. Beat thoroughly then store in a screw-top jar.

SWEET WHITE SAUCE

1 tbsp cornflour
½ pt (315 ml) milk
1 tbsp castor sugar
1 tsp butter

Mix the cornflour to a paste with a little of the milk. Heat the rest of the milk to just below boiling-point; pour over the cornflour, beating constantly, then return to the saucepan. Heat slowly, stirring constantly, to boiling-point. Simmer for 2 minutes. Remove from the heat and stir in the sugar and butter.
Serve with puddings.

FRUIT SAUCE

1 tbsp cornflour
2 tbsps sugar
½ pt (315 ml) fruit juice or syrup
1 dsp lemon juice
1 dsp butter
2 tbsps chopped cherries
a dash of liqueur or sherry

Blend the cornflour and sugar with a little of the fruit syrup. Bring the remaining syrup to the boil and stir it into the cornflour. Return to the pan, and cook gently for 5 minutes, stirring all the time. Remove from the heat, and stir in the lemon juice, butter, and chopped cherries. Add the liqueur or sherry, and stir.
Serve with puddings or ice-cream.

CHOCOLATE SAUCE

1 tbsp cornflour
½ pt (315 ml) milk
2 oz (60 g) grated chocolate
½ tsp vanilla essence
1 tsp butter
1½ tbsps sugar

Mix the cornflour to a paste with a little of the milk. Heat the remaining milk in a saucepan with the chocolate. When the chocolate has melted, pour the hot liquid on to the cornflour, stirring all the time. Return to the pan and bring to the boil, stirring constantly. Add the vanilla, butter, and sugar and continue simmering for 2 or 3 minutes.
Serve with puddings.

LEMON SAUCE

1 tbsp arrowroot or cornflour	a little grated nutmeg
½ pt (315 ml) water	1 dsp butter
3 oz (90 g) sugar	
1 tsp grated lemon rind	
2 tbsps lemon juice	

Mix the arrowroot or cornflour to a smooth paste with a little of the water. Bring the remaining water to the boil and pour it over the arrowroot. Mix until smooth, and return to the saucepan. Add the sugar and lemon rind and juice. Boil for 5 minutes until clear. Stir in the nutmeg and butter.
    Serve with puddings.

JAM SAUCE

1 dsp cornflour or arrowroot	1 dsp lemon juice
¼ pt (150 ml) water	1 tbsp sugar
4 tbsps jam	

Blend the cornflour to a smooth paste with a little of the water. Heat the rest of the water in a saucepan with the jam, lemon juice, and sugar; stir until the sugar has dissolved. Pour the hot liquid gradually over the cornflour, stirring all the time, then return to the pan. Heat, stirring constantly, until the sauce comes to the boil and turns clear. Simmer for 2 or 3 minutes.
    Serve with puddings.

THIN JAM SAUCE

1 cup apricot jam	1 tbsp liqueur
½ cup water	

Heat the jam and water to boiling-point, and simmer for 5 minutes. Strain and flavour with the liqueur.
    Serve with puddings, moulded desserts, or ice-cream.

BUTTERSCOTCH SAUCE

1 tbsp cornflour	4 oz (125 g) brown sugar
½ pt (315 ml) milk	½ tsp vanilla essence
1 tbsp butter	

Mix the cornflour to a paste with a little of the milk. Heat the remaining milk with the butter and sugar, stirring until the sugar has dissolved. Pour over the cornflour, beating all the time, then return to the pan. Bring to the boil, stirring constantly, then add the vanilla and simmer for 2 or 3 minutes.
    Serve hot or cold with puddings or ice-cream.

CARAMEL SAUCE

¼ pt (150 ml) milk	1 tbsp butter
1 cup brown sugar	½ tsp vanilla essence

Heat all the ingredients in a saucepan, stirring until the sugar has dissolved. Bring to the boil and simmer for 5 minutes, stirring all the time.
    Serve with puddings or ice-cream.

APPLE BRANDY SAUCE

1 cup apple jelly (see page 137)	2 tbsps orange juice
½ cup brandy	

Melt the apple jelly in a saucepan and add the brandy and orange juice. Bring quickly to the boil and serve.
    Serve with plain puddings.

BRANDY SAUCE

1 tbsp cornflour	2 tbsps sugar
½ pt (315 ml) milk	2 tbsps brandy

Blend the cornflour to a paste with a little of the milk. Heat the remaining milk with the sugar, stirring until the sugar has dissolved. Pour the hot liquid over the cornflour, stirring all the time, then return to the saucepan. Bring to the boil, stirring constantly. Add the brandy and simmer for 2 or 3 minutes.
    Serve with puddings.

HARD SAUCE

6 oz (185 g) butter	6 fl oz (185 ml) brandy
6 oz (185 g) icing sugar	1 tsp finely grated orange rind
6 oz (185 g) castor sugar	

Cream the butter. Gradually beat in the sugars alternately with the brandy. Continue beating until the mixture is light and creamy. Stir in the orange rind. Chill before serving.
    Serve with Christmas pudding or other fruit puddings.

CUSTARD SAUCE

½ pt (315 ml) milk	a few drops of vanilla essence
2 eggs	
1 tbsp sugar	

Heat the milk to just below boiling-point. Beat the eggs with the sugar then pour in the hot liquid gradually, beating all the time. Transfer to the top of a double saucepan or put the bowl over a pan of simmering water. Cook, stirring frequently, until the custard thickens enough to coat the back of a spoon; do not allow to boil. Stir in the vanilla.
    Serve hot or cold with puddings or fruit.

Duck with cherries (page 35), glazed carrots (page 51), and new potatoes (page 53)

Fruity curry (page 42) and boiled rice

Roast lamb with minted stuffing (page 43) and roast potatoes

Roast pork (page 44) with roast potatoes and carrots

New potatoes (page 53), baked tomatoes (page 54), asparagus (page 51), and glazed carrots (page 51)

Complexion salad (page 56) and mayonnaise (page 62)

Chocolate soufflé (page 78) and pineapple fruit salad (page 78)

Snow-capped apples (page 69)

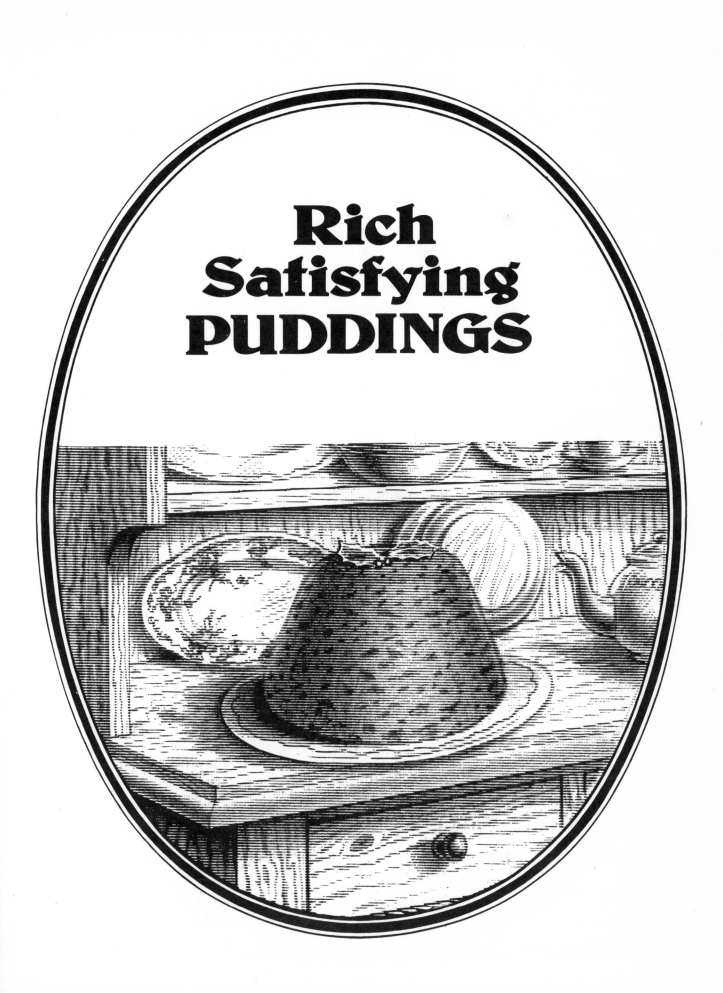

Rich Satisfying PUDDINGS

Steamed Puddings

Before making the pudding mixture, grease the pudding basin and lid or paper cover. Put a large saucepan of water on to heat while you prepare the mixture. Two-thirds fill the pudding basin, leaving room for rising, cover tightly, and lower it into the boiling water, which should reach halfway up the basin. The water must simmer gently for all the cooking time required and should be topped up with more boiling water as necessary.

Boiled Puddings

Scald a pudding cloth and sprinkle it with flour or grease a pudding basin. Put a large saucepan filled with water on to heat while you prepare the mixture. Pour the mixture into the prepared cloth and tie; alternatively, pour the mixture into a pudding basin, cover with greased paper, and tie in a dry scalded cloth. Lower the pudding into the boiling water, which should cover the pudding. The water must boil for all the cooking time required and should be topped up with more boiling water as necessary.

PANCAKES

4 oz (125 g) plain flour   fat
a pinch of salt   sugar
1 egg   lemon juice or jam
½ pt (315 ml) milk

Sift the flour and salt into a mixing bowl. Make a well in the centre, break in the egg, and stir the flour into it with a wooden spoon. Slowly beat in half the milk, until all the flour has been worked in from the sides. Beat thoroughly then add the rest of the milk. Leave to stand for at least half an hour. Pour the batter into a jug. Heat fat in a 6- or 7-inch (15 or 18 centimetre) pan until hot. Fry small quantities of batter at a time, tilting the pan to cover with a thin coating. When each pancake is golden underneath, toss or turn with a palette knife or egg-slice to cook the other side. Turn out on to paper covered with sugar; sprinkle with lemon juice or warmed jam, roll up, and serve at once, sprinkled with more sugar. Alternatively, cook all the pancakes, stacking them as they are prepared on a plate over a saucepan of simmering water, and keeping them covered. Pancakes can be kept in the refrigerator for several days if layered between greaseproof paper; they should be reheated quickly without adding fat to the frying pan.

COCONUT PANCAKES

1 quantity pancake batter (see   sugar
above)   grated nutmeg
shredded coconut   lemon juice

Make the pancakes as described in the recipe above. When cooked, sprinkle with coconut, sugar, and nutmeg. Roll up and serve with a little lemon juice squeezed over.

FRUIT FRITTERS

4 oz (125 g) plain flour   fat or oil
a pinch of salt   castor sugar
1 egg   cinnamon
¼ pt (150 ml) milk or milk
and water
4 cooking apples

Sift the flour and salt into a mixing bowl. Make a well in the centre, break in the egg, and pour in half the liquid. Gradually beat in the flour until it has all been worked in; beat well. Slowly add the rest of the liquid, beating until smooth. Cut the apples into ¼-inch (5-millimetre) thick rings. Dip the apple rings in the prepared batter and deep-fry in fat or oil until golden. Drain on absorbent paper, sprinkle with castor sugar to which a little cinnamon has been added, and serve at once. Small halved bananas or tinned pineapple slices can be prepared in the same way.

SOUFFLE OMELETTE

2 eggs, separated   2 tbsps jam
1 tsp castor sugar   extra castor sugar
1 dsp butter

Beat the egg-yolks with the castor sugar. In another bowl, beat the egg-whites until stiff. Carefully fold the egg-whites into the yolks. Heat the butter until hot in a frying pan. Pour in the egg mixture and cook over moderate heat until the omelette is set and golden underneath. Put the pan under the griller until the top is set and golden. Spread the warmed jam on the omelette, fold in half, and transfer to a heated serving plate. Sprinkle with extra castor sugar and serve at once.

MARMALADE PUDDING

3 oz (90 g) self-raising flour   approx. 1 small cup milk
a pinch of salt   a little brown sugar
2 oz (60 g) sugar
3 oz (90 g) fresh breadcrumbs
3 oz (90 g) finely shredded
suet
4 oz (125 g) marmalade
1 egg, well beaten

Mix the flour with the salt, sugar, breadcrumbs, and suet. Make a well in the centre and add 3 ounces (90 grams) of the marmalade and the egg. Add the milk gradually, mixing to make a soft mixture. Grease an ovenproof dish, and sprinkle with brown sugar. Spread the remaining marmalade on the bottom of the dish. Pour in the pudding mixture. Bake in a moderate oven for about 45 minutes.
    Serve with custard (see page 64).

CHOCOLATE SAUCE PUDDING

4 oz (125 g) butter   2 tbsps cocoa
1 cup sugar   ½ cup milk
1 egg   1½ cups hot water
vanilla essence
1 cup self-raising flour

Cream the butter with ½ cup of the sugar. Add the egg and vanilla essence, beating in well. Fold in the sifted flour and 1 tablespoon of the cocoa alternately with the milk. Pour the mixture into a greased ovenproof dish. Mix together the remaining sugar and cocoa and sprinkle over the top. Gently pour in the hot water. Bake in a moderate oven for 35 to 40 minutes.

FAMILY PUDDING

2 cups plain flour   3 tbsps melted butter
1 dsp baking powder   1 cup milk
½ tsp salt   ¾ cup sultanas (optional)
1 egg
¾ cup sugar

Sift the flour, baking powder, and salt into a mixing bowl. Beat the egg with the sugar, then blend in the butter and milk; pour on to the flour, mixing well. Fold in the sultanas. Transfer the mixture to a well-greased ovenproof dish and bake in a moderate oven for 1 to 1½ hours.

FRUIT SPONGE

2 large cups cherries or
    plums
½ pt (315 ml) water
6 oz (185 g) sugar
2½ oz (75 g) butter

1 egg, well beaten
4 oz (125 g) self-raising flour
a pinch of salt
scant ¼ pt (150 ml) milk

Simmer the fruit in the water with 1½ ounces (45 grams) of the sugar for 15 minutes. Strain, and transfer the fruit to a greased ovenproof dish. Boil the fruit juice with 2 ounces (60 grams) of the remaining sugar until the liquid is reduced to ¼ pint (150 millilitres); pour over the fruit. Cream the butter with the remaining sugar. Add the egg, beating well. Sieve the flour and salt, and add alternately with the milk. Pour this mixture over the fruit. Bake in a moderately slow oven for 40 to 45 minutes.

Serve with top of the milk, mock cream, or sweetened cream cheese made from sour milk.

PUFFED RICE

2 tbsps cooked rice
2 eggs, separated
1 tbsp sugar

1 tbsp sweet sherry
1 tsp cream

Put the rice in an ovenproof dish. Beat the egg-yolks with the sugar, sherry, and cream; add to the rice. Beat the egg-whites until stiff and fold into the rice mixture. Bake in a slow oven for 15 minutes.

RHUBARB UPSIDE-DOWN PUDDING

2 cups chopped rhubarb
4½ oz (140 g) sugar
5 oz (155 g) plain flour
1 tsp cinnamon
rind and juice of 1 orange

1 tsp baking powder
2 oz (60 g) butter
1 egg, lightly beaten
2–3 tbsps milk

Put the prepared rhubarb in an ovenproof dish. Mix together 2 ounces (60 grams) of the sugar, 1 tablespoon of the flour, the cinnamon, and the grated rind; sprinkle over the rhubarb. Sift the remaining flour and the baking powder. Rub in the butter and add 2 ounces (60 grams) of remaining sugar. Beat in the egg. Work in the milk to make a stiffish dough. Spread this over the rhubarb and bake in a moderate oven for half an hour. Mix the orange juice with the remaining sugar; pour this over the pudding and bake a little longer. Remove the pudding from the oven and loosen round the sides of the dish with a knife. Turn out on to a heated serving dish.

RHUBARB PUDDING

2 cups fresh breadcrumbs
5 oz (155 g) sugar
1 dsp lemon juice
1 dsp grated lemon rind

1 egg, well beaten
¾ cup milk
2 cups chopped rhubarb

Mix the breadcrumbs, sugar, lemon juice and rind, egg, and milk together. Add the rhubarb, and mix well. Transfer the mixture to a greased pie-dish, cover with greaseproof paper, and bake in a moderate oven for 1 hour.

LEMON CUSTARD PUDDING

4 oz (125 g) sugar
2 oz (60 g) butter
2 oz (60 g) self-raising flour
grated rind and juice of 1
    lemon

2 eggs, separated
½ pt (315 ml) milk

Beat the sugar into the butter, then mix in the sifted flour. Add the lemon rind and juice, then the beaten egg-yolks and the milk. Beat the egg-whites until stiff and fold into the pudding mixture. Turn into a large ovenproof dish, stand it in a baking tin filled with about 1 inch (2·5 centimetres) of water, and bake in a moderate oven for 45 minutes, or until set.

PEARS AND NUTS BAKED IN GINGERBREAD

5 oz (155 g) self-raising flour
¼ tsp salt
½ tsp bicarbonate of soda
½ tsp mixed spice
1 tsp ground ginger
4 oz (125 g) butter
2 oz (60 g) golden syrup
1 oz (30 g) sugar

1 egg
¼ pt (150 ml) milk
1½ oz (45 g) brown sugar
1 extra tbsp golden syrup
3 pears, peeled, cored, and
    halved
a few shelled walnuts

Sift the flour, salt, soda, spice, and ginger into a mixing bowl. Melt 2 ounces (60 grams) of the butter with the 2 ounces (60 grams) of golden syrup, and the 1 ounce (30 grams) of sugar; bring to the boil. Add to the flour mixture, stirring well. Beat the egg well and add the milk. Stir into the cake mixture. Melt the remaining butter in an 8-inch (20-centimetre) square tin; add the brown sugar and the extra syrup, mixing well. Fill the pear-halves with shelled walnuts, and place cut-side down in the tin, keeping the nuts in place. Pour the gingerbread batter over the pears. Bake in a moderate oven for 60 to 70 minutes. Turn on to a serving dish.

BAKED PEACHES

1 peach per person
butter
ground almonds

sugar
brown sugar
Madeira or sweet sherry

Dip the peaches in boiling water then peel off the skins. Cut in half, and remove the stones. Blend butter with ground almonds and sugar to form a paste. Fill the peach cavities with the paste and join the halves together. Place close together in a small ovenproof dish. Sprinkle with brown sugar and about 1 teaspoon per peach of Madeira or sweet sherry. Bake in a moderate oven until the sugar forms a brown syrup. Baste the fruit.

Serve with whipped cream.

CARAMEL BANANA PUDDING

$\frac{1}{4}$ cup butter
$\frac{1}{2}$ cup brown sugar
3–4 bananas, sliced
1 tbsp raspberry jam
1 cup plain flour
1 tsp baking powder

$\frac{1}{4}$ tsp salt
$\frac{2}{3}$ cup sugar
2 egg-yolks, well beaten
$\frac{1}{2}$ cup milk
$\frac{1}{2}$ tsp vanilla essence

Grease a pie-dish with the butter, and sprinkle with the $\frac{1}{2}$ cup of brown sugar. Cover with the bananas and spread with the raspberry jam. Sift the flour, baking powder, and salt into a mixing bowl with the sugar; make a well in the centre and pour in the egg-yolks, milk, and vanilla essence. Beat the dry ingredients in from the side and continue beating vigorously to form a smooth batter; pour on to the bananas. Bake in a moderate oven for about half an hour. Turn out on to a plate so that the caramelised bananas are on top.

Serve with whipped cream, custard (see page 64), or lemon sauce (see page 64).

SNOW-CAPPED APPLES

Prepare and fill the apples in the same way as for baked apples (see below). About 20 minutes before the apples are expected to be cooked, whisk two egg-whites until stiff, beat in 2 tablespoons of castor sugar and whisk again until stiff; top each apple with some of this meringue mixture and return to the oven until the apples are tender and the topping is golden and crisp.

BAKED APPLES

6 large cooking apples
$\frac{1}{2}$ cup mixed dried fruit
2 tbsps chopped nuts

$\frac{1}{2}$ tsp cinnamon
brown sugar

Core the apples and pare off a strip of peel around the top of each. Mix together the dried fruit (chop dates, apricots, and so on), nuts, cinnamon, and 1 tablespoon of brown sugar. Divide the fruit mixture between the apples, taking care not to pack the stuffing too tightly. Put the apples in a shallow ovenproof dish, or pie-plate, sprinkle over 3 or 4 tablespoons of brown sugar and pour in a cup of water. Cook in a moderately hot oven for an hour, or until the apples are soft.

APPLE CHARLOTTE

1 lb (500 g) cooking apples, peeled, cored, and sliced
1–2 tbsps water
2 heaped tbsps sugar
thin slices of bread or cake
melted butter

bread or cake crumbs
sugar
spice
butter

Stew the apples with the water and sugar. Grease an ovenproof dish and line it with slices of bread (with the crusts removed) or cake, which have been dipped in melted butter. Pour in the puréed apple, and cover with breadcrumbs or cake crumbs. Sprinkle over sugar mixed with a little spice and dot with butter. Bake in a moderate oven for 30 to 45 minutes.

Serve with custard (see page 64) or whipped cream.

FRUIT CRUMBLE

1$\frac{1}{2}$ lb (750 g) fresh fruit
3 oz (90 g) butter
6 oz (185 g) plain flour

3 oz (90 g) castor sugar

Peel and slice the fruit as appropriate and arrange in an ovenproof dish. Rub the butter into the flour in a mixing bowl until it resembles fine breadcrumbs; stir in the sugar. Sprinkle the topping over the fruit and bake in a moderately hot oven for 30 to 40 minutes. Cinnamon, nutmeg, or other spices may be added to the fruit for variation.

Serve with custard (see page 64) or cream.

FRUIT CRISP

1 tin fruit
2 oz (60 g) butter
4 oz (125 g) brown sugar
$\frac{1}{2}$ tsp grated lemon rind
a pinch of grated nutmeg
1 egg, beaten

2 cups buttered dried breadcrumbs

Drain the fruit, reserving the syrup. Cream the butter and sugar with the lemon rind and nutmeg. Beat in the egg. Stir in the breadcrumbs. Put the fruit in a greased ovenproof dish and spread the topping over. Bake in a moderate oven for about 25 minutes. Serve at once with the heated reserved syrup and ice-cream.

BAKED EGG CUSTARD

2 eggs
1 dsp castor sugar

$\frac{1}{2}$ pt (315 ml) milk

Beat the eggs then add the sugar and beat thoroughly. Gradually add the heated milk, whisking in well. Pour into a greased pie-dish. Stand the dish in a pan of hot water, and bake in a slow oven until set, when a knife inserted in the middle of the custard comes out clean.

BREAD AND BUTTER PUDDING

$\frac{1}{3}$-inch (7 mm) thick slices of buttered bread
mincemeat (see page 138) or sultanas and chopped mixed peel
sugar

1$\frac{1}{2}$ pt (940 ml) milk
2 eggs, beaten
vanilla essence
cinnamon

Grease a large pie-dish. Cover the bottom with slices of bread, buttered side uppermost. Cover with a thin layer of mincemeat or sultanas and chopped peel, and sprinkle with sugar. Continue layering thus till the dish is full, ending with a layer of bread. Pour on $\frac{1}{2}$ pint (315 millilitres) of the milk and leave to stand for 10 minutes. Beat the eggs and gradually pour over the remaining milk, stirring all the time; add vanilla essence to taste and pour over the bread. Sprinkle the top generously with sugar and cinnamon. Bake for 2 hours in a slow oven. Raise the temperature to hot to brown the bread for 10 minutes longer.

BAKED BANANA PUDDING

⅓-inch (7 mm) thick slices of
  buttered bread
bananas
4 eggs
½ cup sugar

1 qt (1·25 litres) milk
vanilla essence
desiccated coconut (optional)

Place a layer of bread, buttered side down, in the bottom of a greased pie-dish. Cover with a layer of bananas, cut lengthwise. Continue layering thus until the dish is full, ending with a layer of bread. Beat the eggs in a mixing bowl, beat in the sugar, then gradually whisk in the milk and vanilla. Pour over the pudding. Sprinkle with coconut. Bake in a moderate oven for half an hour, or until set.

RICE PUDDING

2 oz (60 g) rice
1 oz (30 g) sugar
1 oz (30 g) grated suet or
  butter

grated nutmeg
1 pt (625 ml) milk
1 egg, well beaten (optional)

Wash the rice, place in a greased pie-dish and sprinkle with the sugar, suet, and nutmeg. Pour in the milk and stir. Bake in a slow oven for 2 to 3 hours. Stir the pudding two or three times during the first 1½ hours. Do not allow the pudding to boil. The egg should be added half an hour before the end of cooking time. Ground cinnamon, finely grated lemon rind, or a bay-leaf can be used instead of nutmeg to flavour the pudding.

QUEEN PUDDING

¾ pt (475 ml) milk
1 dsp butter
2 heaped tbsps fresh white
  breadcrumbs
1 dsp sugar

1 tsp grated lemon rind
  (optional)
2 eggs, separated
2 tbsps raspberry or other jam
2 oz (60 g) castor sugar

Heat the milk with the butter to boiling-point; pour over the breadcrumbs, the dessertspoon of sugar, and the lemon rind in a mixing bowl and leave to stand for half an hour. Stir in the egg-yolks and pour into a buttered pie-dish. Bake in a moderately hot oven for about half an hour, or until set. Remove from the oven and spread the jam over the top and then pile on the egg-whites, which have been stiffly beaten with the castor sugar. Lower the oven temperature to moderate and return the pudding for about 20 minutes, until the meringue is light golden and crisp.

GINGER PUDDING

1 egg, beaten
a pinch of salt
2 tbsps milk
2 oz (60 g) butter
1 tbsp golden syrup
4 oz (125 g) self-raising flour

1 tsp ground ginger
½ tsp bicarbonate of soda

Beat the egg and salt in a small bowl; beat in the milk. Stir in the butter and golden syrup, which have been melted together. Sift the flour, ginger, and soda into a mixing bowl. Make a well in the centre and pour in the egg mixture; mix thoroughly. Pour the mixture into a greased pudding basin and cover with greased paper. Steam for 1½ hours.

Serve with custard (see page 64).

RICH CABINET PUDDING

3 oz (90 g) seeded raisins
3 oz (90 g) currants
2 pieces of candied peel,
  chopped
slices of stale sponge cake

4 eggs
4 oz (125 g) sugar
nutmeg
1 pt (625 ml) milk

Butter a pudding basin and sprinkle with half the raisins and currants and half the candied peel. Cover with a layer of sliced sponge cake. Mix the remaining peel, raisins, and currants and sprinkle over the cake. Top with another layer of sliced sponge cake. Beat the eggs with the sugar and nutmeg, stir in the milk, and pour over the cake. Leave to stand for half an hour, then cover and place the basin in a saucepan half-filled with boiling water. Steam for 1½ hours.

Serve with sweet white sauce (see page 63). If you prefer a plain pudding, use slices of bread and butter instead of cake.

BROWN STEAMED PUDDING

4 tbsps brown sugar
2 tbsps butter
4 tbsps raspberry jam
8 tbsps plain flour

1 tsp mixed spice
1 tsp bicarbonate of soda
1 cup milk

Cream the butter and sugar; beat in the jam. Add the sifted flour and spice, alternately with the soda dissolved in the milk; mix well. Pour into a greased pudding basin and steam for 2½ hours.

Serve with sweet white sauce (see page 63) flavoured with lemon essence.

GOLDEN PUDDING
(without eggs or sugar)

1 tbsp butter
2 tbsps golden syrup
½ tsp bicarbonate of soda

½ cup milk
1 large cup self-raising flour
a pinch of salt

Cream the butter and golden syrup. Add the soda, which has been dissolved in the milk. Fold in the sifted flour and salt to form a smooth mixture. Place in a greased pudding basin, cover, and steam for 1¾ hours. Dates or sultanas may be added, if you wish.

Serve with sweet white sauce (see page 63) or custard (see page 64).

NOTHING PUDDING

1 tbsp butter
1 cup boiling water
½ cup sugar
1 tsp bicarbonate of soda

1 cup plain flour
1 cup raisins or other dried
  fruit

Melt the butter and dissolve the sugar and soda in the boiling water. Fold in the flour and fruit. Pour the mixture into a greased pudding basin, cover, and steam for 3 hours.

NINA'S PUDDING

1 cup plain flour
1 cup mixed dried fruit
¾ cup sugar
1 tsp mixed spice

1 cup milk
1 tbsp butter
½ tsp bicarbonate of soda

Mix the flour, fruit, sugar, and spice together. Heat the milk, melt the butter in it, and add the soda; stir this into the fruit mixture. Pour into a greased pudding basin, cover, and steam for 2½ hours.

FARMER'S PUDDING

1 large cup plain flour
½ tsp bicarbonate of soda
1 tsp cream of tartar
1 small cup sugar
½ cup dripping

green gooseberries, diced
 rhubarb, or dried fruit
milk

Sift the flour, soda, and cream of tartar into a mixing bowl. Add the sugar. Rub in the dripping. Add the gooseberries, rhubarb, or dried fruit. Mix with enough milk to make a soft consistency. Transfer to a greased pudding basin, cover, and steam for 1½ hours.
Serve with sugar and cream.

TREACLE SPONGE PUDDING

1 cup plain flour
2 tbsps sugar
1 tsp salt
1 tsp bicarbonate of soda
1 heaped tsp ground ginger
1 tbsp butter

2 tbsps treacle
1 cup milk

Sift all the dry ingredients into a mixing bowl then rub in the butter. Make a well in the centre of the mixture. Add treacle, and then pour on the milk gradually. Mix well to form a smooth batter. Steam in a greased pudding basin for 2 hours.

FEATHER DATE PUDDING

2 tbsps butter
2 tbsps golden syrup
½ tsp bicarbonate of soda
¾ cup milk
1 cup self-raising flour

1 level tsp mixed spice
1 cup chopped dates

Melt the butter and golden syrup in a saucepan over gentle heat. Remove from the heat. Dissolve the soda in the milk, and add. Mix in the sifted flour and spice and the dates. Turn the mixture into a greased pudding basin and put a square of greased paper on top. Cover securely with the lid, and steam for 2 hours.

PRUNE PUDDING

1 cup milk
1 tsp bicarbonate of soda
1½ cups chopped prunes
3 tbsps melted butter
3 tbsps honey, golden syrup,
 or treacle
½ cup plain flour
a pinch of salt

1 egg, well beaten
½ tsp almond essence
1 cup rolled oats

Dissolve the soda in the milk. Mix together all the other ingredients, stirring well, then add the milk. Turn the mixture into a greased pudding basin. Cover, and steam for 2½ hours.
Serve with custard (see page 64).

WAGGA WAGGA PUDDING

2 small cups plain flour
2 small cups sugar
1 small cup currants
1 tsp mixed spice

a pinch of salt
1 tsp bicarbonate of soda
2 cups boiling water
1 heaped tbsp butter

Combine the dry ingredients in a mixing bowl. Dissolve the soda in 1 cup of the boiling water and melt the butter in the other. Stir the melted butter mixture into the dry ingredients, then the soda mixture. Pour into a greased pudding basin and steam for 3 hours.
Serve with sweet white sauce (see page 63).

STEAMED APPLE PUDDING
(without eggs)

1 oz (30 g) butter
1 cup sugar
1 cup plain flour
1 tsp mixed spice
1 cup fresh breadcrumbs

1 cup sultanas
1 cup grated apple
1 tsp bicarbonate of soda
1 small cup milk

Beat the sugar into the butter. Sift the flour and spice and add to the creamed mixture. Add the breadcrumbs, sultanas, and apple. Dissolve the soda in the milk and add, mixing well. Steam for 2½ hours in a greased pudding basin or boil in a floured cloth for 2 hours.

STEAMED SAGO PUDDING

½ cup sago
1 cup milk
1 tbsp sugar
1 cup seeded raisins
2 cups fresh breadcrumbs
1 egg, beaten
1 tbsp melted butter

½ tsp bicarbonate of soda
1 tbsp milk

Soak the sago in the cup of milk for 12 hours, or overnight. Mix in the sugar, raisins, breadcrumbs, egg, and butter. Dissolve the soda in the tablespoon of milk, add, and mix thoroughly. Pour into a pudding basin, cover, and steam for 2½ to 3 hours.

BANANA PUDDING

1½ tbsps butter
½ cup sugar
3 eggs, separated
1 cup plain flour

2 bananas, mashed
2½ cups milk

Cream the butter and sugar. Beat the egg-yolks in thoroughly. Stir in the flour, then the bananas. Add the milk. Beat the egg-whites until stiff, and fold in lightly. Place in a greased pudding basin; cover, and steam for 1 to 1¼ hours.
Serve with fruit syrup or sweet sauce (see the chapter 'Superior Sauces and Dressings').

BANANA AND RAISIN PUDDING

½ tsp bicarbonate of soda
a little milk
1 cup fresh breadcrumbs
1 cup seeded raisins
1 egg

2 tbsps plain flour
1 cup mashed bananas

Dissolve the soda in milk. Mix all ingredients together and place in a greased pudding basin. Cover, and steam for 2 hours.
Serve with custard (see page 64).

SAGO PLUM PUDDING

1 cup milk
1 cup fresh breadcrumbs
2 tbsps sago
2 tbsps butter
½ cup sugar
1 cup seeded raisins or other dried fruit

¼ tsp grated nutmeg
½ tsp bicarbonate of soda
1 tsp cold water
1 egg, beaten

Heat the milk and pour it over the breadcrumbs, sago, and butter. Allow to stand for half an hour then add the sugar, fruit, and nutmeg. Dissolve the soda in the cold water and add to the mixture. Stir the egg in lightly but thoroughly. Pour into a greased pudding basin and steam for 2¼ hours.
Serve with custard (see page 64).

STEAMED PLUM PUDDING

2 cups plain flour
1 cup sugar
1 tsp mixed spice
½ tsp grated nutmeg
½ tsp cinnamon

a pinch of salt
2 tbsps dripping
2 cups mixed dried fruit
1 tsp bicarbonate of soda
2 cups warm water

Sift the flour, sugar, spice, nutmeg, cinnamon, and salt into a mixing bowl. Rub in the dripping; add the mixed fruit and the soda dissolved in the warm water; mix, then leave to stand overnight. Next day, steam for 4 hours in a greased pudding basin; alternatively, boil the mixture in a scalded cloth sprinkled with flour.

GOLDEN GLOW DUMPLINGS

1 egg
a little milk
1 cup plain flour
1 tsp baking powder
1 tbsp butter

2 tbsps seeded raisins or dates
1 tsp finely grated lemon rind

Syrup
1 cup hot water
1 tbsp butter

½ cup sugar
1 tbsp golden syrup

Beat the egg with a little milk. Sift the flour and baking powder into a mixing bowl. Rub in the butter then stir in the fruit and lemon rind. Add the egg mixture. Form into small balls and drop into the syrup. Bring the syrup back to boiling-point, then allow the dumplings to simmer for 20 minutes. Take care that they do not burn.
Syrup: Heat all the ingredients in a saucepan, stirring to dissolve the sugar. Bring to the boil.
Serve with custard (see page 64) or cream.

APPLE DUMPLINGS

8 oz (250 g) apples
6 oz (185 g) plain flour
½ tsp baking powder
1 egg

1 oz (30 g) butter
2 oz (60 g) dried breadcrumbs
sugar

Core the unpeeled apples and grate them into the flour in a mixing bowl. Mix, and leave for half an hour. Add the baking powder and egg, mixing well. Drop spoonfuls of this mixture into fast-boiling, salted water; take care that the water does not go off the boil. Cover and boil the dumplings for 15 minutes. Meanwhile, melt the butter in a frying pan, add the breadcrumbs, and stir until crisp. Lift the dumplings out of the pan, and toss them in the buttered breadcrumbs. Sprinkle with sugar, and serve very hot.

PARADISE PUDDING

3 apples, peeled and cored
3 oz (90 g) sugar
3 oz (90 g) currants
4 oz (125 g) fresh breadcrumbs

a little grated nutmeg
3 tbsps brandy or sherry
3 eggs

Mince or grate the apples and combine with the sugar, currants, breadcrumbs, and nutmeg. Beat the eggs with the brandy, and add to the mixture. Pour into a greased pudding basin and steam for 2 hours. Alternatively, boil the pudding in a scalded and floured cloth.

POORMAN'S PUDDING

1 cup finely chopped suet
1 cup plain flour
1 cup milk
1 cup fresh breadcrumbs

1 cup sugar
1 cup mixed dried fruit
1 tsp bicarbonate of soda

Mix all the ingredients together and pour into a greased pudding basin. Cover and boil for 2½ to 3 hours.

GRANDMOTHER'S PUDDING

1 heaped tsp bicarbonate of soda
¾ pt (475 ml) boiling water
1 tbsp butter
2 cups plain flour

a pinch of salt
1 cup sugar
12 oz (375 g) sultanas and currants
1½ oz (45 g) candied peel

Dissolve the soda in half the boiling water and melt the butter in the other half. Pour both into a mixing bowl and stir in the other ingredients. Tie in a floured cloth and boil for 2½ hours.

PLAIN SUET PUDDING

1 lb (500 g) plain flour
1 tsp baking powder
½ tsp salt

8 oz (250 g) finely chopped suet
a little milk or water

Sift the flour, baking powder, and salt into a mixing bowl. Add the suet and mix in enough milk to make a limp dough. Tie the mixture in a scalded, floured pudding cloth, leaving enough room for the pudding to swell. Boil steadily for 1½ hours.
Serve with a sweet sauce (see the chapter 'Superior Sauces and Dressings').

ROLY-POLY PUDDING

8 oz (250 g) plain flour
1 tsp baking powder
½ tsp salt
4 oz (125 g) finely chopped
 suet

a little water
3–4 tbsps jam

Sift the flour, baking powder, and salt into a mixing bowl. Add the suet. Mix in enough water to make a stiff dough. Roll the dough into a rectangle, about ½ inch (1 centimetre) thick. Spread with jam to within an inch (2·5 centimetres) of the edges. Moisten the sides and ends with water. Roll up lightly and seal the edges. Wrap the pudding in a scalded cloth, and secure the ends with string; boil for 1½ to 2 hours. Alternatively, cook the mixture on a greased ovenproof dish in a hot oven for 45 minutes to an hour.
 Serve with custard (see page 64) or jam sauce (see page 64).

FIG PUDDING

6 oz (185 g) finely chopped
 suet
8 oz (250 g) finely chopped
 figs
1 cup plain flour
1 cup fresh breadcrumbs

½ cup sugar
a pinch of salt
a pinch of nutmeg
1 tsp baking powder
2 eggs, well beaten
1¼ cups milk

Mix the suet and figs with the dry ingredients. Add the eggs and milk, mixing well. Pour the mixture into a greased pudding basin. Cover and boil for 3½ hours.

FRUIT PUDDING

2 oz (60 g) butter
1 cup sugar
3 eggs
1 tsp bicarbonate of soda
½ cup milk
1 packet mixed dried fruit

a few chopped dates
1–2 tbsps brandy
1 tsp vanilla essence
2½ cups plain flour
1 dsp baking powder

Blend the sugar into the butter. Add the eggs, one at a time, beating well after each addition. Dissolve the soda in the milk and add to the mixture. Mix in the fruit, dates, brandy, and vanilla. Stir in the sifted flour and baking powder. Mix well and pour into a greased pudding basin. Boil for 3 hours.

AUNT GERT'S FRUIT PUDDING

(without eggs)

1 cup milk
¾ cup sugar
1 tsp grated nutmeg
3 oz (90 g) butter

1 cup mixed dried fruit
1 tsp bicarbonate of soda
1 cup self-raising flour

Combine the milk, sugar, nutmeg, butter, and mixed fruit in a saucepan. Mix well, and bring to the boil over moderate heat. Add the soda and flour, folding in thoroughly. Pour the mixture into a pudding basin, and boil for 1½ to 2 hours.
 Serve with chocolate sauce (see page 63) or custard (see page 64).

DATE PUDDING

(without eggs)

2 cups self-raising flour
a pinch of salt
grated nutmeg
¾ cup sugar
1 lb (500 g) halved dates

½ pt (315 ml) boiling water
1 tbsp butter
1 heaped tsp bicarbonate of
 soda

Sift the flour, salt, and nutmeg into a mixing bowl. Add the sugar and dates. Melt the butter in half the boiling water and dissolve the soda in the other half; mix together, then add to the flour and dates. Tie tightly in a scalded cloth sprinkled with flour. Boil for 2 to 2½ hours.

COLD TEA PLUM PUDDING

2 cups plain flour
a pinch of salt
1 tsp mixed spice
2 tbsps butter
1 cup sugar
½ cup raisins

½ cup sultanas
½ cup currants
1 tsp bicarbonate of soda
1 cup cold tea

Sift the flour, salt, and spice into a mixing bowl. Rub in the butter, then add the sugar and fruit. Stir in the soda dissolved in the cold tea, mixing well. Pour the mixture into a scalded pudding cloth, which has been sprinkled with flour and 2 teaspoons of sugar. Tie tightly, leaving very little space for rising. Plunge into a pan of boiling water. Cover and cook for 2½ hours.
 Serve with custard (see page 64).

CHRISTMAS PUDDING

8 oz (250 g) currants
12 oz (375 g) seeded raisins
8 oz (250 g) sultanas
4 oz (125 g) chopped dates
4 oz (125 g) candied peel
4 oz (125 g) blanched
 almonds
½ tsp grated nutmeg
1 tsp mixed spice

6 tbsps brandy or rum
1 lb (500 g) butter
1 lb (500 g) brown sugar
9 eggs
8 oz (250 g) fresh
 breadcrumbs
8 oz (250 g) plain flour
a pinch of salt
½ tsp bicarbonate of soda

Clean and prepare the fruit then put it in a bowl with the almonds, nutmeg, spice, and brandy; leave to stand overnight. Next day, have ready a large saucepan of boiling water. Cream the butter and sugar. Add the eggs, one at a time, beating well after each addition. Stir in the fruit mixture and the breadcrumbs. Sift the flour with the salt and soda, and mix in thoroughly. Tie the mixture in a strong pudding cloth, which has been scalded and sprinkled with flour; allow a little room for the pudding to swell. Boil for 6 hours. Boil again for 3 hours on the day it is to be eaten.
 Serve with hard sauce (see page 64).

Delectable DESSERTS

Gelatine

Use 1½ level tablespoons of gelatine for every pint (625 millilitres) of liquid, or according to the manufacturer's instructions. In hot weather or if there is no refrigerator available, a little more gelatine will be needed. The gelatine will dissolve without trouble in hot water if it has first been allowed to soak in cold water. Do not add a hot gelatine mixture to milk or it will curdle. A gelatine mixture that is left to become quite cold and to thicken a little can be beaten to a thick froth, provided that there is no fat in the mixture. A jelly that is to be set with fruit or vegetables should also be left to thicken slightly before the solid ingredients are added.

Unmoulding Desserts

Dip the mould quickly into warm water, then wipe dry. Cover with the serving dish, then invert the two on to a stable surface and try to remove the mould; if it does not come away easily, cover the mould with a hot cloth and try again.

LEMON SAGO

2 tbsps sago
1 pt (625 ml) water
1 tbsp treacle
2 tbsps sugar

grated rind and juice of 1
lemon

Boil the sago in the water until soft. Add the treacle, sugar, and lemon rind and juice. Leave to cool.
Serve with custard (see page 64) and cream.

RHUBARB SPECIAL

1 cup sugar
½ cup water
1 bunch of rhubarb, chopped
grated rind and juice of 1
  orange

2 egg-whites
1 tbsp sugar
2 bananas, mashed
3 cups cooked rice

Heat the cup of sugar and the water in a saucepan, stirring until the sugar has dissolved. Add the rhubarb and simmer until soft but not pulpy. Leave to cool. Add the orange rind and juice. In a separate bowl, beat the egg-whites until stiff; fold in the 1 tablespoon of sugar, then the bananas and rice. Combine with the rhubarb and pile into a glass dish.
Serve with whipped cream.

FRUIT JUNKET

2 egg-yolks
1 dsp sugar
1 pt (625 ml) milk
1 junket tablet or 2 tsps
  rennet
sponge cake

2 bananas
fresh or glacé cherries
extra sugar
¼ pt (150 ml) cream
chopped nuts
cinnamon

Beat the egg-yolks thoroughly with the 1 dessertspoon of sugar in a mixing bowl. Heat the milk and pour it on to the egg mixture, beating all the time. Crush the junket tablet with a little water and stir it into the milk. Line four individual dishes with small fingers of sponge cake, a few slices of banana, and sliced cherries. Sprinkle lightly with sugar. Pour the junket into the lined dishes and leave to set. Beat the cream and pile on top of the dishes; decorate with nuts and cherries and sprinkle with cinnamon.

BLANCMANGE

3 tbsps cornflour
1 pt (625 ml) milk

2 tbsps sugar
vanilla or other essence

Blend the cornflour to a thin paste with a little of the milk. Heat the rest of the milk with the sugar until boiling-point is reached. Pour on to the cornflour, stirring all the time. Return to the pan and bring to the boil, stirring constantly. Flavour with vanilla and pour into a mould that has been rinsed with cold water; leave to set. A rich blancmange can be made by adding two egg-yolks and two stiffly beaten egg-whites to the above mixture, as soon as the saucepan is taken off the heat.

CHOCOLATE BLANCMANGE

Make in the same way as for blancmange (see above), adding 1 tablespoon of cocoa to the cornflour.

FRUIT BLANCMANGE

Make in the same way as for blancmange (see this page), adding 1 teaspoon of finely grated orange or lemon rind to the milk before heating it.

PRUNE JELLY

8 oz (250 g) stoned prunes
1 pt (625 ml) water
peeled rind of 1 lemon

4 oz (125 g) sugar
3 tbsps gelatine

Soak the prunes overnight in the water. Next day, cook until tender with the rind and the sugar. Soak the gelatine in cold water until soft, then dissolve it in some of the liquid from the prunes. Press the prunes through a sieve and combine with the gelatine, mixing well. Pour into small moulds that have been rinsed with cold water and leave to set.
Serve with cream.

MILK JELLY

1½ tbsps gelatine
3 tbsps boiling water
1 pt (625 ml) milk
2 oz (60 g) castor sugar
1 tsp vanilla essence

food colouring (optional)

Sprinkle the gelatine over the boiling water and whisk until dissolved. Heat the milk with the sugar and vanilla, stirring to make sure that the sugar has dissolved; leave until lukewarm. Pour the warm milk carefully on to the gelatine, stirring well, and tint with a few drops of food colouring. Pour into a mould that has been rinsed with cold water and leave to set.

CHOCOLATE MILK JELLY

1½ tbsps gelatine
3 tbsps boiling water
1 pt (625 ml) milk
2 oz (60 g) plain chocolate
2 oz (60 g) castor sugar

1 tsp vanilla essence

Make in the same way as for milk jelly (see above), dissolving the chocolate with the sugar in the milk.

LEMON MERINGUE MOULD

¾ cup sugar
¼ cup water
3 tsps gelatine
1 egg-white
juice of ½ lemon
½ pt (315 ml) cream

fresh or tinned fruit

Boil the sugar with the water and gelatine for 5 minutes; leave to cool. When cold, whip until white and frothy. Beat the egg-white until stiff, then fold into the gelatine mixture with the lemon juice. Beat well again. Pour into a buttered ring tin. Leave to set. Tip upside-down on to a serving plate. Put a hot cloth on the tin and the mould should leave the tin easily. Fill and decorate with whipped cream and fruit.

ORANGE BASKETS

4 large oranges   a little cold water
2 tbsps gelatine
2 lb (1 kg) sugar

Cut a small slice from the top of each orange. Taking care not to puncture the skins, scoop out the fruit, using a small spoon. Press the juice from the pulp, strain, and, if necessary, make up to 1 pint (625 millilitres) with water. Soak the gelatine in the juice for 1 hour, then put in a saucepan with the sugar, and slowly bring to the boil, making sure that the sugar has dissolved. Continue cooking for 10 minutes; stir occasionally and skim the mixture. Pour into the orange cups and allow to stand until the jelly is firmly set. Cut the oranges into quarters with a sharp knife.

STRAWBERRY MOULD

2 tbsps gelatine   1–2 cups crushed strawberries
1 cup boiling water   a few drops of red food
1 cup milk   colouring
1 egg, beaten
½ cup sugar
2 tbsps cream

Dissolve the gelatine in the boiling water. Cool to lukewarm then add the milk, egg, sugar, and cream. Stir in the strawberries and colour pink with food colouring. Leave to set.

GRAPE MOULD

1 lb (500 g) green grapes,   3 rounded dsps semolina
   halved and seeded   a few drops of cochineal
a pinch of bicarbonate of soda 1 egg-white
1 tbsp brown sugar
1 dsp honey
juice of 1 lemon

Make the grapes up to 1 pint (625 millilitres) with cold water, then heat to boiling-point; boil for 10 minutes. Add the soda, sugar, honey, and lemon juice and bring to the boil again. Sprinkle in the semolina and boil for 5 minutes. Colour with a few drops of cochineal. Whip the egg-white until stiff and fold into the hot semolina mixture. Pour into a mould that has been rinsed with cold water. Leave to set.

Serve with top of the milk or thin cream.

STRIPED MOULD

Jelly
1 heaped dsp gelatine   1 dsp lemon juice
½ pt (315 ml) pineapple or sugar
   orange juice

Blancmange
approx. ½ pt (315 ml)   1½ tbsps cornflour
   evaporated milk   1 tbsp sugar
   water

Jelly: Soak the gelatine in 2 tablespoons of the pineapple or orange juice. Bring the rest of the juice to the boil and pour over the soaked gelatine. Stir until the gelatine has dissolved, and add the lemon juice and sugar. Leave to cool but not to set. Pour half the blancmange into a mould that has been rinsed with cold water and leave until cool. Pour half the cooled jelly over and leave to set. Whip the rest of the blancmange and pour it over the jelly. Soften the remaining jelly by putting the bowl over hot water; pour over the blancmange. Put the mould in the refrigerator, and allow to set.

Blancmange: Add a couple of tablespoons of water to the evaporated milk. Mix the cornflour with a little of the milk. Bring the rest of the milk to the boil, add the sugar, and stir to prevent burning. Pour on to the cornflour, stirring until smooth. Return the mixture to the saucepan and bring to the boil, stirring all the time. Cook gently for 4 or 5 minutes. Stir until cool.

PASSIONFRUIT CREAM

1 cup chilled evaporated milk ½ cup hot water
¾ cup sugar   pulp of 6–8 passionfruit
1 dsp gelatine

Whisk the milk to a stiff froth and then gradually add the sugar. Add the gelatine, which has been dissolved in the hot water, and whisk again. Stir in the passionfruit pulp. Leave for 1 hour to set.

PASSIONFRUIT FLUMMERY

1 cup sugar   1 tbsp plain flour
1 tbsp gelatine   juice of 1 lemon
1½ cups hot water   pulp of 12 passionfruit

Dissolve the sugar and gelatine in the hot water. Mix the flour to a paste with a little water, and add to the liquid. Allow to cool. Beat for 10 minutes and, when setting, add the lemon juice and the passionfruit pulp.

ANGEL'S FOOD

1½ tbsps gelatine   a few drops of vanilla essence
1 pt (625 ml) milk
juice and peeled rind of 1
   lemon
½ cup sugar
2 eggs, separated

Soak the gelatine in a little of the milk. Heat the rest of the milk with the lemon peel to boiling-point; stir in the gelatine; add the sugar and bring to the boil again, stirring to make sure that the sugar has dissolved. Stir the egg-yolks in carefully. Pour into a bowl, add the lemon juice, and leave to cool, stirring from time to time. When the mixture is beginning to set, fold in the egg-whites, which have been stiffly beaten, and the vanilla. Pour into a mould that has been rinsed with cold water and refrigerate until set.

BANANA CREAM

3 tsps gelatine   1 tbsp brandy
½ pt (315 ml) cream
6 bananas
½ cup sugar

Leave the gelatine to soak in the cream. Mash the bananas and beat with the sugar until creamy. Combine the banana and cream mixtures and fold in the brandy. Pour into a mould that has been rinsed with cold water and leave to set.

SPANISH CREAM

1½ tbsps gelatine
1 pt (625 ml) milk
3 eggs, separated

2 oz (60 g) sugar
1 tsp vanilla essence

Soak the gelatine in the milk until soft. Heat gently until the gelatine dissolves and boiling-point is reached. Beat the egg-yolks with the sugar and pour the hot liquid on slowly, beating all the time. Return to the pan and heat gently until almost boiling, stirring constantly. Remove from the heat and fold in the stiffly beaten egg-whites and the vanilla. Pour into a mould that has been rinsed with cold water and leave to set.

FRUIT SPONGE

2½ tbsps gelatine
½ pt (315 ml) water
1 pt (625 ml) orange juice
grated rind of 3 oranges
4 oz (125 g) sugar

3 eggs, separated

Soak the gelatine in the water. Heat the juice with the rind and sugar; bring to the boil then add the soaked gelatine. Beat the egg-yolks in a mixing bowl; slowly pour the hot liquid on, stirring all the time. Return to the pan and heat, stirring, until the mixture thickens—do not allow to boil. Pour into a bowl and leave until it is starting to set. Beat the egg-whites until stiff and fold into the orange mixture. Pour into a mould that has been rinsed with cold water and leave to set.

STRAWBERRY MOUSSE

1 lb (500 g) strawberries
1 tbsp orange juice
2 oz (60 g) castor sugar
½ pt (315 ml) cream

2 egg-whites

Wash and hull the strawberries, reserving about ten for decoration. Crush the remaining strawberries and mix with the orange juice and castor sugar. Beat the cream until stiff and beat the egg-whites separately until stiff. Fold the cream into the strawberry mixture, then fold in the egg-whites. Pile into individual serving dishes and chill. Decorate with the reserved strawberries before serving.

CHOCOLATE SOUFFLE

1 tbsp gelatine
1 tbsp cocoa
1 tbsp sugar
milk or water
1 chilled tin evaporated
    milk

a few nuts

Mix the gelatine with the cocoa and sugar in a small saucepan; blend to a thick cream with a little milk or water. Heat gently until the gelatine has dissolved. Leave to cool. Whip the evaporated milk until thick, fold the cooled gelatine mixture in, then pour into a glass bowl or soufflé dish to set. Decorate with nuts.

FRUIT SHERBET

1 tbsp gelatine
6 tbsps boiling water
1 tbsp sugar
¼ pt (150 ml) sieved preserved
    fruit

1 tbsp lemon juice
2 egg-whites

Sprinkle the gelatine over the boiling water and whisk until dissolved. Stir in the sugar, fruit, and lemon juice. Beat the egg-whites until stiff and fold into the mixture. Pile into individual serving dishes and chill until set. Decorate if you wish with whipped cream, chopped nuts, and so on.

APPLE SNOW

4 large cooking apples, peeled,
    cored, and sliced
juice and peeled rind of a
    lemon
4 oz (125 g) sugar

4 egg-whites

Stew the apples gently with the lemon juice and rind and the sugar until soft. Remove the rind and mash the apples; leave to cool. Beat the egg-whites until stiff. Fold the whites into the apples and beat together until the mixture has a sponge-like consistency. Chill before serving.

FRUIT FOOL

1 lb (500 g) gooseberries,
    raspberries, blackberries,
    rhubarb, or apples

4 oz (125 g) castor sugar
½ pt (315 ml) cream

Prepare the fruit as appropriate and stew until soft with the sugar and just enough water to keep it from burning. Rub through a sieve and leave to cool. Whip the cream until thick and fold into the fruit purée. Pour into a glass serving bowl or individual dishes and chill. Before serving, decorate with a little extra cream.

PINEAPPLE FRUIT SALAD

1 ripe pineapple
4 oranges, chopped
2 bananas, sliced
2 apples, chopped
pulp of 3 passionfruit
8 oz (250 g) cherries or grapes
8 oz (250 g) strawberries

4 oz (125 g) castor sugar
2 tbsps brandy or liqueur

Cut the pineapple in half lengthwise, scoop out the flesh and chop. Combine the chopped pineapple with the other prepared fruit, the castor sugar, and the brandy. Fill the pineapple halves with the fruit mixture and chill well before serving. Any combination of fresh or tinned fruits may be used, depending on what is available.
    Serve with whipped cream.

STRAWBERRY ROYAL DESSERT

4 cups strawberries
castor sugar
2 tbsps curaçao
2 tbsps brandy
1 pt (625 ml) vanilla ice-
    cream

1 cup sweetened whipped
    cream

Combine the strawberries with the sugar, curaçao, and brandy in a serving bowl. Beat together the softened ice-cream and the whipped cream. Pour over the strawberries and return to the refrigerator for a time before serving.

STRAWBERRY TRIFLE

1 lb (500 g) strawberries
2 tbsps castor sugar
1/4 pt (150 ml) brandy or
    orange juice
1 layer of sponge cake
1 1/2 pt (940 ml) cold custard
    (see page 64)

1/2 pt (315 ml) cream, whipped
chopped nuts

Wash, hull, and slice the strawberries, reserving about twelve for decoration. Sprinkle over the castor sugar and soak for a few hours in the brandy or orange juice. Drain the strawberries and pour the liquid over the cake in a glass bowl. Arrange half the sliced strawberries on top, then pour in half the custard. Make another layer with the remaining sliced strawberries, then pour in the rest of the custard. Sweeten the whipped cream with a little castor sugar and pile on top of the trifle. Decorate with the reserved whole strawberries and chopped nuts.

BISCUIT TRIFLE

1 cup butter
1 1/2 cups icing sugar
3 eggs, well beaten
1 tsp vanilla essence or coffee
    essence

1/2 cup chopped nuts
1/2 cup chopped cherries
1 packet sugar biscuits
1/2 cup port or sherry
1/2 pt (315 ml) cream

Cream the butter and icing sugar until soft and white. Add the eggs gradually, then the essence, nuts, and cherries. Line a loose-bottomed cake-tin with buttered greaseproof paper. Dip the biscuits in the wine. Put a layer of biscuits in the cake-tin, then a layer of the mixture. Continue until all the ingredients are used. Cover the tin with a plate and leave in the refrigerator for 24 hours. Turn out and decorate with whipped cream before serving.

Mouth-watering PASTRIES and PIES

There are several points essential to good pastry-making:

* Everything involved, including the kitchen, should be cool—hands, utensils, ingredients, and the surface used for rolling out—a marble slab is ideal.
* The mixing and rolling should be done as quickly and lightly as possible—over-handling will make the pastry tough.
* The water used for mixing should be ice-cold and added with great care—the exact amount needed will depend on the type of flour; too much will make the dough sticky and difficult to handle and the baked pastry tough, whereas too little will leave the dough crumbly and the baked pastry dry.
* The oven should be pre-heated to hot, varying according to the type of pastry, and the pastry cooked quickly. The richer the pastry, the hotter the oven needs to be.

Butter is the fat normally used for pastry-making but equal amounts of butter and lard are also suitable for some types of shortcrust pastry. For the various kinds of basic pastry, rub the fat in quickly with the fingertips until the mixture is like fine breadcrumbs, then sprinkle over the liquid, mixing with a knife. Form the dough into a ball and chill for half an hour to make it more workable. Flour the pastry board or other surface (and the rolling pin) sparingly, or the extra flour will toughen the pastry. A glass or china rolling pin is useful for pastry-making, as it is cooler than wooden varieties. Roll the dough out quickly and lightly, rolling away from you, and lifting and turning the dough at intervals. Try to avoid rolling the dough out twice.

Note: The weight of pastry specified in a recipe refers to the amount of flour used in the pastry, not to its total weight.

Basic Types of Pastry

Shortcrust: This is the basic pastry for sweet and savoury pies and tarts. Rich shortcrust has a higher fat content and is suitable for the same variety of dishes.

Flan Pastry: This is a very stiff pastry containing an egg, or egg-yolk, and sugar and is used for sweet flans, tarts, and pies.

Cheese Pastry: This is a savoury pastry with grated cheese, egg, and flavourings such as mustard and cayenne pepper added. It is used for making biscuits, small savouries—for example, cheese straws—and savoury tarts and pies.

Flaky Pastry: This is a rich pastry with a high butter content that is suitable for savoury and sweet dishes. It must not be over-handled, treated roughly, or allowed to get warm before use. Flaky and puff pastry are suitable for prolonged cooking, as they take longer to harden than other varieties.

Puff Pastry: This is the richest and lightest of pastries, with a very high butter content that produces an even, flaky, crisp pastry. It is very time-consuming to make and should be prepared the day before baking and chilled so that it is firm and cool to use. It is generally reserved for luxury dishes such as vol-au-vents and cream-filled sweet pastries.

Rough Puff Pastry: This is a version of puff pastry that is quicker and easier to make; it is suitable for pies, sausage rolls, and turnovers.

Choux Pastry: This is made by heating the fat with the liquid, briskly beating in the flour, then cooling and gradually adding eggs, to form a glossy firm mixture. It is used for special foods—savoury and sweet puffs, éclairs, and so on.

Hot-water Crust Pastry: This is used for making 'raised' pies such as veal and ham, pork, and game, which are often eaten cold. It is exceptional in that the water used must be heated and the dough kept warm until use. It is very flexible when warm and is moulded to the required shape.

Suet Crust Pastry: This is used for sweet or savoury dishes that need slow cooking, often involving boiling or steaming. It is unusual among pastry in that it always contains a raising agent.

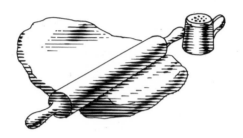

SHORTCRUST PASTRY

8 oz (250 g) plain flour   4 oz (125 g) butter
¼ tsp salt   2–3 tbsps cold water

Sift the flour and salt into a mixing bowl. Cut the butter into the flour with a knife then rub it in with the fingertips until the mixture resembles fine breadcrumbs. Sprinkle the water over and mix in first of all with a knife then with the fingertips. Knead quickly until smooth. Roll out lightly on a floured surface, using a floured rolling pin.

BAKED SHORTCRUST PASTRY CASE

Put a flan-ring on an oven tray. Roll out the specified quantity of shortcrust pastry to make a circle about ⅛ to ¼ inch (3 to 5 millimetres) thick and about 2 inches (5 millimetres) bigger than the flan-ring to be used; do not stretch the dough. Ease the pastry on to a rolling pin, lower it over the tin, and press gently into it. Roll over the top with the rolling pin to remove surplus pastry, or cut it away with a sharp knife. Crimp the edges of the pastry if you wish. Prick the base of the pastry with a fork, cover with a circle of greaseproof paper, and fill with dried haricot beans or rice. Bake in a hot oven for 15 minutes. Remove the paper and the beans and return the case to the oven for 5 minutes, until golden. Remove the flan-ring and return the case to the oven if it is still pale. Cool on a wire rack then use as required.

RICH SHORTCRUST PASTRY

Make in the same way as for shortcrust pastry (see above) but use 5 ounces (155 grams) of butter and only 1 tablespoon of water. Chill for half an hour in the refrigerator before rolling out.

CHEESE PASTRY

4 oz (125 g) plain flour   2 oz (60 g) finely grated
a pinch of salt   Cheddar cheese
a pinch of dry mustard   1 egg-yolk
a pinch of cayenne pepper   approx. 1 dsp cold water
2 oz (60 g) butter

Sift the flour, salt, mustard, and cayenne into a mixing bowl. Cut in the butter with a knife then rub it in with the fingertips until the mixture resembles fine breadcrumbs. Add the cheese, tossing with the flour. Mix to a stiff dough with the egg-yolk and water. Turn out on to a lightly floured surface. Knead quickly and lightly until the dough is smooth. Wrap in a clean tea-towel and chill for at least half an hour before using.

Brush beaten egg-white over a fruit pie that is nearly cooked and sprinkle with a little sugar before returning to the oven to brown.

ROUGH PUFF PASTRY

8 oz (250 g) plain flour   a squeeze of lemon juice
a pinch of salt   ¼ pt (150 ml) cold water
6 oz (185 g) diced chilled
   butter

Sift the flour and salt into a mixing bowl. Stir the butter into the flour. Mix to a stiff dough with the lemon juice and water. Turn on to a floured surface and roll out to a rectangle three times as long as it is wide. Fold the top third down and the bottom third up. Seal the edges by pressing firmly with a rolling pin. Wrap in a clean tea-towel and leave for half an hour. Turn the pastry to the left so that the folds are at the sides. Continue the rolling, folding, chilling, and turning processes until you have completed them four times altogether. Chill well before using.

PUFF PASTRY

8 oz (250 g) plain flour   approx. ¼ pt (150 ml) cold
a pinch of salt   water
a squeeze of lemon juice   8 oz (250 g) softened butter

Sift the flour and salt into a mixing bowl. Mix in the lemon juice and water to form a soft dough. Knead lightly on a floured surface until smooth. Shape the butter into a flat brick and roll the pastry out to a rectangle twice as long as it is wide. Put the butter on the lower half of the rectangle. Fold the top half of the pastry down and press the edges together firmly with a rolling pin to seal. Wrap in a clean tea-towel and chill in the refrigerator for half an hour. Place the pastry on a floured surface with the fold on the right and roll out to a rectangle three times as long as it is wide. Fold the bottom third up and the top third down and press the edges together firmly with a rolling pin, to seal. Chill again. Repeat the processes of turning, rolling, folding, and chilling until you have completed them six times altogether. Chill thoroughly before using.

SUET CRUST PASTRY

8 oz (250 g) plain flour   approx. ¼ pt (150 ml) cold
½ tsp salt   water
1 tsp baking powder
4 oz (125 g) finely shredded
   suet

Sift the flour, salt, and baking powder into a mixing bowl. Add the suet, tossing lightly with the flour. Mix to a soft dough with the water. Turn out on to a floured surface and knead until smooth. Roll out and use as required.

CHOUX PASTRY

2 oz (60 g) butter   4 oz (125 g) plain flour
¼ pt (150 ml) water   4 eggs

Heat the butter and water in a small saucepan until boiling-point is reached. Add the flour and continue cooking, beating until the mixture forms a ball. Remove from the heat and leave to cool slightly. Add the eggs, one at a time, beating well after each addition. Beat for several minutes until smooth and shiny. Use at once as required.

FLAKY PASTRY

8 oz (250 g) plain flour
a pinch of salt
6 oz (185 g) butter

approx. ¼ pt (150 ml) cold
water
a squeeze of lemon juice

Sift the flour and salt into a mixing bowl. Cream the butter and divide it into four equal portions. Rub one portion into the flour and mix to a soft dough with the water and lemon juice. Roll out the pastry on a floured board and knead well until smooth. Wrap in a clean tea-towel and chill in the refrigerator for an hour. Roll out into a rectangle three times as long as it is wide. Spread small flakes of the second portion of butter on to the top two-thirds of the pastry. Sprinkle lightly with flour. Fold the top third of the pastry down and fold the bottom third up. Press the open edges firmly with the rolling pin to seal. Chill again for half an hour. Turn the pastry so that the folds are at the sides. Roll out to a rectangle again and spread with flakes of the third portion of butter. Fold and seal as before and chill for half an hour. Roll out to a rectangle again and spread with flakes of the last portion of butter. Roll out, fold, and seal. Chill before rolling out and using as required.

HOT-WATER CRUST PASTRY

1 lb (500 g) plain flour
1 tsp salt
4 oz (125 g) lard

¼ pt (150 ml) water or milk
and water

Sift the flour and salt into a mixing bowl; form a well in the centre. Heat the lard and liquid in a saucepan until boiling-point is reached. Pour the hot liquid into the well in the dry ingredients and beat to a dough with a wooden spoon. Turn out on to a lightly floured surface and knead quickly until smooth. Put in a bowl over a pan of hot water, cover with a clean tea-towel, and leave to stand for half an hour. Use as required. For a pie, cut off one-quarter of the dough to use as the lid, and keep it warm over hot water until needed.

CHEESE STRAWS

6 oz (185 g) cheese pastry
(see page 83)

Roll the pastry out thinly on a floured surface. Cut into thin, 4-inch (10-centimetre) strips. Roll out the trimmings and cut, using two different-sized round cutters, about twelve rings. Bake until golden on greased oven trays in a moderate oven. When cool, form into bundles by putting about six straws in each ring.

ASPARAGUS LOGS

4 oz (125 g) self-raising flour
a pinch of salt
a pinch of cayenne pepper
1 tbsp grated cheese
1 dsp butter
2 tbsps liquid from the
asparagus

cooked asparagus stems
1 egg, beaten
plain flour
dried breadcrumbs
fat or oil

Sift the flour, salt, and cayenne into a mixing bowl; mix in the cheese. Lightly rub in the butter. Mix to a stiff dough with the asparagus liquid. Turn on to a lightly floured surface, and roll out thinly. Cut into strips about 3 inches (8 centimetres) long and 1 inch (2·5 centimetres) wide. Brush with the egg, put an asparagus stem on each strip, and roll the pastry around the asparagus. Dip

each log first in flour, then in egg, and finally in breadcrumbs. Deep-fry in hot fat until golden. Drain on absorbent paper, and serve hot or cold.

SHRIMP BOATS

8 oz (250 g) shortcrust pastry
(see page 83)

Filling
½ tsp gelatine
2 tbsps warm water
½ cup mayonnaise (see page
62)

8 oz (250 g) chopped fresh or
tinned shrimps
parsley or cooked peas

Roll the pastry out thinly and line small patty tins. Place rounds of greaseproof paper in them and fill with rice or dried beans. Bake in a moderately hot oven for about 10 minutes. Remove the rice and paper.
Filling: Dissolve the gelatine in the water and mix with the mayonnaise; mix in the shrimps. Pour into the cases. Cover with chopped parsley or peas, or fix a cucumber 'sail' in the mixture when almost set. Fresh or tinned salmon can be used instead of shrimps.

SAUSAGE ROLLS

4 oz (125 g) flaky pastry (see
this page) or shortcrust
pastry (see page 83)
6 oz (185 g) sausage-meat
salt and pepper

beaten egg or milk

Roll the pastry out thinly on a floured surface to a rectangular shape twice as long as it is wide. Trim the edges and halve lengthwise. Season the sausage-meat, dust with flour, and divide into two equal portions. Form each piece of meat into a roll the same length as the two pieces of pastry. Put the meat on the dough, moisten the edge of one long side of the dough, and fold over the meat, pressing down to seal. Cut each roll into six small rolls using a sharp knife. Make two cuts in the top of each roll, brush with egg or milk, and arrange them on an oven tray. Bake in the upper half of a hot oven for 15 minutes; reduce the temperature to moderate and continue cooking for a further 10 to 15 minutes.

SAVOURY PUFFS

½ cup water
¼ cup butter
a pinch of salt

¼ cup rolled oats
½ cup plain flour
2 eggs

Heat the water with the butter and salt until the butter has melted. Add the oats and flour and stir constantly over low heat until the mixture forms a ball. Remove from the heat. Leave to cool. Add the eggs, one at a time. Beat well. Drop small teaspoons of the mixture on a greased oven tray, leaving space between each to allow for puffing. Bake in a hot oven for 20 minutes. Leave to cool.

Fill with any savoury filling.

A little lemon juice added to dough with the cold water will help to make the pastry light.

VEGETABLE FLAN

1 oz (30 g) butter
2 medium potatoes, finely diced
1 medium onion, finely diced
½ green pepper, finely diced
4 eggs
¼ tsp dried mixed herbs
¼ tsp salt
pepper
3 medium tomatoes, peeled and finely diced
1 baked 10-inch (25 cm) shortcrust pastry case (see page 83)

Melt the butter and add the potatoes, onion, and green pepper; fry gently for 5 minutes. Beat the eggs with the herbs, salt, and pepper in a large mixing bowl. Stir in the tomatoes and the fried vegetables. Pour the mixture into the pastry case. Bake in a moderate oven until the egg is set and the top is golden.

CHEESE TART

1 tbsp butter
1 tbsp plain flour
1 cup milk
½ cup grated matured cheese
1 small onion, grated
salt
cayenne pepper
1 egg, separated
1 baked shortcrust pastry case (see page 83)

Melt the butter, and blend in the flour; cook gently for 2 or 3 minutes without browning. Gradually add the milk, and heat, stirring constantly, until thick. Add the cheese, onion, salt, and cayenne. Beat the egg-yolk into the mixture, then fold in the egg-white, which has been stiffly beaten. Pour into the pastry case, and bake in a moderate oven until golden.

CHEESE PIE

6 oz (185 g) shortcrust pastry (see page 83)
1 cup hot milk
a knob of butter
1 cup fine fresh breadcrumbs
2 oz (60 g) grated cheese
1 tsp grated onion (optional)
1 egg, beaten
salt and pepper

Roll out half the pastry to line a greased pie-plate. Mix the other ingredients, season to taste, and pour into the pie-plate. Cover with the remaining pastry and decorate with the pastry trimmings. Bake in a moderate oven for about 40 minutes. Serve hot or cold.

TOMATO PIE

4–5 tomatoes, sliced
8 oz (250 g) macaroni, broken into small pieces
1 small onion, sliced
1 tbsp chopped bacon fat
1 oz (30 g) butter
2 oz (60 g) grated cheese
salt and pepper
6 oz (185 g) shortcrust pastry (see page 83)

Cook the tomatoes with a little salt in a covered pan over low heat to extract the juice; sieve and set aside. Meanwhile cook the macaroni in a large saucepan of boiling salted water until tender, about 20 minutes; strain. Fry the onion and bacon in a little fat. Mix this into the macaroni. Add the butter and the cheese. Season with salt and pepper and add the tomato purée; mix well. Line a pie-dish with half the pastry and add the mixture. Top with the remaining pastry and cover with greased paper; bake in a moderate oven for about 20 minutes, or until the pastry is golden.

FARMER'S PIE

8 oz (250 g) shortcrust pastry (see page 83)
Filling
1 potato, finely chopped
2 tomatoes, peeled and sliced
2 oz (60 g) grated cheese
1 small apple, finely chopped
1 ham or bacon rasher (or left-over meat), diced
salt and pepper
1 egg, beaten

Roll out half the pastry to line a deep pie-plate. Fill with the potato, tomatoes, cheese, apple, ham, and seasoning; pour over the egg. Cover with the remaining pastry. Bake for 20 minutes in a hot oven then reduce heat to moderate and cook for about an hour.

Roll the bottom layer of a double-crusted pie slightly thicker than the covering layer.

PICNIC PIE

4 oz (125 g) shortcrust pastry (see page 83)
1 small onion, chopped
butter
3–4 bacon rashers, chopped
½ cup mashed potatoes
1 dsp parsley
milk
salt and pepper
2–3 eggs

Line a pie-plate with the pastry. Fry the onion in butter until tender. Add the bacon, and cook for a few minutes. Remove from the heat and add the potatoes and parsley; stir in enough milk to make a smooth mixture and season with salt and pepper. Pour into the pastry case. Beat the eggs until fluffy, season, and pour over potato mixture. Bake in a moderate oven until set and golden. Serve hot or cold.

SALMON ROLL

1 lb (500 g) rough puff pastry (see page 83) or flaky pastry (see page 84)
1 egg, beaten
2 hard-boiled eggs, chopped finely
Filling
1 lb (500 g) tinned salmon
1 cup cooked peas
1 cup diced cooked celery
approx. 1 cup white sauce (see page 60)

Roll out the pastry to form a ¾-inch (2-centimetre) thick rectangle. Spread the salmon mixture evenly over the dough, to within an inch (2·5 centimetres) of the edge. Roll up carefully, moistening and sealing the edges. Slide the roll on to a well-greased oven tray and brush with egg. Bake in a hot oven for 10 minutes, then reduce the heat to slow and bake for 35 minutes. Heat the remaining sauce, add the hard-boiled eggs, and serve as a sauce.
Filling: Flake the salmon and mix with the peas, celery, and enough sauce to bind.

Brush egg-white over a pastry base to prevent liquid from seeping through.

STEAK AND KIDNEY PUDDING

8 oz (250 g) suet crust pastry (see page 83)
1½ lb (750 g) diced good-quality steak
1 ox kidney or 2–3 sheep kidneys, chopped
2 large onions, finely chopped

2 tbsps plain flour
marjoram
thyme
savory
salt and pepper
1 cup cold water or stock

Roll out about three-quarters of the dough on a floured surface into a circle large enough to line a pudding basin, allowing a generous amount to overlap the sides of the basin. Roll out the remaining dough to use to cover the pudding. Combine in a mixing bowl the steak, kidneys, and onions. Toss in the flour, seasoned with herbs to taste and salt and pepper. Transfer to the lined basin and add the water. Fold the overlapping section of pastry over the filling, moisten, and cover with the pastry lid; make sure that it is well sealed. Cover with greaseproof paper and a scalded cloth, tying tightly with string. Lower into a large pan with enough boiling water to cover the basin. Steam for about 4 hours, topping up the boiling water as necessary.

VEAL OLIVE PIE

1½ lb (750 g) veal fillet
6 oz (185 g) ham or bacon
¼ pt (150 ml) stock or water
8 oz (250 g) rough puff pastry (see page 83) or flaky pastry (see page 84)

beaten egg

Seasoning
4 oz (125 g) fresh breadcrumbs
2 tbsps chopped parsley
1 tbsp butter

grated rind of ½ lemon
a little grated nutmeg
salt and pepper
2 tbsps milk

Cut the veal into thin slices about 3 by 2 inches (8 by 5 centimetres). Cut rind from the ham or bacon and cut to the same shape as the veal pieces. Put a piece of ham on each slice of veal and divide the seasoning between them. Roll up and arrange in a pie-dish; pour in the stock. Roll out the pastry to cover the pie-dish. Glaze with beaten egg. Bake in a hot oven for 10 to 20 minutes, until the pastry has risen, then lower the temperature to moderate and continue cooking for about 1½ hours.
Seasoning: Mix the breadcrumbs with the parsley, butter, lemon rind, nutmeg, salt, and pepper; bind with the milk.

SEA PIE

1½ lb (750 g) topside steak
1 onion, finely diced
1 carrot, finely diced
1 turnip, finely diced
1 pt (625 ml) water
1 tsp salt
pepper

6 oz (185 g) suet crust pastry (see page 83)

Cut the meat into small pieces and put in a saucepan with the vegetables, water, and salt and pepper. Bring to the boil then simmer gently for an hour. Roll out the pastry to the size of the saucepan lid and place carefully over the meat. Cover with the lid and continue to simmer slowly for an hour. Cut the pastry into four or six pieces and arrange around a heated serving dish; put the meat in the centre and pour over the gravy.

CORNISH PASTIES

1 lb (500 g) lean steak, finely chopped
1 lb (500 g) potatoes, finely diced
1 turnip, finely diced
1 onion, finely chopped
salt and pepper
12 oz (375 g) shortcrust pastry (see page 83)

beaten egg or milk

Combine the meat and vegetables in a mixing bowl and season. Divide the pastry into six equal portions. Knead each piece into a ball and roll out on a floured surface to a circle of about ¼-inch (5-millimetre) thickness. Divide the mixture between the pastry rounds, moisten the edges with cold water, and fold the edges together, pressing to seal. Crimp the edges with the fingers. Prick the pasties with a fork, brush with beaten egg or milk, and arrange on a greased oven tray. Cook in a hot oven for 10 minutes then reduce the temperature to moderate and continue cooking for about half an hour.

MUTTON PIE

1 tbsp butter
1 dsp plain flour
a little grated nutmeg
a little cayenne pepper
salt
1 lb (500 g) leg chops
approx. ¼ pt (150 ml) stock or water

6 oz (185 g) shortcrust pastry (see page 83) or flaky pastry (see page 84)
beaten egg

Blend together the butter, flour, nutmeg, cayenne, and salt until the mixture resembles fine breadcrumbs. Press some of the mixture on to both sides of the chops and arrange them in a pie-dish. Pour over the stock or water. Roll out the pastry to cover the dish; trim the edges and use the trimmings to decorate the pie. Brush with beaten egg and make a hole in the middle of the pie to allow steam to escape. Bake in a hot oven for 10 to 20 minutes, until the pastry has risen, then reduce the temperature to moderate and continue cooking for about 1½ hours.

RAISED PORK PIE

1½ lb (750 g) chopped pork
1 lb (500 g) hot-water crust pastry (see page 84)

1 tbsp chopped parsley
salt and pepper
beaten egg

Put the pork in a saucepan and cover with water; simmer gently for 1 hour, or until tender. Drain, reserving the stock, and leave to cool. Mould three-quarters of the warm pastry by hand around a large jam-jar, to form a round pie-case. Fill with the cold pork, sprinkle in the parsley, and season. Moisten the edges of the pastry and cover with the remaining pastry for the lid; press the edges together well to seal. Make a hole in the centre to allow the steam to escape, trim the edges, and use the trimmings to decorate the pie. Brush with beaten egg and pin a band of greased paper around the pie. Bake in the centre of a moderately hot oven for about half an hour then remove the paper, lower the temperature to moderate, and continue cooking for about an hour. Leave to cool. Melt ½ pint (315 millilitres) of the reserved stock and pour through the steam-hole into the pie. Leave to set before cutting.

RABBIT PIE

1 rabbit, jointed	¼ pt (150 ml) stock or water
4 oz (125 g) chopped bacon rashers	8 oz (250 g) rough puff pastry (see page 83) or flaky pastry (see page 84)
2 hard-boiled eggs, quartered	
1 dsp finely chopped parsley	beaten egg
salt and pepper	

Arrange the rabbit joints in a pie-dish with the bacon, eggs, parsley, and seasoning. Pour in the stock. Roll out the pastry to cover the dish. Trim the edges and use the trimmings to decorate the pie. Make a hole in the middle to allow the steam to escape. Brush with beaten egg and bake in a hot oven for 10 to 15 minutes, until the pastry has risen. Lower the temperature to moderate and cook for about 1½ hours.

PIGEON PIE

1 lb (500 g) sliced rump steak	1 dsp chopped parsley
4 pigeons, cut in quarters	8 oz (250 g) puff pastry (see page 83), rough puff pastry (see page 83), or flaky pastry (see page 84)
salt and pepper	
2 tbsps plain flour	
2 tbsps butter	
1 pt (625 ml) stock	
4 hard-boiled eggs, sliced	beaten egg or milk
1 shallot, finely chopped	

Dredge the steak and the pigeon pieces in seasoned flour. Brown in the hot butter then stir in the stock and stew for about half an hour. Strain off the gravy and reserve. Leave to cool then transfer to a pie-dish with the eggs, shallot, parsley, and seasoning. Pour over the reserved gravy. Roll out the pastry to cover and brush with beaten egg or milk. Bake in a hot oven for about an hour, covering with greased paper when the crust has browned.

Brush savoury pies with beaten egg-yolk for a shiny, golden crust.

APPLE CRUMB FLAN

4 oz (125 g) shortcrust pastry (see page 83)	1 dsp butter
	½ tsp mixed spice
1 lb (500 g) apples, peeled, cored, and sliced	1 large cup fresh breadcrumbs
	½ cup mixed dried fruit, cleaned and chopped
2 oz (60 g) sugar	

Line a flan-tin with the pastry. Stew the apples in as little water as possible. When cooked, beat to a smooth pulp and add the sugar, butter, spice, breadcrumbs, and fruit; mix well. Allow to cool, then pour into the pastry case. Bake for about 20 minutes in a moderate oven. Serve hot or cold.

APPLE PIE

8 oz (250 g) shortcrust pastry (see page 83), rough puff pastry (see page 83), or flaky pastry (see page 84)	3–4 cloves (optional)
	beaten egg or milk
1 lb (500 g) apples, peeled, cored, and sliced	
3 oz (90 g) sugar	
1 tsp finely grated lemon rind	

Line a pie-plate with half the pastry. Layer the apples in the plate, sprinkling sugar, lemon rind, and cloves between the layers; heap the fruit up a little in the centre to support the pastry. Moisten the edges of the pastry with water and roll out the remaining pastry to form a lid. Cover and press the edges together to seal. Crimp the edges and brush the top with egg or milk. Make two slits in the top to allow steam to escape. Bake in the centre of a hot oven for 15 minutes then reduce the temperature to moderate and cook for about 30 to 45 minutes.

Serve with cream or custard (see page 64).

LEMON MERINGUE PIE

4 oz (125 g) shortcrust pastry (see page 83)	2 heaped tbsps cornflour
	⅓ cup cold water
1½ cups water	2 eggs, separated
1 cup sugar	2 oz (60 g) butter
finely grated rind of 2 lemons	a pinch of salt
½ cup lemon juice	4 oz (125 g) castor sugar

Roll the pastry out thinly to line an 8-inch (20-centimetre) pie-plate. Prick with a fork, cover with a circle of greaseproof paper, and fill with dried haricot beans or rice; bake in a hot oven for 15 minutes. Remove the beans and bake for 5 or 10 minutes longer. Leave to cool. Heat the 1½ cups of water with the sugar and lemon rind and juice until boiling. Blend the cornflour with the ⅓ cup of cold water and stir into the liquid. Stir until the mixture thickens then simmer for 3 or 4 minutes, stirring all the time. Remove from the heat and leave to cool slightly. Beat in the egg-yolks and return to the heat for 2 minutes. Add the butter. Pour into the pastry case. Beat the egg-whites with the salt until stiff. Gradually beat in half the castor sugar and continue beating until smooth and glossy. Fold in the remaining sugar. Pile over the filling in the pastry case. Bake in a moderate oven for 15 minutes.

CURLY WIGS

1½ cups self-raising flour	¾ cup sugar
a pinch of salt	½ cup butter
2 tbsps butter	1 cup boiling water
1 stick of rhubarb	

Sift the flour and salt into a mixing bowl. Rub in the 2 tablespoons of butter until the mixture resembles fine breadcrumbs. Mix in enough water to form a stiff dough. Roll out on a floured surface to form a rectangle. Put the stick of rhubarb on the dough and sprinkle with a little sugar and water. Roll the dough over the rhubarb and cut into 1½-inch (4-centimetre) lengths. Stand the rolls in an ovenproof dish. Mix the ¾ cup of sugar with the ½ cup of butter and the cup of boiling water; stir until the butter has melted. Pour the sauce over the curly wigs and bake for 1 hour in a moderate oven. Sprinkle with sugar.

Serve with ice-cream or cream.

RASPBERRY SHORTBREAD

1 cup self-raising flour   raspberry jam
½ cup sugar   coconut
½ cup butter
milk

Sift the flour and sugar into a mixing bowl. Rub in the butter with the fingertips until the mixture resembles breadcrumbs. Mix in a little milk to form a stiff dough. Press the dough into the base of a greased slab-tin. Spread with raspberry jam. Sprinkle with coconut. Bake in a moderate oven for about 20 minutes. Cut into slices when cool.

SPICED RAISIN PIE

4 oz (125 g) shortcrust pastry   1 tsp cinnamon
   (see page 83)   1 tsp allspice
2 tbsps butter   1 tsp ground cloves
2 cups sugar   1 cup chopped raisins
4 eggs, separated
3 tbsps vinegar

Roll out the pastry to line a pie-plate. Cream the butter and sugar. Add the beaten egg-yolks and vinegar, then the spices and raisins. Beat well and fold in the stiffly beaten egg-whites. Pour into the pastry case. Cook in a slow oven until firmly set.

APRICOT SHORTCAKE

3 oz (90 g) butter   2 cups self-raising flour
4 oz (125 g) sugar   1 small tin apricots
1 egg, beaten   icing sugar
2 tbsps milk
Sauce
syrup drained from the apricots   2 tbsps sugar
½ cup water   butter
1 tbsp custard powder

Cream the butter and sugar. Beat in the egg and milk. Gradually add the flour, mixing carefully. Turn on to a floured board and divide into halves. Roll out one half to line a pie-plate. Drain the apricots, reserving the syrup. Arrange the apricots on the pastry. Roll out the remaining pastry to cover the apricots. Bake in a moderate oven for 20 minutes. When cooked, sprinkle with icing sugar and serve with the sauce.
Sauce: Heat the apricot syrup in a saucepan with the water. Blend the custard powder with a little water; stir into the liquid and cook for 1 minute. Stir in the sugar and a knob of butter; heat gently to boiling-point.

Leave cooked pastry dishes in a draught-free place to cool gradually after removing from the oven.

CARAMEL TART

Pastry
1 cup self-raising flour   1 egg
1½ tbsps butter
Caramel Filling
2 tbsps butter   1 cup milk
1 heaped tbsp plain flour   a pinch of salt
1 cup brown sugar   vanilla essence
2 egg-yolks

Pastry: Sift the flour into a mixing bowl. Rub the butter in with the fingertips until the mixture resembles breadcrumbs. Mix in the egg to form a stiff dough. Roll out on a floured board to line a pie-plate or flan-tin. Prick the base with a fork and cover with a circle of greaseproof paper. Fill with dried haricot beans or rice and bake in a hot oven for 15 to 20 minutes. Remove the paper and beans and bake for 5 minutes longer. Leave to cool.
Caramel Filling: Melt the butter in a saucepan. Stir in the flour, sugar, egg-yolks, milk, salt, and vanilla; stir until the mixture thickens, then pour into the pastry case.

CUSTARD TART

4 oz (125 g) shortcrust pastry   ½ pt (315 ml) milk
   (see page 83)   grated nutmeg
2 eggs
2 tbsps sugar

Roll out the pastry to line a 7-inch (18-centimetre) pie-plate. Stand on an oven tray. Beat the eggs with the sugar; gradually beat the heated milk into the egg mixture. Strain the custard into the pastry case and sprinkle with nutmeg. Bake in a pre-heated moderately hot oven for about 15 minutes, until the pastry begins to brown. Lower the heat to moderate and cook for about half an hour, or until the custard is set.

RASPBERRY WALNUT TART

Pastry
1 cup self-raising flour   1 egg-yolk
½ cup plain flour   raspberry jam
a pinch of salt
3 oz (90 g) butter
3 oz (90 g) castor sugar
1 dsp cold water
a squeeze of lemon juice

Filling
2 oz (60 g) butter   ½ cup desiccated coconut
¼ cup castor sugar   1 egg-white, stiffly beaten
1 tsp vanilla essence   a little extra castor sugar
1 egg, beaten
¾ cup self-raising flour
a pinch of salt
1 tsp cinnamon
1 tsp spice
1½ tbsps milk
2 oz (60 g) chopped walnuts

Pastry: Sift the flours and salt into a mixing bowl. Rub in butter until the mixture resembles breadcrumbs. Add the castor sugar and mix to a dough with the water, lemon juice, and egg-yolk. Roll out to fit a Swiss-roll tin. Spread with raspberry jam.

Filling: Cream the butter and castor sugar. Beat in the vanilla and the egg. Fold in the sifted flour, salt, cinnamon, and spice, alternately with the milk. Add the walnuts and coconut. Spread the filling over the pastry. Pile the egg-white on top. Sprinkle with castor sugar. Bake in a moderate oven for 25 to 30 minutes.

MINCE PIES

8 oz (250 g) shortcrust pastry (see page 83), rough puff pastry (see page 83), or puff pastry (see page 83)

8–12 oz (250–375 g) mincemeat (see page 138)
beaten egg
icing sugar or castor sugar

Roll out the pastry thinly and divide it in half. Cut out 2½-inch (6-centimetre) rounds to fit patty tins and fill with about 1 dessertspoon of mincemeat. Roll out the remaining pastry and cut out 2-inch (5-centimetre) lids for the pies. Moisten the edges of the pies with water and cover with the lids, pressing the edges together to seal. Brush with egg, make a slit in the top of each, and bake in a hot oven for about 20 minutes. Remove and cool. Dredge with sugar.

CREAM PUFFS

2 oz (60 g) choux pastry (see page 83)

whipped cream
icing sugar or melted chocolate

Pipe the pastry into 2-inch (5-centimetre) rounds several inches apart on an ungreased oven tray; alternatively drop teaspoonfuls on to an oven tray. Cover with a baking tin and bake in the centre of a hot oven for 45 to 50 minutes; do not lift the cover during this time or the puffs will collapse. Remove the puffs, slit to allow steam to escape, and cool on a rack. Fill with cream and dust with icing sugar or brush with melted chocolate.

ECLAIRS

2 oz (60 g) choux pastry (see page 83)
whipped cream or thick custard

chocolate glacé icing (see page 124) or melted chocolate

Put the pastry into a forcing bag with a plain ½-inch (1-centimetre) nozzle. Pipe in 3- to 4-inch (8- to 10-centimetre) fingers on to an oven tray. Bake in the upper half of a moderately hot oven for 30 to 40 minutes, until golden, crisp, and risen. Remove, slit down each side to allow the steam to escape, and cool on a wire rack. Fill with cream or custard and ice on top with chocolate glacé icing or melted chocolate.

Oven–fresh BREAD, LOAVES, and SCONES

The essence of bread-making is yeast and its proper treatment. There are two forms of yeast—compressed and dried—and a number of steps for their use in recipes. Compressed yeast is a moist, putty-like substance with the one disadvantage that it will keep for only one or two days, although refrigerated it will last for several weeks. It must be kept in a cool place until use, when it should be creamed with a little sugar to start it working, then combined with the specified liquid, which should be at blood-temperature.

You need only half as much yeast in dried form, which consists of small granules, easily obtainable in packets or tins; it can be stored for about six months. Dried yeast should be sprinkled over some of the warm liquid and left in a warm place for 10 to 15 minutes until dissolved and bubbling.

When working with yeast, it is important that the atmosphere and all utensils should be warm and away from draughts, to nurture the yeast, which will be prevented from working or killed altogether by extremes of temperature.

Basic Steps in Bread-making

First, the dry ingredients are mixed together in a warmed mixing bowl. The yeast is then activated as described above. The yeast and liquid is added to the bowl and the mixture is kneaded in the bowl or on a floured surface until it is firm and pliable, about 10 minutes. The prepared dough is then covered and put to rise until doubled in bulk: this will take 24 hours in a refrigerator, if a very slow rising time is wanted; overnight in a cold room; or about 1 hour in a warm place. The dough is then turned out, kneaded for a few minutes, shaped, and put into greased tins or trays. The dough should be covered and left to rise until doubled in size before baking; bread is usually started in a very hot oven and the temperature is reduced after about half an hour. Rich mixtures generally need a lower temperature to prevent them from burning.

Scones

Scones, like pastry, need to be prepared quickly and lightly. The utensils and ingredients used should be cool. The mixing should be done with a round-bladed knife and the mixture should be light but slightly sticky; 1 tablespoon of cornflour in the mixture will help to achieve a light result. If the dough is too dry, the scones will be tough; if it is too wet they will spread. Over-mixing will result in leathery scones. The scones should be cooked in a hot oven as soon as the mixture is ready. If the oven is too slow, the scones will be tough; if it is too quick, they will be soggy. They may be wrapped in a cloth to keep them warm after baking but this may make them a little doughy; if they are put on wire racks to cool they will be more crisp. Scones should be broken rather than cut before buttering.

ACID YEAST

1 medium potato
1½ tbsps sugar
½ tsp citric or tartaric acid

1 cup warm water
1 dsp plain flour

Boil the potato and mash it. Leave to cool. Mix in the other ingredients. Bottle, and cork tightly. Keep in a warm place for 12 hours in a bottle that has recently been used for yeast, or for 24 hours in a new bottle.

WHITE BREAD

3½ lb (1·75 kg) plain flour
1 tsp salt
1 oz (30 g) compressed yeast

1 tsp sugar
approx. 1½ pt (940 ml) tepid water

Sift the flour and salt into a warm mixing bowl; make a well in the centre. Cream the yeast with the sugar, then add the warm water. Pour the yeast mixture into the well in the dry ingredients and mix thoroughly with the fingertips, kneading for about 10 minutes, until it is no longer sticky. Lightly flour the bowl and cover with a damp tea-towel. Leave in a warm place until the dough has doubled in bulk, about 1 hour. Warm and grease loaf-tins or oven trays. Pre-heat the oven to very hot. Turn the dough on to a floured surface and knead for a few minutes. Form into loaves to three-quarters fill the tins; put in a warm place for 15 to 20 minutes, until the dough rises to the top of the tins. Bake for 15 minutes, then reduce the temperature to hot and continue baking until the loaves are well risen, golden, and sound hollow when tapped with the knuckles.

QUICK WHITE BREAD

1 lb (500 g) plain flour
1 tsp salt
½ oz (15 g) compressed yeast

1 tsp sugar
½ pt (315 ml) tepid water
1 tsp butter, melted

Sift the flour and salt into a mixing bowl. Cream the yeast and sugar in a warm bowl; add the water and butter. Make a well in the centre of the flour and add the liquid. Mix to a soft dough. Turn on to a floured surface and knead thoroughly. Form into a loaf. Leave in a warm place for 40 minutes, or until doubled in size. Bake in a moderate oven for 40 minutes.

EASY MILK BREAD

1 lb (500 g) self-raising flour
1 tsp salt

approx. ½ pt (315 ml) milk

Sift the flour and salt into a mixing bowl. Mix to a dough with the milk. Pour into a well-greased, 7-inch (18-centimetre) round, 3-inch (8-centimetre) deep cake-tin. Bake in a moderate to hot oven for about 1 hour.

WHOLEMEAL BREAD

3 lb (1·5 kg) wholemeal plain
 flour
1 dsp salt
2 oz (60 g) butter
2 oz (60 g) compressed yeast

1 tsp sugar
½ pt (315 ml) warm milk
approx. 1 pt (625 ml)
 warm water

Mix the flour with the salt; rub in the butter. Cream the yeast with the sugar, then add a little of the warm liquid. Make a well in the centre of the dry ingredients and mix in the yeast, milk, and enough of the water to form a soft dough. Turn on to a lightly floured surface and knead for about 10 minutes, until the dough is no longer sticky. Flour the mixing bowl lightly, return the dough to it, and cover with a damp tea-towel. Leave in a warm place to rise until doubled in size. Grease four small loaf-tins or two large tins and pre-heat the oven to hot. Turn the dough out on to a floured surface and knead for several minutes. Divide the dough into as many portions as needed and half-fill the tins. Cover and leave for about 20 minutes, or until the dough rises to the top of the tins. Bake for about 15 minutes, then reduce the temperature to moderate and continue cooking until the loaves shrink slightly from the sides of the tin and sound hollow when tapped with the knuckles. Turn out and cool on a wire rack.

WALNUT BREAD

3 cups self-raising flour
1 cup roughly chopped
 walnuts
1 cup sugar
1 cup sultanas

a little nutmeg
a pinch of salt
1 egg
milk

Combine all the dry ingredients in a mixing bowl. Beat the egg in a cup and then fill the cup with milk. Add this cup of liquid, and another ½ pint (315 millilitres) of milk, to the dry ingredients and beat. Pour into a greased tin and bake for 1¼ to 1½ hours in a moderate oven.

HONEY LUNCH BREAD

9 oz (280 g) honey
9 oz (280 g) brown sugar
1 tsp allspice
a few drops of aniseed or 1 tsp
 caraway seed

1 egg, beaten
2 oz (60 g) butter
1 cup milk
18 oz (560 g) plain flour
1 tbsp baking powder

Mix the honey, sugar, allspice, aniseed or caraway seed, and the egg in a bowl. Heat the butter and milk in a saucepan, and bring to the boil. Stir the liquid into the honey mixture. Sift the flour and baking powder three times, and fold into the mixture. Pour into a large tin. Bake in a moderate oven for 2 hours.

DELICIOUS ORANGE BREAD

1 oz (30 g) compressed yeast
¼ cup tepid water
1 cup orange juice
grated rind of 1 orange
grated rind of 1 lemon
1 tsp salt
1 tbsp melted butter
3 tbsps sugar

2 egg-yolks, well beaten
4 cups plain flour

Soften the yeast in the tepid water and add to the orange juice and grated rinds. Add the salt, melted butter, sugar, and egg-yolks. Stir in the flour gradually. Knead well until the dough is smooth and elastic. Cover and set aside for 2 hours in a warm place. Knead once more very lightly and make into two loaves. Set aside again until they are doubled in size. Bake in a moderate oven for 1 hour.

BILLY BREAD

1 cup wholemeal
1 cup plain flour
1 dsp baking powder
a pinch of salt

1 tbsp golden syrup
approx. 1 cup milk

Sift the dry ingredients into a mixing bowl. Stir in the golden syrup. Mix to a soft dough with milk. Put in a billycan and bake for 1½ hours in a hot oven. Leave for half an hour before turning out.

MUFFINS

1 lb (500 g) plain flour
1 tsp salt
approx. ½ pt (315 ml) warm
    water
1 oz. (30 g) compressed yeast
1 egg, beaten

1 oz (30 g) butter, melted

Sift the flour and salt into a mixing bowl; make a well in the centre. Mix the yeast with a little of the liquid then add to the dry ingredients with the egg, the butter, and enough of the remaining warm water to form a soft dough. Turn out on to a well-floured surface and knead for about 10 minutes, until the dough is no longer sticky. Flour the mixing bowl lightly, return the dough to it, and cover with a damp tea-towel. Stand in a warm place until the dough has doubled in size. Turn out on to a floured surface and knead for several minutes. Roll out to ½-inch (1-centimetre) thickness and cut into rounds. Transfer to a floured oven tray, dust with flour, cover, and leave to rise until doubled in size. Bake in a hot oven for about 5 minutes. Remove from the oven, turn, and bake for another 5 minutes.
  Serve toasted, split, and buttered.

SALLY LUNN MUFFINS

2 lb (1 kg) plain flour
1 tbsp sugar
1 tsp salt
1 oz (30 g) dried yeast
1 tbsp lard or butter

1 egg, beaten
1¼ pt (780 ml) milk

Sift the flour, sugar, salt, and yeast into a mixing bowl. Rub in the cold lard. Mix to a stiff batter with the egg and milk. Two-thirds fill cold, well-greased muffin pans. Leave in a warm place until the dough rises to the top of the tins. Bake in a hot oven for 15 minutes.

CRUMPETS

1 lb (500 g) plain flour
½ oz (15 g) compressed yeast
approx. 1 pt (625 ml) warm
    milk and water
a pinch of bicarbonate of soda

1 tsp salt

Sift the flour into a mixing bowl; make a well in the centre. Cream the yeast with a little of the liquid. Add to the flour with the remaining liquid. Beat with the hand for 5 minutes. Cover with a damp tea-towel and stand in a warm place for at least 1 hour, until doubled in size. Dissolve the soda and salt in a little extra warm water and beat into the mixture. Cover and return to a warm place for about 45 minutes. Grease and heat a girdle (or a heavy frying pan); grease some crumpet rings and heat them on the girdle at the same time. Pour in enough batter to cover the bottom of the rings and cook gently until the top is set. Remove the rings, turn the crumpets, and cook for a few minutes on the other side.

HOT CROSS BUNS

1 lb (500 g) plain flour
1 oz (30 g) yeast
1 tsp sugar
approx. ½ pt (315 ml) warm
    milk and water
2 oz (60 g) castor sugar
½ tsp salt
½ tsp mixed spice
½ tsp cinnamon
Glaze
2 tbsps sugar

½ tsp grated nutmeg
1 oz (30 g) candied peel
2 oz (60 g) currants
2 oz (60 g) sultanas
2 oz (60 g) butter, melted
1 egg, beaten

4 tbsps milk and water

Sift one-quarter of the flour into a large mixing bowl. Cream the yeast with the 1 teaspoon of sugar and mix with the warm liquid. Add the liquid to the flour, mixing well. Cover with a tea-towel and leave for about 20 minutes until frothy. Meanwhile sift together the remaining flour, the 2 ounces (60 grams) of castor sugar, the salt, spice, cinnamon, and nutmeg. Stir the sifted ingredients into the yeast mixture, then the fruit, and then the melted butter and beaten egg. Mix to a soft dough by hand. Turn out on a floured surface and knead until smooth. Cover with a damp tea-towel and stand in a warm place for about 1 hour, until doubled in size. Turn the dough out on to a floured surface and knead for a few minutes. Divide the dough into about twelve pieces and shape into buns. Arrange them on a greased and floured oven tray, leaving plenty of room for spreading. Cover and leave in a warm place for 20 to 30 minutes. Pre-heat the oven to very hot. Cut a cross on top of each bun with a sharp knife. Bake for about 15 minutes. Remove and brush with the hot glaze.

Glaze: Heat the sugar with the milk and water, stirring to make sure that the sugar has dissolved. Bring to the boil.

DATE BUNS

3¾ cups plain flour
¾ cup sugar
1 tbsp cream of tartar
1 dsp bicarbonate of soda

1 cup chopped dates
1 egg, beaten
1 cup milk
2 tbsps melted butter

Mix all the dry ingredients together; add the dates. Beat the egg with the milk; pour on to the dry ingredients and mix well. Add the melted butter. Divide the mixture into twelve pieces and place in a well-greased roasting tin. Bake in a moderate oven for 20 minutes.

COCONUT LOAF

½ cup desiccated coconut
½ cup sugar
1 cup self-raising flour

¾ cup milk
lemon essence (optional)

Combine the coconut, sugar, and flour in a mixing bowl. Mix to a soft dough with the milk. Pour into a greased tin and bake in a moderate oven for about 20 minutes.

BROWNIE

3 cups plain flour	2 cups hot water
1 dsp baking powder	1 tsp bicarbonate of soda
a pinch of salt	1 dsp mixed spice
1 cup sugar	2 eggs, well beaten
2 tbsps butter	
1 packet mixed dried fruit	

Sift the flour, baking powder, and salt into a mixing bowl. Add the sugar; rub in the butter. In a separate bowl, mix the fruit with the hot water, soda, and spice; when cool, add the eggs. Mix the fruit mixture into the dry ingredients. Bake in a well-greased, 9- by 8-inch (23- by 20-centimetre) tin in a moderate oven for 1 hour.

Serve sliced and buttered.

EGGLESS DATE LOAF

½ cup sugar	a handful of chopped mixed
1 cup chopped dates	nuts
1 tsp ground ginger	a few walnuts, chopped
½ tsp mixed spice	1½–2 cups self-raising flour
½ tsp grated nutmeg	a pinch of salt
1 tbsp butter	
½ tsp bicarbonate of soda	
1 tsp cinnamon	
1 cup boiling water	

Combine the sugar, dates, ginger, mixed spice, nutmeg, butter, soda, and cinnamon in a mixing bowl. Pour over the boiling water, the mixed nuts, and the walnuts; beat well. Fold in the flour and salt. Pour into a greased tin and bake in a moderate oven for half an hour.

CURRANT LOAF

1 cup cold black tea	a pinch of salt
1 cup currants	
1 small cup sugar	
2 cups self-raising flour	

Mix the tea with the currants and sugar in a bowl. Leave to stand for 2 or 3 hours, stirring occasionally. Sift the flour and salt, and stir into the currant mixture. Pour into a greased, 8- by 4-inch (20- by 10-centimetre) loaf-tin. Bake in a moderate oven for about 1 hour. Leave to cool.

Serve sliced and buttered.

HONEY FRUIT LOAF

3 oz (90 g) butter	4 oz (125 g) self-raising flour
½ large cup honey	2 oz (60 g) plain flour
1 egg, lightly beaten	4 tbsps milk
6 oz (185 g) mixed dried fruit	

Cream the butter and honey. Beat the egg in thoroughly. Stir in the mixed fruit and the sifted flours. Add the milk and mix well. Line the bottom of a greased loaf-tin with greaseproof paper, and pour in the mixture. Bake in the middle of a moderate oven for 1 to 1¼ hours.

MOIST FRUIT LOAF

1 packet port wine jelly	1 packet mixed dried fruit
crystals	1 cup walnuts (optional)
2 cups boiling water	3 tsps bicarbonate of soda
½ cup sugar	3 cups plain flour
2 tbsps golden syrup	3 tsps baking powder
4 oz (125 g) butter	

Grease two loaf-tins. Pre-heat the oven to moderate. Make the jelly in the usual way with the 2 cups of boiling water. Stir into the hot liquid the sugar, golden syrup, butter, fruit, walnuts, and soda. Sift the flour and baking powder and fold in carefully. Pour the mixture into the prepared tins and bake for about 1 hour.

LEMON NUT LOAF

2 oz (60 g) butter	¾ cup milk
¾ cup sugar	½ cup finely chopped walnuts
1 dsp grated lemon rind	2 oz (60 g) grated cheese
2 eggs	
2 cups self-raising flour	
a pinch of salt	

Cream the butter with the sugar and lemon rind. Add the eggs, one at a time, beating well after each addition. Sift the flour and salt, and add to the creamed mixture, alternately with the milk. Fold in the walnuts and cheese. Turn into a greased loaf-tin. Bake in a moderate oven for 1 hour. Test with a skewer before removing.

MALT LOAF

3 cups self-raising flour	½ cup sultanas, currants, or
2 tbsps sugar	raisins
¾ cup malt and golden syrup	milk
or honey, mixed	
1 egg, beaten	

Mix the dry ingredients. Add the malt and syrup, then the egg, and finally the dried fruit. Mix to a soft dough with milk. Bake in a greased tin in a moderate oven.

NUT LOAF

1 cup chopped dates	1 egg, beaten
1 tsp bicarbonate of soda	2 cups plain flour
1 cup boiling water	1 tsp baking powder
1 tbsp butter	1 cup chopped walnuts
1 cup sugar	

Grease three small loaf-tins. Pre-heat the oven to moderately hot. Put the dates in a bowl and sprinkle with the soda. Pour over the boiling water and leave to stand for half an hour. Cream the butter and sugar with the egg. Sift the flour with the baking powder. Stir the date mixture into the creamed ingredients, then fold in the flour and nuts. Pour into the prepared tins and bake for 40 to 45 minutes.

FRENCH SCONE

a pinch of salt
1 egg, separated
½ cup sugar
½ cup milk
½ tsp vanilla essence

1 cup self-raising flour
1 tbsp melted butter
a little extra melted butter
1 tsp sugar
½ tsp cinnamon

Grease a 7-inch (18-centimetre) sandwich tin. Pre-heat the oven to moderate. Add the salt to the egg-white in a mixing bowl and beat until stiff. Gradually beat in the sugar. Fold in the beaten egg-yolk, the milk and vanilla, then the sifted flour. Carefully stir in the tablespoon of melted butter. Pour the mixture into the prepared tin and bake for 20 to 25 minutes. Remove from the tin and, while the cake is still warm, brush with melted butter and sprinkle over the teaspoon of sugar and the cinnamon.

Serve sliced and buttered.

PLAIN SCONES

8 oz (250 g) self-raising flour
½ tsp salt
1–2 oz (30–60 g) butter

approx. ¼ pt (150 ml) milk
beaten egg or milk

Pre-heat the oven to very hot. Sift the flour and salt into a mixing bowl. Rub in the butter with the fingertips until the mixture resembles fine breadcrumbs. For sweet scones, add 2 tablespoons of castor sugar at this stage. Add enough milk to make a soft, but not sticky, dough, mixing with a knife. Turn out on to a lightly floured surface and roll out lightly to ½-inch (1-centimetre) thickness. Cut into squares with a floured knife or into rounds with a floured biscuit cutter. Arrange on a floured oven tray and brush with egg or milk. Bake in the hottest part of the oven for 10 to 12 minutes, or until well risen and golden.

RICH BUTTER SCONES

2 cups self-raising flour
2 tbsps icing sugar
2 tbsps powdered milk
1 tsp baking powder
a pinch of salt

4 tbsps butter
1 egg
approx. 1 cup water
milk or melted butter

Pre-heat the oven to hot. Sift the flour with the icing sugar, powdered milk, baking powder, and salt. Rub in the butter thoroughly with the fingertips. Beat the egg with the water. Mix the dry ingredients to a soft dough with the egg and water. Turn on to a floured surface and knead lightly. Roll out and cut into shapes. Arrange on an oven tray and brush with milk or melted butter. Bake for about 12 to 15 minutes.

QUICK-MIX SCONES

2 tbsps butter
1½ tbsps sugar
2 eggs, beaten
2 cups self-raising flour
a pinch of salt

½ cup milk
½ cup sultanas

Pre-heat the oven to hot. Cream the butter and sugar. Beat in the eggs. Add the sifted flour and salt, alternately with the milk. Mix to a soft dough. Add the sultanas. Turn on to a floured surface, knead slightly, and roll out gently. Cut into rounds and arrange on an oven tray. Bake for 7 to 10 minutes.

PUMPKIN SCONES

1 egg
1 heaped tbsp butter
1 cup mashed pumpkin
½ cup sugar
3 cups self-raising flour

½ tsp salt
milk

Pre-heat the oven to hot. Beat the egg with the butter, pumpkin, and sugar. Add the sifted flour and salt. Add enough milk to form a soft dough. Knead and roll out on a floured surface. Cut into rounds and arrange on an oven tray. Cook for 10 minutes.

POTATO SCONES

8 oz (250 g) plain flour
a pinch of salt
2 oz (60 g) butter

8 oz (250 g) mashed potatoes
milk or water

Pre-heat the oven to hot. Sift the flour and salt into a mixing bowl. Rub in the butter with the fingertips. Add the potatoes and mix to a soft dough with milk or water. Turn on to a floured surface, knead slightly, then roll out to about ½-inch (1-centimetre) thickness. Cut into rounds and arrange on a floured oven tray. Brush with milk and bake for about 10 minutes.

Serve split and buttered.

SAVOURY SCONES

1 quantity plain scone dough (see this page)
2 hard-boiled eggs, finely chopped
1 tbsp butter, melted
1 tbsp anchovy essence

a little lemon juice
a pinch of white pepper
finely grated cheese

Pre-heat the oven to hot. Make the scone dough and roll out thinly on a floured surface; cut into halves. Mix together the chopped eggs, melted butter, anchovy essence, lemon juice, and pepper. Spread the egg mixture over one-half of the dough and cover with the remaining half. Cut into rounds, sprinkle with grated cheese, and arrange on an oven tray. Bake for about 10 minutes.

CHEESE SCONES

2 tbsps butter
2 oz (60 g) grated cheese
2 eggs, beaten
½ tsp dry mustard
¼ tsp salt

2 cups self-raising flour
½ cup milk
a little extra milk
paprika pepper

Pre-heat the oven to hot. Cream the butter with the cheese. Beat in the eggs, mustard, and salt. Add the sifted flour. Mix to a soft dough with the milk. Knead slightly then roll out on a floured surface and cut into rounds. Arrange on a greased oven tray, brush with milk, and sprinkle with a little paprika. Bake for 7 to 10 minutes.

DATE AND ORANGE SCONES

2 tbsps butter
2 tbsps sugar
grated rind of 1 small orange
1 egg, beaten
½ cup chopped dates or
  raisins

2 cups self-raising flour
a pinch of salt
½ cup milk
¼ cup orange juice

Pre-heat the oven to hot. Cream the butter with the sugar and the orange rind. Beat the egg in thoroughly then add the dates. Fold in the sifted flour and salt, alternately with the milk and orange juice. Turn on to a floured surface and roll out to ½-inch (1-centimetre) thickness. Cut into squares or rounds with a floured knife or cutter. Arrange on an oven tray. Bake for 10 to 12 minutes.

PIKELETS

8 oz (250 g) self-raising flour
a pinch of salt
1 tbsp sugar

1 egg, beaten
approx. ½ pt (315 ml) milk
1 tbsp butter

Sift the flour and salt into a mixing bowl; stir in the sugar. Mix to a thick, smooth batter with the egg and the milk. Heat a heavy frying pan, grease with the butter, and pour in small spoonfuls of the batter. When golden underneath and bubbling on top, turn carefully and cook on the other side. As the pikelets are cooked, transfer them to a wire rack.

Serve hot or cold with butter and syrup or jam.

GIRDLE SCONES

12 oz (375 g) plain flour
a pinch of salt
¼ tsp bicarbonate of soda

¼ pt (150 ml) milk

Sift the flour and salt into a mixing bowl. Dissolve the soda in the milk and pour into the sifted ingredients, mixing to a soft dough. Roll out on a floured surface and cut into rounds. Cook on a hot, greased girdle (or a heavy frying pan) for about 5 minutes on each side.

Serve hot, split and buttered.

AUNT NELLIE'S DROP CAKES

½ cup butter
1 cup sugar
3 eggs, well beaten
1 cup plain flour
1 cup cornflour

1 tsp baking powder

Pre-heat the oven to moderately hot. Cream the butter and sugar. Beat in the eggs. Sift the flours and baking powder and add to the creamed mixture. Place teaspoons of the mixture on a well-greased oven tray. Bake for about 15 minutes.

When cold, sandwich together with jam or other filling.

WELSH CAKES

8 oz (250 g) self-raising flour
3 oz (90 g) butter
3 oz (90 g) currants
3 oz (90 g) sugar

1 egg, beaten
a little milk or water
extra sugar

Sift the flour into a mixing bowl. Rub in the butter with the fingertips until the flour resembles fine breadcrumbs. Stir in the currants and sugar. Mix to a stiff dough with the egg and milk or water. Roll out on a floured surface to ¼-inch (5-millimetre) thickness. Cut into rounds and cook on a hot girdle (or a heavy frying pan) for about 5 minutes on each side. When cooked, dredge with sugar.

PUFTALOONS

3 cups plain flour
3 tsps baking powder
1 tsp salt

1 cup milk and water
fat

Sift the flour, baking powder, and salt into a mixing bowl. Add the liquid to make a firm dough. Roll out dough to ½-inch (1-centimetre) thickness and cut into squares. Deep-fry the squares in fat until golden. Drain on absorbent paper.

Serve with golden syrup.

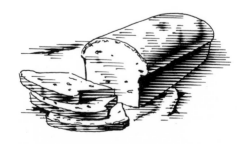

Biscuit trifle (page 79)

Above: Christmas pudding (page 73), caramel slice (page 103), shortbread (page 102), mince pies (page 89), and Christmas cake (page 118). *Below:* Mint julep (page 146), pineapple egg-nog (page 144), and claret cup (page 145)

A basket of assorted breads, including quick white bread (page 92), easy milk bread (page 92), and wholemeal bread (page 92), with nut loaf (page 94), and eggless date loaf (page 94)

Above: Apple pie (page 87) made with shortcrust pastry (page 83) and shortcrust turnovers with mincemeat (page 138). *Below:* A selection of pickles, jams, and preserved fruit

Sponge butterflies (page 106) with snowballs (page 106); cherry cakes (page 107) with glacé icing
(page 124) and variously decorated patty cakes (page 106) and gem cakes (page 106)

Foundation cake (page 112), lamingtons (page 113), and chocolate sandwich cake (page 113) with
chocolate glacé icing (page 124)

Ginger fluff sandwich (page 120)

Coconut ice (page 130), French jellies (page 130), toffees (page 131), and assorted creams (page 130)

Crunchy Sumptuous
BISCUITS
and SLICES

Many of the rules and hints for pastry-making apply equally to dough-based biscuits. Plain rolled biscuits can be iced and decorated as you wish or sandwiched together and filled (see the chapter 'Luscious Icings and Fillings').

Generally, dough for rolled biscuits should be fairly stiff. Dough that has too much liquid will be sticky and difficult to handle and the biscuits will tend to spread; half an hour in the refrigerator will, however, make it more manageable. A mixture that is to be put through a biscuit forcer should be a little softer or the shapes will break as they come out of the forcer, which will be difficult to operate. Ideally, all biscuits should be cut from an even first rolling, using cutters or small glasses or cups. If the mixture has been handled a great deal or re-rolled it will produce heavy biscuits. Biscuits can be shaped easily by breaking off pieces of dough and rolling them into small balls with the hands; arrange them on oven trays and press flat with a fork.

Rich biscuit mixtures with a high fat content may be arranged on cold ungreased oven trays but those containing little fat should be baked on well-greased trays. For even baking, biscuits should be of uniform size and thickness.

After baking, which is generally done in a moderately hot oven until the biscuits are golden, they should be removed to wire racks to cool; if the mixture is rich and the biscuits are soft when baked, they need to be left to firm before being moved to finish cooling.

Fill and ice if necessary and store the biscuits in airtight containers.

SHREWSBURY BISCUITS

4 oz (125 g) butter
4 oz (125 g) sugar
vanilla essence
1 egg

7 oz (220 g) self-raising flour
a pinch of salt

Cream the butter and sugar with the vanilla. Beat the egg in thoroughly. Stir in the sifted flour and salt to make a fairly stiff dough. Form the mixture into small balls. Arrange on greased oven trays, allowing room for spreading. Press down with a floured fork. Bake in a moderate oven for about 15 to 20 minutes.

BACHELOR'S BUTTONS

8 oz (250 g) plain flour
1 dsp baking powder
a pinch of salt
4 oz (125 g) butter
1 egg
4 oz (125 g) sugar

1 tsp vanilla essence
extra sugar

Sift the flour, baking powder, and salt into a mixing bowl. Rub in the butter until the mixture resembles breadcrumbs. Beat the egg with the sugar and vanilla. Mix the dry ingredients to a dough with the egg mixture. Form into small balls, roll in sugar, and arrange on greased oven trays. Bake in a moderate oven for about 10 minutes.

BURNT BUTTER BISCUITS

8 oz (250 g) butter
8 oz (250 g) sugar
vanilla essence
2 eggs, well beaten
10 oz (315 g) self-raising
    flour

a pinch of salt
halved blanched almonds

Heat the butter slowly in a saucepan until it is light brown. Allow to cool, then beat in the sugar and the vanilla. Beat the eggs in thoroughly, then fold in the flour, which has been sifted with the salt. Form into small balls and arrange on greased oven trays, leaving room for spreading. Press half an almond into the top of each and bake in a moderate oven for 12 to 15 minutes.

MALT BISCUITS

4 oz (125 g) butter
4 oz (125 g) sugar
1 tbsp golden syrup
1 tbsp malt
8 oz (250 g) self-raising flour

1 egg
2 tbsps chopped almonds

Heat the butter, sugar, golden syrup, and malt, stirring until the sugar has dissolved. Remove from the heat and add the flour, then the egg and nuts. Arrange teaspoons of the mixture on greased oven trays, leaving room for spreading, and bake in a moderate oven for about 10 minutes.

GINGER BISCUITS

1 cup butter
2 cups sugar
1 cup treacle or golden syrup
1 cup milk
1 dsp bicarbonate of soda
5 cups plain flour

½ tsp salt
1 dsp ground ginger

Heat the butter, sugar, treacle, milk, and soda in a saucepan, stirring until the butter melts and the sugar dissolves. Remove from the heat and leave to cool slightly. Stir in the sifted flour, salt, and ginger. Drop teaspoons of the mixture on to greased oven trays, leaving room for the biscuits to spread. Bake in a moderately hot oven for 15 to 20 minutes.

GINGERNUTS

2 tbsps butter
8 oz (250 g) sugar
1 egg
½ cup treacle or golden syrup
8 oz (250 g) plain flour

1 dsp baking powder
1 tbsp ground ginger

Cream the butter and sugar. Beat in the egg. Add the treacle, then the flour, which has been sifted with the baking powder and ginger. Roll into balls the size of walnuts. Place on greased oven trays, allowing room for the biscuits to spread, and bake in a moderate oven for 12 to 15 minutes, until brown.

COCKLES

2 eggs
the weight of the eggs in plain
    flour
the weight of the eggs in
    cornflour

the weight of the eggs in castor
    sugar
1 dsp baking powder
4 oz (125 g) butter

Replace 1 tablespoon of flour with 1 tablespoon of desiccated coconut. Sift the flours and baking powder. Cream the butter and sugar. Beat the eggs into the creamed mixture, one at a time, beating well after each addition. Fold in the sifted dry ingredients. Arrange small teaspoons of the mixture on a greased oven tray. Bake in a moderately hot oven for 7 to 10 minutes. Leave to cool.

Sandwich pairs of the biscuits together with jam, ice with vanilla icing (see the chapter 'Luscious Icings and|Fillings'), and sprinkle with coconut.

JAM-SANDWICH BISCUITS

½ cup butter
¾ cup sugar
1 egg
⅓ cup desiccated coconut
1 tsp bicarbonate of soda

⅓ cup milk
1 dsp golden syrup
2 cups plain flour
a pinch of salt

Cream the butter and sugar. Beat the egg in thoroughly. Mix in the coconut. Dissolve the soda in the milk and add to the creamed mixture with the golden syrup. Fold in the flour, which has been sifted with the salt. Drop spoonfuls of the mixture on to greased oven trays, and press flat with a fork. Bake in a moderately hot oven for 10 to 12 minutes. Leave to cool.

Sandwich together with white icing mixed with raspberry jam.

RAW PEANUT BISCUITS

½ cup butter
1 cup brown sugar
1 egg
1½ cups self-raising flour
1 dsp cocoa

1 cup chopped raw peanuts

Cream the butter and sugar. Beat the egg in thoroughly. Sift in the flour and cocoa. Add the nuts. Place teaspoons of the mixture on greased oven trays. Bake in a moderate oven for 12 to 15 minutes.

PEANUT CRISPIES

½ cup butter
¾ cup sugar
1 egg
1 large cup self-raising flour
1 tsp cocoa

1 tsp salt
1 large cup unroasted peanuts

Cream the butter and sugar. Beat the egg in thoroughly. Mix in the flour, cocoa, salt, and peanuts. If the mixture is too dry to be workable, add a little milk. Form into balls the size of walnuts and arrange on cold oven trays, leaving room for spreading. Bake in a moderate oven until golden.

BUTTERNUTS

4 oz (125 g) butter
1 cup sugar
1 egg
½ tsp vanilla essence
2 tbsps golden syrup
1 tbsp milk
1½ cups plain flour

½ tsp salt
½ tsp bicarbonate of soda
1 tsp cream of tartar
1 cup desiccated coconut
2 oz (60 g) finely chopped nuts, or mixed dried fruit

Cream the butter and sugar. Beat in the egg and vanilla, then add the golden syrup and milk, mixing well. Sift together the flour, salt, soda, and cream of tartar; add with the coconut to the creamed mixture. Fold in the nuts. Drop teaspoons of the mixture on to greased oven trays, allowing room for spreading. Bake in a moderate oven for about 12 to 15 minutes, until golden.

ANZACS

¾ cup desiccated coconut
1 cup rolled oats
1 cup sugar
1 cup plain flour
a pinch of salt

½ cup butter
1 tbsp golden syrup
1 dsp bicarbonate of soda
1½ tbsps boiling water

Combine the coconut, oats, sugar, flour, and salt in a mixing bowl. Melt the butter and golden syrup in a saucepan. Dissolve the soda in the boiling water and add to the syrup. Mix the liquid into the dry ingredients. Arrange teaspoons of the mixture on greased oven trays and flatten with a floured fork. Bake in a slow oven for 20 to 30 minutes.

CHERRY BISCUITS

4 oz (125 g) butter
4 oz (125 g) sugar
1 egg
8 oz (250 g) self-raising flour

glacé cherries

Cream the butter and sugar. Beat in the egg. Sift the flour, then mix into the creamed mixture to make a fairly stiff dough. Place teaspoons of the mixture on greased oven trays and press a cherry on top of each. Bake in a moderate oven for about 15 minutes, until golden.

CRUNCHIES

4 oz (125 g) butter
3 oz (90 g) sugar
1 tsp golden syrup
1 tbsp boiling water
a few drops of vanilla essence
4 oz (125 g) self-raising flour

1 cup rolled oats

Cream the butter and sugar. Add the golden syrup, boiling water, and vanilla essence. Stir in the flour and oats, mixing well. Roll into balls and arrange on greased oven trays. Bake in a moderate oven for 15 to 20 minutes. Leave to cool.

Decorate with a little icing.

ROLLED OAT BISCUITS

¼ cup dripping
1 tsp bicarbonate of soda
2 tbsps water
2 cups rolled oats

¾ cup brown sugar
1 cup plain flour

Heat the dripping, soda, and water in a saucepan to boiling-point. Combine the oats and sugar in a mixing bowl, then add the flour. Stir the soda mixture into the dry ingredients with a knife. Allow to stand for 10 minutes. Roll the mixture into small balls, arrange on greased oven trays, allowing room to spread, and press down with a fork. Bake in a moderate oven for about 20 minutes.

OATMEAL BISCUITS

8 oz (250 g) loaf sugar
8 oz (250 g) butter
1 lb (500 g) fine oatmeal

2 eggs
cold water

Pound the sugar. Add the butter, oatmeal, and eggs. Mix to a stiff dough with a little cold water. Roll out on a floured surface into small balls. Arrange on greased oven trays, and flatten with a fork. Bake in a moderate oven for about 15 minutes, until crisp and pale golden.

BRANDY SNAPS

2 oz (60 g) butter
2 oz (60 g) golden syrup
2 oz (60 g) sugar
2 oz (60 g) plain flour

½ tsp ground ginger
½ tsp grated lemon rind
½ tsp lemon juice or brandy

Melt the butter with the syrup and sugar in a saucepan; stir to dissolve the sugar. Remove from the heat and stir in the flour, ginger, lemon rind, and juice. Drop small teaspoons of the mixture on to greased oven trays, leaving plenty of room for spreading. Bake in a slow oven for 15 to 20 minutes. Remove from the oven and leave for a couple of minutes. When slightly set, roll up quickly around the handle of a wooden spoon. Cool on a wire rack.

Fill with whipped cream before serving.

WALNUT WAFERS

4 oz (125 g) butter
4 oz (125 g) golden syrup
3 oz (90 g) sugar
4 oz (125 g) self-raising flour
3 oz (90 g) chopped nuts

1 dsp ground ginger
1 tsp baking powder

Heat the butter, syrup, and sugar gently in a saucepan until the butter has melted. Remove from the heat and add the other ingredients, mixing well. Drop teaspoons of the mixture on to greased oven trays. Bake in a moderate oven for 10 minutes. Leave to cool for a few minutes before removing from the tray, then lift off with a knife. The wafers may then be quickly rolled like brandy snaps if you wish. Working quickly, roll the warm wafers around the greased handle of a wooden spoon. Leave to cool on a wire rack.

Fill with whipped cream before serving.

COCONUT MACAROONS

3 egg-whites
a pinch of salt
8 oz (250 g) castor sugar
2 cups desiccated coconut
1 dsp cornflour

2 oz (60 g) chopped blanched
almonds
½ tsp vanilla essence

Beat the egg-whites with the salt until stiff. Gradually beat in the sugar, with the bowl standing over hot water, until a crust forms on the bottom. Remove the bowl from the hot water and fold in the coconut, cornflour, almonds, and vanilla. Drop small teaspoons of the mixture on to an oven tray covered with greased paper. Bake in a slow oven for 30 to 40 minutes.

FOAM BISCUITS

½ cup milk
1 cup sugar
1 tsp bicarbonate of soda
3 cups plain flour

a pinch of salt
1 cup butter

Heat the milk with the sugar in a saucepan, stirring to make sure that the sugar has dissolved. Bring to the boil, stir in the soda, and remove from the heat. Leave to cool. Sift the flour and salt into a mixing bowl, then rub in the butter until the mixture resembles breadcrumbs. Pour in the cooled liquid and mix to a firm dough. Roll out on a floured surface and cut into shapes. Bake in a moderately hot oven for 10 to 15 minutes.

GERMAN BISCUITS

1 lb (500 g) plain flour
1 tsp cream of tartar
1 tsp bicarbonate of soda
4 oz (125 g) butter
8 oz (250 g) light brown
  sugar

1 egg, well beaten
2 tbsps treacle

Sift the flour with the cream of tartar and soda. Cream the butter and sugar. Beat in the egg and treacle. Fold in the sifted dry ingredients. Roll out on a floured surface and cut into shapes. Arrange on oven trays. Bake in a moderate oven until light golden.

While still hot, sandwich pairs of biscuits together with jam; ice with vanilla icing (see the chapter 'Luscious Icings and Fillings').

OLD-FASHIONED BISCUITS

2 cups plain flour
½ cup butter
½ cup sugar
1 tsp baking powder

a pinch of salt
2 eggs, well beaten
essence (optional)
a little desiccated coconut

Sift the flour into a mixing bowl. Rub in the butter with the fingertips. Stir in the sugar, baking powder, and salt. Mix to a stiff dough with the eggs and essence. Knead on a lightly floured board and roll out until the dough is very thin. Sprinkle with coconut. Cut out shapes with a cutter or a glass. Arrange on greased oven trays and bake in a moderate oven until light brown.

SUNBEAMS

1 cup self-raising flour
a pinch of salt
2 tbsps sugar

1 tbsp butter
1 egg, beaten
apricot jam

Sift the flour and salt into a mixing bowl. Add the sugar and rub in the butter. Mix to a stiff dough with the egg. Roll out on a floured surface and trim to an oblong shape. Spread lightly with jam, and roll up tightly, as for a Swiss roll. Cut into ½-inch (1-centimetre) slices and arrange on a greased oven tray. Bake in a moderate oven until golden.

SPICED PIN-WHEELS

½ cup butter
½ cup sugar
1 egg-yolk
½ tsp vanilla essence
1¾ cups self-raising flour
a pinch of salt

3 tbsps milk
1 tbsp treacle
½ tsp grated nutmeg
½ tsp cinnamon
½ tsp ground ginger
1 tbsp self-raising flour

Cream the butter and sugar. Beat in the egg-yolk and vanilla. Sift the 1¾ cups of flour and the salt; fold into the creamed mixture, alternately with the milk. Mix until smooth. Transfer half the mixture to another bowl; add the treacle, nutmeg, cinnamon, and ginger; stir well and add the extra tablespoon of flour. Roll the plain mixture out on a floured board to form a rectangle. Roll the spiced mixture to a rectangle of the same size, and lay on top of the plain dough. Roll up tightly, as for a Swiss roll. Cut in ¼-inch (5-millimetre) slices and arrange, cut side up, on a greased oven tray, allowing room for spreading. Bake for 10 minutes in a moderately hot oven.

SAVOURY BISCUITS

3 cups plain flour
1 tsp salt
½ cup butter
water

Sift the flour and salt into a mixing bowl. Rub in the butter with the fingertips until the mixture resembles breadcrumbs. Mix to a firm dough with water. Knead lightly on a floured surface and roll out thinly. Cut into rounds or squares and arrange on greased oven trays; prick the biscuits well with a fork. Bake in a moderate oven until light golden, about 15 minutes.

SHORTBREAD

7 oz (220 g) butter
3 oz (90 g) castor sugar
9 oz (280 g) plain flour
2 oz (60 g) cornflour or rice
  flour
½ tsp baking powder
¼ tsp salt
sugar

Cream the butter and castor sugar. Gradually work in the sifted flour, cornflour, baking powder, and salt. Press evenly into a greased 8-inch (20-centimetre) sandwich tin. Pinch a frill around the edge, and prick the mixture with a fork. Mark into eight sections with a knife. Bake in a moderate oven for 20 to 30 minutes. Turn out and sprinkle with sugar.

MARSHMALLOW SHORTBREAD

½ cup butter
½ cup sugar
1 egg
1 tsp vanilla essence
Marshmallow
1 cup sugar
¾ cup water
2 cups self-raising flour
apricot jam
a few dates, halved

1 dsp gelatine

Cream the butter and sugar. Beat the egg in thoroughly. Add the vanilla. Sift in the flour and mix to a dry dough. Roll out on a floured surface to a rectangular shape; cut into halves. Line a greased shallow tin with one half. Spread apricot jam on the top. Sprinkle over the dates, which have been pressed flat, and cover with the remaining pastry. Bake in a moderate oven for 20 to 25 minutes, then leave to cool.
Marshmallow: Boil the sugar with the water and gelatine for a few minutes. Allow to cool, then beat until thick. Spread over the shortbread. Leave to set. Ice with chocolate icing (see the chapter 'Luscious Icings and Fillings').

BISCUIT SLICE

4 oz (125 g) butter
¾ cup sugar
1 tbsp cocoa
½ packet seeded raisins
2 oz (60 g) chopped walnuts
1 tsp vanilla essence
2 small eggs, well beaten
8 oz (250 g) crushed plain
  biscuits

Melt the butter in a saucepan, then remove from the heat and add all the other ingredients except for the biscuit crumbs; mix well. Return the saucepan to the heat and bring the mixture to boiling-point. Remove from the heat and mix in the crushed biscuits. Put into a paper-lined slab-tin and press down well. Leave to set.
  Ice when cold with chocolate icing (see the chapter 'Luscious Icings and Fillings'). Cut into bars when the icing is set.

FRUIT WEDGES

4 oz (125 g) butter
1 cup brown sugar
1 egg
1½ cups self-raising flour
a pinch of salt
½ cup mixed dried fruit

Cream the butter and sugar. Beat the egg in thoroughly. Add the sifted flour and salt and the mixed fruit. Press into a greased slab-tin. Bake in a moderate oven for 25 to 30 minutes. Allow to cool in the tin, then mark and cut into blocks.

RASPBERRY SLICE

4 oz (125 g) butter
1 cup sugar
2 eggs
1½ cups self-raising flour
warm raspberry jam
1 cup desiccated coconut

Cream the butter with ½ cup of the sugar. Beat in one of the eggs. Add the sifted flour and mix well. Press the mixture into a greased slab-tin and spread with raspberry jam. Beat the remaining egg with the remaining ½ cup of sugar and the coconut. Spread over the mixture in the tin. Bake for 15 to 20 minutes in a moderate oven.

OLD ENGLISH MATRIMONIALS

1½ cups self-raising flour
¾ cup brown sugar
½ cup rolled oats
1 cup desiccated coconut
6 oz (185 g) butter
¾ cup raspberry jam

Sift the flour into a mixing bowl. Stir in the sugar, rolled oats, and coconut, mixing well together. Melt the butter and pour into the mixture, stirring well. Press half the mixture into a greased slab-tin. Spread with the jam, which has been warmed. Crumble the remaining mixture over the jam. Bake in a moderate oven for half an hour. Leave to cool in the tin, then cut into slices or fingers.

APRICOT OAT BARS

4 oz (125 g) butter
½ cup sugar
Topping
6 oz (185 g) chopped dried
  apricots
2 eggs
1 cup brown sugar
1 cup plain flour
½ cup rolled oats

⅓ cup self-raising flour
1 cup desiccated coconut

Melt the butter, remove from the heat, and mix with the sugar, flour, and oats. Press into a greased 9-inch (23-centimetre) square tin. Bake in a moderate oven for 15 minutes. Remove from the oven and spread over the topping. Return to the oven and bake for a further 20 to 25 minutes. Leave in the tin to cool, then cut into bars.
Topping: Cover the apricots with hot water; leave to stand for 10 minutes and then drain. Meanwhile, beat the eggs, and beat in the sugar, flour, and coconut; fold in the apricots.

LEMON SLICE

8 oz (250 g) crushed plain biscuits
1 cup desiccated coconut
4 oz (125 g) butter, melted
½ tin condensed milk
juice and grated rind of ½ lemon

Mix all the ingredients well together. Press into a greased slab-tin. Cover with lemon icing (see the chapter 'Luscious Icings and Fillings'). Chill in the refrigerator. Slice when set.

PASSIONFRUIT FINGERS

1 cup icing sugar
¾ cup butter
pulp of 4 passionfruit, strained
1½ cups self-raising flour
1 cup cornflour
a pinch of salt

Cream the icing sugar and butter. Beat in the passionfruit pulp. Mix in the sifted flour, cornflour, and salt. Press into a greased slab-tin, and cook in a moderate oven for half an hour. Cut into squares while hot. Leave to cool.

Ice with 'Vienna fruit icing (see page 124), made with passionfruit pulp.

GINGER CRUNCHIES

4 oz (125 g) butter
2 oz (60 g) sugar
1 cup plain flour
1 tsp ground ginger
Topping
3 tbsps icing sugar
1 tsp ground ginger
1½ tbsps butter
1 tsp baking powder

1 dsp golden syrup

Cream the butter and sugar. Mix in the sifted dry ingredients. Press into a greased slab-tin. Bake in a moderate oven for about 20 minutes, or until light brown. Leave to cool until warm, then spread with the topping. Cut into fingers.
Topping: Heat all the ingredients in a small saucepan over a low heat. Stir well to blend; bring to the boil.

WALNUT FINGERS

4 oz (125 g) butter
1 cup sugar
1 egg, separated
6 oz (185 g) plain flour
½ tsp baking powder
a pinch of salt
1 egg
1 cup desiccated coconut
1 cup chopped walnuts
2 oz (60 g) chopped glacé cherries
1 tsp vanilla essence

Cream the butter with ½ cup of the sugar. Beat in the egg-yolk, then mix in the flour, which has been sifted with the baking powder and salt. Press into a greased slab-tin. Beat the egg-white with the egg and remaining sugar; add the coconut, walnuts, cherries, and vanilla. Spread over the mixture in the tin and bake in a moderate oven for 20 to 30 minutes.

When cold, ice as you wish (see the chapter 'Luscious Icings and Fillings') and cut into fingers.

CHOCOLATE SLICE

1 cup self-raising flour
¾ cup sugar
1 cup desiccated coconut
1 tbsp cocoa
4 oz (125 g) butter, melted

Combine all the dry ingredients in a mixing bowl. Pour in the melted butter and mix well. Press into a greased slab-tin. Bake for 10 minutes in a moderate oven.

While still warm, ice with chocolate icing (see the chapter 'Luscious Icings and Fillings') and cut into squares.

CARAMEL SLICE

1 cup self-raising flour
¾ cup brown sugar
1 cup desiccated coconut
4 oz (125 g) butter, melted
½ tsp vanilla essence

Sift the flour into a mixing bowl. Stir in the sugar and coconut. Add the butter and the vanilla. Press into a greased slab-tin and bake in a moderate oven for 20 minutes.

Ice with chocolate icing (see the chapter 'Luscious Icings and Fillings') while still warm.

CARAMEL SQUARES

4 oz (125 g) butter
4 oz (125 g) brown sugar
1 egg
1 cup self-raising flour
a pinch of salt
¾ cup chopped walnuts
¾ cup chopped dates
½ tsp vanilla essence

Cream the butter and sugar. Beat in the egg. Add the sifted flour and salt, then the nuts, dates, and vanilla essence. Spread into a greased slab-tin. Bake in a moderate oven for about 15 minutes. When cold, cut into squares.

FUDGE SLICE

½ cup butter
2 tbsps sugar
1 egg, lightly beaten
1 tbsp cocoa
8 oz (250 g) crushed biscuits
½ cup chopped nuts
vanilla essence
desiccated coconut

Heat the butter and sugar together gently; bring to the boil and continue cooking for a few minutes. Cool slightly. Mix in the egg, then the cocoa, biscuits, nuts, and vanilla. Press into a greased Swiss-roll tin. Sprinkle with coconut, and leave for 2 hours to set. Serve sliced. Store in the refrigerator in very hot weather.

FUDGE FINGERS

1 cup self-raising flour
¾ cup sugar
4 oz (125 g) butter
⅓ cup chopped mixed nuts
⅓ cup chopped mixed dried
   fruit
⅓ cup chopped dates

a little preserved ginger, finely
   chopped
1 dsp desiccated coconut
1 dsp cocoa
a pinch of salt
1 egg, beaten

Sift the flour into a mixing bowl. Stir in the sugar, then rub in the butter with the fingertips. Mix in the nuts, mixed fruit, dates, ginger, coconut, cocoa, and salt. Mix to a stiff dough with the egg. Press with the hand into a well–greased slab-tin. Bake in a moderate oven for 20 to 25 minutes. Cut into strips while still hot, and leave in the tin until cool.

NUTTIES

½ cup butter
½ cup brown sugar
½ cup desiccated coconut

½ cup salted peanuts
1 cup self-raising flour

Melt the butter, remove from the heat, and add the sugar, coconut, peanuts, and flour. Press into a greased slab-tin and cook in a moderate oven for about 25 minutes. Leave to cool.

Ice with lemon icing or chocolate icing (see the chapter 'Luscious Icings and Fillings') and cut into bars.

Perfect
LITTLE CAKES

PATTY CAKES

4 oz (125 g) butter	2 eggs
4 oz (125 g) sugar	8 oz (250 g) self-raising flour
½ tsp vanilla essence	a pinch of salt
1 tbsp hot water	approx. ¼ pt (150 ml) milk

Pre-heat the oven to hot. Cream the butter and sugar. Add the vanilla essence and hot water; beat until fluffy. Add the eggs, one at a time, beating well after each addition. Sift the flour with the salt, and add to the mixture, alternately with the milk. Put paper patties in the patty tins before baking. (This saves greasing the pans, and keeps the cakes a good shape.) Put a dessertspoon of the mixture into each paper. Bake in the hottest part of the oven for 12 to 15 minutes.

When cool, ice as you wish (see the chapter 'Luscious Icings and Fillings').

GEM CAKES

2 oz (60 g) butter	4 oz (125 g) self-raising flour
2 oz (60 g) castor sugar	a pinch of salt
½ tsp vanilla essence	3–4 tbsps milk
1 egg	

Heat gem trays in a moderately hot oven. Cream the butter with the sugar and vanilla. Beat the egg in thoroughly. Sift the flour and salt and fold into the mixture, alternately with enough milk to give a soft dropping consistency. Grease the gem trays and three-quarters fill with the cake mixture. Bake for 10 to 12 minutes. Turn out on a wire rack and leave to cool.

QUEEN CAKES

4 oz (125 g) butter	6 oz (185 g) self-raising flour
4 oz (125 g) sugar	a pinch of salt
1 tsp finely grated lemon rind	3 oz (90 g) sultanas
3 eggs	

Pre-heat the oven to moderately hot. Cream the butter with the sugar and lemon rind. Beat in the eggs, one at a time, beating well after each addition. Sift the flour and salt and fold into the mixture with the sultanas. If necessary, add a little milk to make a dropping consistency. Drop dessertspoons of the mixture into paper patties arranged on cold oven trays and bake for 12 to 15 minutes.

SNOWBALLS

4 oz (125 g) butter	8 oz (250 g) self-raising flour
6 oz (185 g) sugar	approx. ¼ pt (150 ml) milk
3 eggs	

Pre-heat the oven to hot. Cream the butter and sugar. Add the eggs, one at a time, beating well after each addition. Fold in the sifted flour, alternately with the milk. Half-fill greased small gem trays with the mixture and bake for about 7 minutes. Cool on a wire rack.

Ice with chocolate icing (see the chapter 'Luscious Icings and Fillings'). Roll in coconut and sandwich together with whipped cream.

JELLY CAKES

1 packet jelly crystals	2 eggs
4 oz (125 g) butter	8 oz (250 g) self-raising flour
4 oz (125 g) sugar	approx. ¼ pt (150 ml) milk
1 tsp vanilla essence	desiccated coconut

Dissolve the jelly crystals in ½ pint (315 millilitres) of boiling water. Pour into a shallow tin or dish and leave to begin setting. Heat gem trays in a moderately hot oven. Cream the butter with the sugar and vanilla. Beat the eggs in, one at a time, beating well after each addition. Sift the flour and fold into the mixture, alternately with enough milk to make a soft dropping consistency. Grease the gem trays well and two-thirds fill with the mixture. Bake for 12 to 15 minutes. Turn out on a wire rack to cool. Holding the cakes with a skewer, dip them in the partly set jelly and then roll in coconut. Return to a wire rack until set.

SPONGE BUTTERFLIES

3 eggs	1 tsp baking powder
3 oz (90 g) castor sugar	jam
3 oz (90 g) plain flour	whipped cream
a pinch of salt	icing sugar

Pre-heat the oven to moderately hot. Grease small patty tins. Beat the eggs vigorously with the castor sugar for 5 minutes, or until thick and light coloured. Sift the flour with the salt and baking powder and fold carefully into the egg mixture. Half-fill the prepared tins with the mixture and bake for about 10 minutes. Cool on a wire rack. Cut a round from the top of each cake. Fill the cakes with a little jam and cream. Cut the tops in half and replace on the cakes to resemble wings. Sprinkle with icing sugar.

CHOCOLATE CAKES

4 oz (125 g) butter	6 oz (185 g) self-raising flour
4 oz (125 g) castor sugar	1 oz (30 g) cocoa
1 tsp vanilla essence	approx. ¼ pt (150 ml) milk
2 eggs	

Pre-heat the oven to moderately hot. Cream the butter with the sugar and vanilla. Beat in the eggs, one at a time, beating well after each addition. Sift the flour with the cocoa and fold into the mixture, alternately with enough milk to make a soft dropping consistency. Arrange paper patties on cold oven trays. Two-thirds fill the paper cases with the mixture and bake for about 15 minutes in the hottest part of the oven. Leave to cool on a wire rack before removing from the paper cases.

Ice with chocolate icing (see the chapter 'Luscious Icings and Fillings') and sprinkle with coconut or nuts.

FRUIT AND NUT CAKES

4 oz (125 g) butter	1 dsp marmalade
4 oz (125 g) sugar	1 oz (30 g) seeded raisins
1 tsp finely grated lemon rind	1 oz (30 g) currants
1 egg	½ oz (15 g) chopped walnuts
6 oz (185 g) self-raising flour	approx. ¼ pt (150 ml) milk

Heat gem trays in a hot oven. Cream the butter and sugar with the lemon rind. Beat the egg in thoroughly. Sift the flour and fold in alternately with the marmalade, fruit, nuts, and enough milk to give a soft dropping consistency. Grease the gem trays well and two-thirds fill with the cake mixture. Bake for 10 to 15 minutes.

CHERRY CAKES

4 oz (125 g) butter
4 oz (125 g) castor sugar
2 eggs
4 oz (125 g) self-raising flour

2 oz (60 g) chopped glacé
  cherries
a little milk

Pre-heat the oven to moderately hot. Cream the butter and sugar. Beat in the eggs, one at a time, beating well after each addition. Sift the flour and fold in with the cherries. If necessary, add enough milk to give a dropping consistency. Arrange paper patties on cold oven trays and half-fill with the mixture. Bake in the hottest part of the oven for about 15 minutes. Allow to cool in the paper cases.

RASPBERRY BUNS

8 oz (250 g) self-raising flour
3 oz (90 g) butter
3 oz (90 g) castor sugar
grated rind of 1 lemon

1 egg, beaten
approx. ¼ pt (150 ml) milk
raspberry jam

Sift the flour into a mixing bowl. Rub in the butter with the fingertips until the mixture resembles breadcrumbs. Stir in the castor sugar and lemon rind. Mix to a stiff dough with the egg and milk. Turn out on to a floured surface and knead lightly until smooth. Roll out to ¾-inch (2-centimetre) thickness and cut into large rounds. Put a teaspoon of jam on each round, moisten the edges of the dough, and bring up to enclose the jam, pressing with the fingers to seal. Arrange on a greased and floured oven tray and bake for 15 to 20 minutes in a moderately hot oven.

SPICED APPLE CAKES

1 cup plain flour
1 tsp baking powder
a pinch of salt
½ tsp cinnamon
½ tsp ground ginger

¼ cup sugar
2 oz (60 g) butter
1 egg, well beaten
stewed apple

Sift the flour, baking powder, salt, and spices into a mixing bowl. Add the sugar, then rub in the butter. Mix to a dough with the egg. Roll out and cut into small rounds to line greased gem trays. Fill with a little stewed apple and cover with another round. Bake for 15 minutes in a moderate oven.

Ice with lemon icing (see the chapter 'Luscious Icings and Fillings').

MADELEINES

4 oz (125 g) butter
4 oz (125 g) castor sugar
2 eggs
4 oz (125 g) plain flour

½ tsp baking powder
jam
desiccated coconut
glacé cherries

Pre-heat the oven to moderately hot. Cream the butter and sugar. Beat in the eggs, one at a time, beating well after each addition. Sift the flour with the baking powder and fold into the mixture. Grease dariole moulds and two-thirds fill them with the mixture. Bake for 15 to 20 minutes. Turn out and cool on a wire rack. Trim the bottoms, so that the cakes will stand evenly. Brush with warm jam and roll in coconut. Stick a cherry on top of each with a little jam.

APRICOT CAKES

approx. 24 dried apricots
4 oz (125 g) butter
4 oz (125 g) castor sugar
1 tsp vanilla essence

2 eggs
7 oz (220 g) self-raising flour
a pinch of salt
approx. ¼ pt (150 ml) milk

Stew the apricots with water to cover and sugar to taste. When tender, drain and leave to cool. Pre-heat the oven to moderately hot. Cream the butter with the castor sugar and vanilla. Beat in the eggs, one at a time, beating well after each addition. Sift the flour and salt and fold into the mixture, alternately with enough milk to make a soft dropping consistency. Arrange twenty-four paper patties on cold oven trays. Put a heaped teaspoon of cake mixture in each paper case and then put a drained apricot on top of each. Cover with another teaspoon of cake mixture. Bake in the hottest part of the oven for about 15 minutes. Leave to cool before removing from the paper cases.

Ice with butter cream (see page 124) and sprinkle with coconut.

COCONUT CAKES

8 oz (250 g) self-raising flour
4 oz (125 g) butter
4 oz (125 g) sugar

1 cup desiccated coconut
2 eggs
castor sugar

Sift the flour into a mixing bowl. Rub in the butter until the mixture resembles breadcrumbs. Mix in the sugar and coconut. Mix to a firm dough with the eggs—if too stiff, add a little milk. Knead and roll into small balls. Dip in castor sugar and arrange on oven trays. Bake in a moderate oven for about 15 minutes.

GINGER CAKES

1 lb (500 g) plain flour
1 oz (30 g) ground ginger
4 oz (125 g) butter

8 oz (250 g) sugar
1 tsp lemon essence
8 oz (250 g) treacle

Pre-heat the oven to moderately hot. Sift the flour and ginger into a mixing bowl. Rub in the butter with the fingertips until the mixture resembles breadcrumbs. Stir in the sugar. Add the lemon essence and mix to a stiff dough with the treacle. Knead on a floured surface until smooth. Roll out and cut into shapes. Arrange on greased oven trays and bake for 10 to 15 minutes.

ORANGE ROCK CAKES

4 oz (125 g) plain flour
1 tsp baking powder
3 oz (90 g) butter
4 oz (125 g) sugar

grated rind and strained juice
  of 2 oranges
1 egg

Pre-heat the oven to moderately hot. Sift the flour and baking powder into a mixing bowl. Rub in the butter with the fingertips. Mix in the sugar and the orange rind. Add the egg and enough orange juice to make a stiff dough. Knead and break into pieces. Bake on a greased oven tray for about 15 minutes.

ROCK CAKES

8 oz (250 g) plain flour
1 tsp baking powder
3 oz (90 g) butter
3 oz (90 g) sugar

½ tsp ground ginger
½ cup sultanas
1 egg, beaten
3 tbsps milk

Pre-heat the oven to hot. Sift the flour and baking powder into a mixing bowl. Rub the butter in lightly with the fingertips. Add the sugar, ginger, and sultanas. Mix to a stiff dough with the egg and milk. Drop small spoonfuls of the mixture on to a greased oven tray. Bake for 10 to 15 minutes.

POWDER PUFFS

6 oz (185 g) castor sugar
3 eggs
2 oz (60 g) plain flour
2 oz (60 g) cornflour
½ tsp cream of tartar

½ tsp baking powder
1 tsp vanilla essence
whipped cream
icing sugar

Pre-heat the oven to moderately hot. Beat the castor sugar with the eggs until thick and light coloured. Sift the flours with the cream of tartar and the baking powder several times. Fold carefully into the egg mixture, then fold in the vanilla. Place small spoonfuls of the mixture on greased oven trays, leaving room for spreading. Bake for 5 to 7 minutes. Put on a wire rack to cool. When cold, sandwich pairs together with whipped cream. Put in an airtight tin for an hour before serving. Sprinkle with icing sugar and serve at once. Do not return the puffs to the airtight tin.

MERINGUES

2 egg-whites
a pinch of salt

4 oz (125 g) castor sugar
1 tsp vanilla essence

Beat the egg-whites with the salt until they are stiff and dry. Gradually beat in the sugar until the mixture is again very stiff. Fold in the vanilla. Arrange teaspoons of the mixture on cold greased oven trays and bake in the coolest part of a slow oven for about 1½ to 2 hours, until quite dry.

LARGE CAKES
For Special Treats

Basic Cake-making Methods

Creaming Method: This method involves beating butter and sugar together until they are pale, smooth, and without any sugary grittiness. Eggs are then gradually and thoroughly added to the mixture and finally dry ingredients and liquid are folded in. Many plain cakes and fruit cakes are made by the creaming method.

Sponge Method: Cakes made in this way are light and fluffy. First, eggs are beaten with castor sugar until light-coloured and thick. The sifted dry ingredients and liquid are then folded in gently.

Rubbing-in Method: Many plain cakes, rock cakes, and tea cakes are made in this way, which is similar to pastry-making in that the fat is rubbed into the dry ingredients until they resemble fine breadcrumbs. Other dry and liquid ingredients are then added to make a workable cake mixture, but it is important not to mix too vigorously, or the cake will be heavy.

Melting Method: This is the method for heavy, moist-textured cakes such as gingerbreads. Syrup, sugar, and butter are heated and poured into the dry ingredients. The mixture must not be too dry, or the cake will burn during the long cooking time. These cakes are fairly heavy and should be left to cool in the tins before turning out.

One-stage Method: This is a quick and simple way of making cakes by beating all the required ingredients together briskly for about 5 minutes. For success, it is necessary to use softened butter or other fat.

Basic Steps in Cake-making

Pre-heat the oven to the specified temperature. Prepare the tins by brushing with melted butter and lining, if the cake is heavy and slow-cooking. Cut greaseproof paper a little larger than the inside of the tin and 2 inches (5 centimetres) higher; snip the bottom edge of the paper and press it into the tin. Cut a round or square of paper to the exact size of the bottom of the tin and press it in. Brush the lining paper with melted butter. Two layers of paper are needed for fruit cakes, as well as a double band of brown paper tied around the outside of the tin to prevent burning. Tins should generally be two-thirds filled with the cake mixture. If the tins are over-filled, the mixture will rise above the tins and overflow into the oven; if the tins have too little mixture in them, the cake will form a hard crust.

Exact cooking times will vary according to the mixture, the oven temperature, and the position of the tins in the oven, but generally cooking times are as follows:

Sponges and Sandwich Cakes: 20–35 minutes in a moderate to moderately hot oven.
Large Plain Cakes: 40–60 minutes in a moderately slow to moderate oven.
Large Light Fruit Cakes: $1\frac{1}{4}$–2 hours in a slow to moderately slow oven.
Large Rich Fruit Cakes: $1\frac{1}{2}$–$4\frac{1}{2}$ hours in a very slow oven.

To test when sponges and sandwich cakes are cooked, press lightly with the finger; if the cake is done, it should spring back at once. The cake should be golden and shrinking slightly from the sides of the tin. Leave in the tin for a few minutes then turn out carefully on a wire rack and leave to cool.

To test when fruit cakes are cooked, insert a fine skewer or toothpick in the centre; if it comes out clean, with no mixture sticking to it, the cake is ready. Leave in the tin to cool.

Common Faults in Cake-making

Fruit Sinking to the Bottom: This generally means that too much liquid or baking powder has been used.

Heaviness: This can be caused by using too much flour, butter, or liquid; slow baking; or not cooking for long enough.

Sinking in the Middle: This can be caused by slamming the oven door while the cake is still rising; having the oven temperature too high; using too much raising; opening the oven door too soon; or not cooking for long enough.

Coarseness: This can be caused by insufficient creaming, not beating the eggs enough, or using too much raising or too much liquid.

Dryness: This generally means that the cake has been cooked for too long or at too high a temperature, or that too little liquid was used.

Cracking: This can be caused by having too stiff a mixture, too small a tin, or the oven temperature too high.

APPLE CAKE

1½ cups self-raising flour
½ cup butter
½ cup sugar
2 eggs, beaten

3 tbsps milk
2 cooking apples, stewed and
    unsweetened

Grease an 8-inch (20-centimetre) round cake-tin. Pre-heat the oven to moderate. Sift the flour into a mixing bowl. Rub in the butter until the mixture resembles fine breadcrumbs. Stir in the sugar. Beat the milk into the eggs and then into the cake mixture to form a batter. Spread three-quarters of the mixture into the prepared tin. Cover with the apple and then spread over the remaining cake mixture. Cook for about half an hour. Leave to cool.

Ice with lemon icing (see the chapter 'Luscious Icings and Fillings').

APPLE TEA CAKE

1 cup self-raising flour
½ cup sugar
1 tsp butter
1 egg, beaten
a little milk

1 apple, thinly sliced
sugar
grated nutmeg

Grease a 6-inch (15-centimetre) sandwich tin. Pre-heat the oven to moderate. Sift the flour and sugar into a mixing bowl. Rub in the butter, then add the egg and milk to form a fairly soft mixture. Pour into the prepared tin. Arrange the apple on top of the mixture. Sprinkle with sugar and nutmeg and bake for half an hour.

BUTTER CAKE

4 oz (125 g) butter
5 oz (155 g) castor sugar
2 eggs
8 oz (250 g) self-raising flour

a pinch of salt
½ cup milk
vanilla essence

Cream the butter and castor sugar. Add the eggs, one at a time, beating well after each addition. Fold in the flour, which has been sifted with the salt, alternately with the milk and essence. Pour the mixture into a greased 7-inch (18-centimetre) tin. Bake for about 40 minutes in a moderate oven.

Ice as you wish (see the chapter 'Luscious Icings and Fillings').

GOOD PLAIN CAKE

6 oz (185 g) butter
6 oz (185 g) castor sugar
2 eggs, well beaten
8 oz (250 g) plain flour
1 tsp baking powder

a pinch of salt
2 tbsps milk
finely grated rind of 1 lemon

Grease a 7-inch (18-centimetre) square tin generously. Pre-heat the oven to moderate. Cream the butter and castor sugar until light and fluffy. Gradually beat in the eggs. Add the sifted flour, baking powder, and salt, alternately with the milk, which has been mixed with the lemon rind. Pour into the prepared tin and bake for 1 hour. Turn out on a wire rack to cool.

Ice with lemon icing (see the chapter 'Luscious Icings and Fillings') and sprinkle with coconut.

ECONOMICAL PLAIN CAKE

1 tbsp butter
½ cup sugar
1 egg

1 cup self-raising flour
½ cup milk

Grease a small loaf-tin. Pre-heat the oven to moderate. Cream the butter and sugar. Add the egg, beating in thoroughly. Fold in the sifted flour and then the milk. Pour into the prepared tin and bake for half an hour. Turn out on a wire rack to cool.

Ice as you wish (see the chapter 'Luscious Icings and Fillings').

CUP CAKE

1 cup butter
1 cup sugar
3 eggs, well beaten
1 dsp cream of tartar
1 cup milk
1 tsp bicarbonate of soda
3 cups plain flour

1 cup currants
1 cup sultanas
1 cup candied peel

Cream the butter and sugar. Beat in the eggs. Put the cream of tartar in the milk and stir in the soda until it froths. Mix into the creamed mixture. Gradually stir in the flour, then the fruit, and mix thoroughly. Turn into a well-buttered tin and bake in a moderate oven for 2 hours.

FOUNDATION CAKE

6 oz (185 g) butter
6 oz (185 g) sugar
3 eggs, well beaten
6 tbsps milk
vanilla essence
10 oz (315 g) self-raising
    flour

a pinch of salt

Cream butter and sugar. Beat in the eggs gradually; then the milk and essence. Lightly fold in the sifted flour and salt. Pour into a greased slab-tin. Bake for about 35 minutes in a moderate oven.

Ice as you wish (see the chapter 'Luscious Icings and Fillings').

Variations

Small Cakes: Cut the baked cake into small fancy shapes, and ice as you wish (see the chapter 'Luscious Icings and Fillings').

Sandwich Cake: Bake the foundation mixture in small sandwich tins for about 25 minutes. Sandwich together with filling or cream and ice as you wish (see the chapter 'Luscious Icings and Fillings').

Marble Cake: Divide the mixture into two and add 1 tablespoon of sifted cocoa to one half. Put alternating spoonfuls of the two mixtures in a greased round cake-tin and bake as for foundation cake. Ice as you wish (see the chapter 'Luscious Icings and Fillings').

Ribbon Cake: Divide the mixture into three; colour one-third pink with cochineal; add 1 dessertspoon of sifted cocoa to another third; and leave the remaining mixture plain. Put alternating spoonfuls of the three mixtures in two greased 8-inch (20-centimetre) sandwich tins and bake for about 25 minutes. Leave to cool, then sandwich together with jam and ice with chocolate glacé icing (see page 124).

Lamingtons: Leave the foundation cake to cool. Cut into squares, dip in chocolate icing (see the chapter 'Luscious Icings and Fillings') and then in coconut. Leave to set.

Orange Cake: Add the grated rind of one orange to the mixture with the milk and essence. Ice with fruit icing (see the chapter 'Luscious Icings and Fillings').

Chocolate Sandwich Cake: Use only 9 ounces (280 grams) of flour and sift with 1 ounce (30 grams) of cocoa. Bake in well-greased sandwich tins for about 25 minutes. Leave to cool then sandwich the cakes together with mock cream (see page 126).

NUMBER CAKE

1 egg	5 tbsps self-raising flour
2 tbsps butter·	
3 tbsps sugar	
4 tbsps milk	

Grease a 7-inch (18-centimetre) cake-tin. Pre-heat the oven to moderate. Cream the butter and sugar. Beat in the egg. Add the sifted flour, alternately with the milk. Pour into the prepared tin and bake for half an hour. Leave to cool.

Ice as you wish (see the chapter 'Luscious Icings and Fillings').

MADEIRA CAKE

15 oz (470 g) butter	$\frac{1}{4}$ pt (150 ml) Madeira
12 oz (375 g) sugar	
7 eggs	
18 oz (560 g) plain flour	
1 tsp baking powder	

Pre-heat the oven to moderate. Grease and line a 9-inch (23-centimetre) cake-tin. Cream the butter and sugar. Add the eggs, two at a time, beating for 5 minutes after each addition. Fold in the flour, which has been sifted with the baking powder. Add the wine, mixing to a smooth batter of moderate stiffness. Pour into the prepared tin and bake for about $1\frac{1}{4}$ hours. Remove from the oven.

Ice carefully while still warm with transparent icing (see page 125).

SEED CAKE

4 oz (125 g) butter	8 oz (250 g) plain flour
4 oz (125 g) sugar	1 tsp baking powder
2 eggs	
lemon essence	
6 tbsps milk	
1 dsp caraway seeds	

Grease a loaf-tin. Pre-heat the oven to moderate. Cream the butter and sugar. Add the eggs, one at a time, beating well after each addition. Add the lemon essence, milk, and caraway seeds then fold in the sifted flour and baking powder. Pour into the prepared tin and bake for 30 to 35 minutes. Leave to cool.

Ice if you wish (see the chapter 'Luscious Icings and Fillings').

CHOCOLATE CAKE

$\frac{1}{2}$ cup butter	2 cups plain flour
1 cup sugar	a pinch of salt
1 egg	1 dsp baking powder
1 tsp bicarbonate of soda	$1\frac{1}{2}$ tbsps cocoa
$\frac{3}{4}$ cup milk	
1 tsp vanilla essence	

Cream the butter and sugar. Beat in the egg. Dissolve the soda in the milk and add to the mixture with the vanilla. Sift the flour with the salt, baking powder, and cocoa three times. Fold into the mixture. Bake in a moderate oven for about 45 minutes. Leave to cool.

Ice with chocolate icing (see the chapter 'Luscious Icings and Fillings').

CHOCOLATE CAKE (without eggs)

4 oz (125 g) butter	1 tsp bicarbonate of soda
4 oz (125 g) sugar	3–4 tbsps cocoa
2 tbsps golden syrup	a pinch of salt
vanilla essence	$1\frac{1}{2}$ cups milk
10 oz (315 g) self-raising flour	

Cream the butter and sugar. Add the golden syrup and vanilla essence. Sift the dry ingredients and add, alternately with the milk. Pour into two 8-inch (20-centimetre) sandwich tins. Bake in a moderate oven for 35 to 40 minutes. Turn out on a wire rack to cool.

Fill and ice as you wish (see the chapter 'Luscious Icings and Fillings').

KENTISH CHOCOLATE CAKE

4 oz (125 g) butter	2 tbsps desiccated coconut
$\frac{3}{4}$ cup sugar	2 tbsps chopped sultanas
vanilla essence	$\frac{1}{4}$ cup milk
2 eggs	
2 tbsps cocoa	
1 cup self-raising flour	

Cream the butter and sugar. Add the vanilla essence, then the eggs, one at a time, beating well after each addition. Add the cocoa, which has been sifted with the flour, the coconut, sultanas, and milk. Bake in a moderate oven for about 45 minutes.

CHOCOLATE FUDGE CAKE

$\frac{1}{2}$ cup butter	$1\frac{3}{4}$ cups self-raising flour
$\frac{3}{4}$ cup sugar	$\frac{1}{2}$ cup cocoa
2 eggs, separated	$\frac{3}{4}$ cup milk

Cream the butter and sugar. Add the egg-yolks, one by one, beating well after each addition. Sift the flour and cocoa, and add to the mixture alternately with the milk. Fold in the egg-whites, which have been stiffly beaten. Pour into a greased 9-inch (23-centimetre) square cake-tin or two small sandwich tins. Bake in a slow oven for 30 to 45 minutes. Turn out on a wire rack to cool.

Ice with chocolate icing (see the chapter 'Luscious Icings and Fillings').

CHOCOLATE SHORTY

5 oz (155 g) butter
2 heaped tbsps castor sugar
6 oz (185 g) plain flour

1 tbsp cocoa
2 heaped tbsps plain biscuit
   crumbs or dried breadcrumbs

Cream the butter and sugar in a mixing bowl. Work in the other ingredients. Turn into two greased sandwich tins. Flatten the mixture by kneading. Bake in a moderate oven for 20 to 30 minutes. Leave to cool in the tins.

Sandwich the cakes together with chocolate icing (see the chapter 'Luscious Icings and Fillings').

CHOCOLATE WINE CAKE

8 oz (250 g) butter
8 oz (250 g) castor sugar
4 eggs
8 oz (250 g) self-raising flour
1½ cups ground rice
3 tbsps cocoa
a pinch of salt

1 tsp vanilla essence
½ cup sherry
2 oz (60 g) chopped walnuts

Grease a 9-inch (23-centimetre) cake-tin. Pre-heat the oven to moderate. Cream the butter and castor sugar thoroughly. Add the eggs, one at a time, beating well after each addition. Sift the flour, rice, cocoa, and salt and add to the mixture, alternately with the vanilla and sherry. Stir in the nuts. Pour into the prepared tin and bake for 1½ hours.

CHOCOLATE AND PEPPERMINT LAYER CAKE

4 oz (125 g) butter
4 oz (125 g) sugar
2 eggs, beaten
½ tsp vanilla essence

5 oz (155 g) self-raising flour
2 tbsps cocoa
water

Peppermint Filling

1 oz (30 g) butter
2 oz (60 g) castor sugar
1 dsp hot water
1 dsp top of the milk

peppermint essence
a few drops of green food
   colouring

Cream the butter and sugar. Beat in the eggs and vanilla essence. Fold in the sifted flour and cocoa. Mix with enough water to make a soft dropping consistency. Pour into two greased sandwich tins and bake for about half an hour in a moderate oven. Leave to cool. Sandwich the cakes together with peppermint filling and ice with chocolate icing (see the chapter 'Luscious Icings and Fillings'). Decorate with silver cachous if you wish.
Peppermint Filling: Cream the butter and castor sugar. Add the water drop by drop, then the milk, drop by drop (if you add the liquid too quickly the mixture will curdle). Add the peppermint essence and beat well. Colour a delicate green with food colouring.

HONEY-TOPPED CAKE

4 oz (125 g) butter
8 oz (250 g) sugar
3 eggs, beaten
½ cup milk

10 oz (315 g) self-raising
   flour
a pinch of salt

Topping

2 oz (60 g) butter
2 oz (60 g) sugar
2 oz (60 g) honey

approx. 1 tbsp water
3 oz (90 g) desiccated coconut

Grease a slab-tin. Pre-heat the oven to moderate. Cream the butter and sugar. Gradually beat in the eggs, the milk, and then the flour, which has been sifted with the salt. Spoon into the prepared tin. Bake for 20 to 25 minutes. Remove from the oven, spread with the topping, and bake for 5 to 10 minutes, or until golden brown.
Topping: Boil the butter with the sugar, honey, and water for 10 minutes. Add the coconut, and mix well. Increase the amount of topping if you are using an especially large tin.

AUNT JANE'S CAKE

7 oz (220 g) sultanas
2 oz (60 g) mixed candied
   peel
8 oz (250 g) butter
7 oz (220 g) castor sugar
2 eggs
10 oz (315 g) plain flour
1½ tsps baking powder
a pinch of salt

a little milk
1 tsp lemon essence
1 tsp vanilla essence

Grease and line an 8-inch (20-centimetre) cake-tin. Pre-heat the oven to moderate. Sift a little flour over the sultanas and peel and leave until needed. Cream the butter and castor sugar. Add the eggs, one at a time, beating well after each addition. Gradually mix in the flour, which has been sifted with the baking powder and salt, alternately with the fruit. Add milk and essences to form a soft consistency. Pour into the prepared tin and bake for about 1½ hours. Leave to cool.

Ice with lemon icing (see the chapter 'Luscious Icings and Fillings') if you wish.

APPLE NUT CAKE (without eggs)

4 oz (125 g) butter
1 cup sugar
½ tsp vanilla essence
2 small tsps bicarbonate of
   soda
1½ cups warm unsweetened
   stewed apples
½ cup seeded raisins

½ cup walnuts
2 cups self-raising flour
3 dsps cocoa
½ tsp cinnamon
½ tsp grated nutmeg
½ tsp mixed spice
walnuts

Grease a Swiss-roll tin. Pre-heat the oven to moderate. Cream the butter and sugar with the vanilla. Dissolve the soda in the apples, mixing well, then add to the creamed mixture. Mix in the raisins and nuts then the flour, which has been sifted with the cocoa and spice. Beat lightly. Spread the mixture in the prepared tin and bake for about 45 minutes. Leave in the tin to cool.

Ice with chocolate icing (see the chapter 'Luscious Icings and Fillings') and decorate with walnuts.

APPLE CAKE

2 oz (60 g) butter	¼ cup milk
2 oz (60 g) sugar	1 cup drained stewed apple
1 egg, beaten	½ tsp ground ginger
1 cup self-raising flour	½ tsp cinnamon

Pre-heat the oven to moderate. Cream the butter and sugar. Beat in the egg. Sift the flour, and fold into the mixture, alternately with the milk. Turn half the batter into a greased 7-inch (18-centimetre) tin. Spread over the stewed apple and pour in the remaining batter. Bake for half an hour. Leave to cool.

Ice with lemon icing (see the chapter 'Luscious Icings and Fillings') and sprinkle with the ginger mixed with the cinnamon.

ORANGE CAKE

6 tbsps butter	2 eggs, separated
1 cup sugar	2 cups self-raising flour
juice and grated rind of 1 orange	¼ tsp salt
	½ cup milk

Grease a 7-inch (18-centimetre) cake-tin. Pre-heat the oven to moderate. Cream the butter and sugar. Add the orange juice and rind. Beat the egg-yolks, then beat into the creamed mixture. Fold in the sifted flour and salt alternately with the milk. Fold in the stiffly beaten egg-whites. Pour into the prepared tin and cook for 40 to 45 minutes. Leave to cool.

Ice as you wish (see the chapter 'Luscious Icings and Fillings').

ORANGE TEA CAKE

1 tbsp butter	1 tsp cream of tartar
½ cup sugar	½ tsp bicarbonate of soda
1 egg	¼ pt (150 ml) milk
grated rind of 1 orange	
2 drops of lemon essence	
1 cup plain flour	

Grease a 7-inch (18-centimetre) sandwich tin. Pre-heat the oven to moderate. Beat the butter and sugar together. Add the egg and beat the mixture well. Add the orange rind and lemon essence. Sift in the flour, cream of tartar, and soda. Mix in the milk. Pour into the prepared tin and bake for 15 to 20 minutes. Leave to cool.

Ice with orange icing (see the chapter 'Luscious Icings and Fillings') if you wish.

GINGER SANDWICH

1 tbsp butter	3 small tsps ground ginger
½ cup sugar	1 dsp cinnamon
1 egg, beaten	1 tsp bicarbonate of soda
½ cup treacle	¼ cup boiling water
½ cup milk	
1½ cups plain flour	

Grease two sandwich tins. Pre-heat the oven to moderate. Cream the butter and sugar; beat in the egg. Stir in the treacle and milk. Sift the flour with the ginger and cinnamon and add to the mixture. Dissolve the soda in the boiling water and add. Pour into the prepared tins and bake for 20 minutes. Turn out on a wire rack to cool.

Sandwich the cakes together with mock cream (see page 126).

BANANA CAKE

4 oz (125 g) butter	1¾ cups plain flour
1 cup sugar	1 tsp baking powder
2 eggs	½ tsp bicarbonate of soda
3 small ripe bananas, well mashed	a little milk
	walnuts, halved

Grease a round cake-tin. Pre-heat the oven to moderate. Cream the butter and sugar. Beat in the eggs thoroughly. Stir in the bananas, then add the sifted flour, baking powder, and soda. Mix to a batter with milk. Pour into the prepared tin and bake for about 45 minutes. Turn out on a wire rack to cool.

Ice with butter cream (see page 124) and decorate with halved walnuts.

RAISIN CAKE

2 cups self-raising flour	½ cup finely chopped seeded raisins
¼ tsp salt	2 eggs, well beaten
4 oz (125 g) butter	½ cup milk
½ cup brown sugar	
½ cup white sugar	

Grease a loaf-tin. Pre-heat the oven to moderate. Sift the flour and salt into a mixing bowl. Rub in the butter then add the brown and the white sugar and the raisins. Fold in the eggs, which have been beaten thoroughly with the milk, and mix well. Pour the mixture into the prepared tin. Bake for 45 to 50 minutes.

CHERRY COCONUT CAKE

4 oz (125 g) butter	vanilla essence
1 cup brown sugar	milk
1 egg	1 cup desiccated coconut
1 cup self-raising flour	1 cup chopped glacé cherries
1 tbsp cocoa	

Cream the butter and sugar. Beat in the egg. Fold in the flour, which has been sifted with the cocoa, alternately with the vanilla and enough milk to make a soft dropping consistency. Pour half of this mixture into a greased tin. Mix the coconut with 1 tablespoon of milk and the cherries; spread over the cake mixture. Cover the cherries with the remaining cake mixture. Bake in a moderate oven for 25 minutes.

Ice while still warm with chocolate icing (see the chapter 'Luscious Icings and Fillings'); mark out squares but do not remove from the tin until cold.

FRUIT AND NUT CAKE

½ cup butter	1½ cups plain flour
1 cup sugar	1 tbsp cocoa
1 egg	1 tsp baking powder
½ cup chopped mixed dried fruit	½ tsp bicarbonate of soda
½ cup walnut pieces	1 cup milk
	desiccated coconut

Grease a 7-inch (18-centimetre) cake-tin. Pre-heat the oven to moderate. Cream the butter and sugar. Add the egg, beating well. Add the fruit and nuts. Fold in the flour, which has been sifted with the cocoa and baking powder, alternately with the soda dissolved in the milk. Pour into the prepared tin and bake for 45 minutes to an hour. Leave to cool.

Cover with warm chocolate icing (see the chapter 'Luscious Icings and Fillings') and sprinkle with coconut.

CHERRY FRUIT CAKE

½ cup water	¼ tsp cinnamon
½ cup sherry	2 cups plain flour
4 oz (125 g) butter	1 tsp baking powder
1 cup sugar	1 tsp bicarbonate of soda
1 lb (500 g) chopped mixed dried fruit	a pinch of salt
	4 oz (125 g) stewed cherries
1 tsp mixed spice	2 eggs, well beaten

Grease an 8-inch (20-centimetre) cake-tin and line with greased greaseproof paper. Pre-heat the oven to moderate. Put the water, sherry, butter, sugar, dried fruit, and spices in a saucepan and heat to boiling-point. Remove from the heat and stir in the flour, which has been sifted with the baking powder, soda, and salt, the cherries, and the eggs. Pour into the prepared tin and bake for 1¼ to 1½ hours. This cake improves considerably if kept for a few days before cutting.

WALNUT COFFEE CAKE

4 oz (125 g) butter	½ tsp vanilla essence
1 cup sugar	
2 eggs, separated	
1½ cups self-raising flour	
salt	
½ cup milk	

Filling

½ cup brown sugar	2 oz (60 g) softened butter
1 dsp cinnamon	
2 tbsps plain flour	
1 cup chopped walnuts	

Grease an 8-inch (20-centimetre) round cake-tin. Pre-heat the oven to moderate. Cream the butter and sugar. Add the egg-yolks, beating in well. Add the sifted flour and salt, alternately with the milk and vanilla. Fold in the stiffly beaten egg-whites. Put half the mixture in the prepared tin. Cover with the filling. Pour in the remaining cake mixture and bake for 45 minutes to an hour.
Filling: Mix all the ingredients together well.

SOUTHERN CAKE

1 cup butter	1 tsp bicarbonate of soda
1 cup sugar	1 cup milk
3 eggs	1 packet mixed dried fruit
3 cups plain flour	

Grease a 7-inch (18-centimetre) cake-tin. Pre-heat the oven to slow to moderate. Cream the butter and sugar. Add the eggs, one by one, beating well after each addition. Add half the flour, then gradually mix in the soda, which has been dissolved in the milk. Add the remaining flour and the fruit. Pour into the prepared tin and bake for 2 hours.

SHOW CAKE

8 oz (250 g) butter	½ tsp cinnamon or mixed spice
8 oz (250 g) light brown sugar	2 oz (60 g) chopped nuts
4 eggs	1 lb (500 g) mixed dried fruit
8 oz (250 g) plain flour	2 oz (60 g) glacé cherries
2 oz (60 g) self-raising flour	3 tbsps brandy or sherry
salt	

Grease an 8-inch (20-centimetre) square cake-tin and line with two layers of greased greaseproof paper. Pre-heat the oven to slow. Cream the butter and sugar. Add the eggs, one at a time, beating well after each addition. Add the plain and self-raising flours, which have been sifted with the salt and spice. Add the nuts, fruit, and brandy. Pour into the prepared tin and bake for 2 hours.

POUND CAKE

4 oz (125 g) mixed candied peel	1 lb (500 g) currants
20 oz (625 g) plain flour	1 lb (500 g) butter
ground mace (optional)	1 lb (500 g) castor sugar
2 oz (60 g) chopped blanched almonds	8 eggs

Grease and line two 7-inch (18-centimetre) cake-tins. Pre-heat the oven to moderate. Shred the peel very finely. Sieve the flour and mace on to a piece of paper and add the peel, almonds, and currants. Beat the butter in a mixing bowl until creamy. Add the castor sugar and cream together. Add the eggs, one at a time, beating well after each addition. Fold in the flour and fruit mixture. Mix in a little milk if necessary to make a good consistency. Pour into the prepared tins and bake for 1½ to 2 hours.

SOLDIER'S POUND CAKE

1 lb (500 g) plain flour	12 oz (375 g) seeded raisins
4 oz (125 g) self-raising flour	12 oz (375 g) currants
a little grated nutmeg	4 oz (125 g) chopped dates
1 tsp cinnamon	4 oz (125 g) mixed candied peel
1 tsp mixed spice	
¼ tsp salt	1 dsp treacle
1 lb (500 g) butter	2 tbsps brandy or rum
1 lb (500 g) sugar	½ tsp bicarbonate of soda
8 eggs	1 dsp boiling water
1½ lb (750 g) sultanas	

Grease a 12-inch (30-centimetre) cake-tin and line with two layers of greased greaseproof paper. Tie two thicknesses of brown paper around the outside of the tin. Pre-heat the oven to slow. Sift the flours with the nutmeg, cinnamon, spice, and salt. Cream the butter and sugar. Beat in the eggs, one at a time, beating well after each addition. Add the sifted dry ingredients alternately with the fruit. Add the treacle, brandy, and then the soda, which has been dissolved in the boiling water. Pour into the prepared tin and bake for 3 to 4 hours.

Dried fruit, unless bought in packets stating it to have been cleaned, should be thoroughly prepared before use: wash and dry the fruit thoroughly, pick it over to remove stems and so on, then sprinkle it with flour, tossing to cover completely.

PUMPKIN FRUIT CAKE

1 large cup cooked pumpkin
4 oz (125 g) butter
1 large cup sugar
2 eggs
1 tsp vanilla essence
1 lb (500 g) mixed dried fruit
2 cups self-raising flour

Grease an 8-inch (20-centimetre) cake-tin and line with two layers of greased greaseproof paper. Pre-heat the oven to moderate. Mash the pumpkin while still warm. Cream the butter and sugar. Beat in the eggs, then mix in the vanilla and pumpkin. Add the fruit, alternately with the sifted flour. Pour into the prepared tin and bake for 1 hour.

PARRAMATTA PLUM CAKE

6 oz (185 g) butter
6 oz (185 g) sugar
3 eggs
8 oz (250 g) self-raising flour
½ tsp bicarbonate of soda
¼ tsp salt
1 tsp mixed spice
¼ cup rum
12 oz (375 g) chopped seeded raisins
6 oz (185 g) currants
2 oz (60 g) mixed candied peel
1 oz (30 g) chopped ginger
2 oz (60 g) chopped walnuts
2 oz (60 g) chopped almonds
1 dsp golden syrup
3 tbsps blackcurrant jam

Grease a 7-inch (18-centimetre) cake-tin and line with two layers of greased greaseproof paper. Tie two thicknesses of brown paper around the outside of the tin. Pre-heat the oven to hot. Cream the butter and sugar until light and fluffy. Add the eggs, one at a time, beating well after each addition. Add the sifted dry ingredients, alternately with the rum. Add the fruit and nuts, golden syrup, and blackcurrant jam. Pour into the prepared tin. Bake for 15 minutes, then reduce the heat to very slow and cook for 3 hours.

LIGHT FRUIT CAKE

8 oz (250 g) butter
8 oz (250 g) sugar
3 eggs
1 tsp vinegar
½ tsp golden syrup
10 oz (315 g) plain flour
1½ tsps baking powder
1 lb (500 g) mixed dried fruit
¼ pt (150 ml) milk

Pre-heat the oven to moderate. Grease a 7-inch (18-centimetre) cake-tin and line with greased greaseproof paper. Cream the butter and sugar. Beat in the eggs, vinegar, and golden syrup. Sift the flour and baking powder, and add to the fruit. Mix into the creamed mixture alternately with the milk. Pour into the prepared tin and bake for about 1½ hours.

BOILED FRUIT CAKE

¾ cup water
1 cup sugar
4 oz (125 g) butter
1 tsp mixed spice
1 packet mixed dried fruit
2 eggs, beaten
1 cup self-raising flour
1 cup plain flour
1 tsp bicarbonate of soda
a pinch of salt

Grease and line a 6-inch (15-centimetre) cake-tin. Pre-heat the oven to moderate. Place the water, sugar, butter, spice, and fruit in a saucepan. Bring to the boil and simmer for 5 minutes. Remove from the heat, leave to cool, and add the eggs and the sifted flours, soda, and salt. Pour into the prepared cake-tin. Bake for 1 to 1½ hours.

BOILED FRUIT CAKE (without eggs)

4 oz (125 g) butter
1 cup sugar
12 oz (375 g) mixed dried fruit
2 tbsps desiccated coconut
¼ tsp salt
2 cups water
3 cups plain flour
1½ level tsps bicarbonate of soda
½ tsp mixed spice
¼ tsp nutmeg

Pre-heat the oven to moderate. Grease a 7-inch (18-centimetre) cake-tin and line with two layers of greased greaseproof paper. Tie two thicknesses of brown paper around the outside. Heat the butter with the sugar, mixed fruit, coconut, salt, and water; bring to the boil and boil for 5 minutes. Leave to cool. Add the flour, which has been sifted with the soda, spice, and nutmeg. Mix well and pour into the prepared tin. Bake for 2¼ hours.

CUSTARD FRUIT CAKE

8 oz (250 g) butter
1 lb (500 g) plain flour
8 oz (250 g) sugar
2 lb (1 kg) mixed dried fruit
1 tsp bicarbonate of soda
½ pt (315 ml) milk
3 eggs, well beaten
½ tsp vanilla essence

Rub the butter into the flour in a mixing bowl. Add the sugar, fruit, and soda. Leave to stand overnight. Grease an 8-inch (20-centimetre) round cake-tin and line with two layers of greased greaseproof paper. Tie two thicknesses of brown paper around the outside of the tin. Boil the milk and pour over the beaten eggs, beating constantly. Transfer to the top of a double saucepan, or stand the bowl over simmering water and cook, stirring frequently, until the custard thickens. Do not allow to boil. Put aside to cool and add the vanilla essence. Mix the custard into the dry ingredients and beat until smooth. Transfer the mixture to the prepared tin and bake in a slow oven for 3½ to 4 hours.

HONEY FRUIT CAKE

8 oz (250 g) butter
1 cup honey
5 eggs, separated
2½ cups plain flour
1 tbsp mixed spice
1 dsp baking powder
2 cups chopped raw peanuts
1 cup chopped almonds
2 cups currants
2 cups seeded raisins
4 oz (125 g) mixed candied peel
8 oz (250 g) glacé cherries
4 oz (125 g) chopped glacé pineapple

Grease a 9-inch (23-centimetre) cake-tin and line it with two layers of greased greaseproof paper. Tie a double layer of brown paper around the outside of the tin. Pre-heat the oven to slow. Cream the butter in a mixing bowl; add the honey, beating well. Add the well-beaten egg-yolks. Sift the flour and sift half of it again twice with the spice and baking powder; add to the creamed mixture. Fold in the stiffly beaten egg-whites. Roll the nuts, currants, raisins, and peel in the remaining flour, and add to the mixture. Add the cherries and pineapple. Transfer to the prepared tin and bake for 2 to 2½ hours.

MOIST FRUIT CAKE (without eggs)

¾ cup butter
1 cup sugar
2 cups self-raising flour
1 cup ground rice
1 tsp grated nutmeg
1 tsp mixed spice
a pinch of salt
1 cup chopped dates
1 cup chopped seeded raisins
a little candied peel
1 dsp bicarbonate of soda
2 tbsps vinegar
1 cup hot milk

Pre-heat the oven to moderate. Grease an 8-inch (20-centimetre) cake-tin and line with two layers of greased greaseproof paper. Tie two thicknesses of brown paper around the outside of the tin. Cream the butter and sugar in a mixing bowl. Rub in the flour, which has been sifted with the rice, nutmeg, spice, and salt, then add the fruit. Dissolve the soda in the vinegar. Make a well in the cake mixture and pour in the vinegar mixture. Draw a little flour over the liquid, and cover the bowl with a clean cloth. Leave in a warm place for half an hour. Thoroughly mix in the milk. Pour into the prepared tin and bake for about 2 hours.

RUM AND DATE CAKE

2½ cups plain flour
a good pinch of salt
¼ tsp bicarbonate of soda
4 oz (125 g) raisins
4 oz (125 g) sultanas
4 oz (125 g) currants
4 oz (125 g) mixed candied peel
2 oz (60 g) chopped blanched almonds
2 oz (60 g) finely chopped dates
2 oz (60 g) finely chopped preserved ginger
8 oz (250 g) butter
8 oz (250 g) brown sugar
6 eggs
1 tbsp golden syrup
grated rind of 1 orange
1 tsp molasses
3 tbsps rum or brandy

Grease an 8-inch (20-centimetre) cake-tin and line with two layers of greaseproof paper. Pre-heat the oven to slow. Sift the flour with the salt and soda. Mix together the raisins, sultanas, currants, candied peel, almonds, dates, and ginger. Cream the butter and sugar. Beat in the eggs, one by one, beating well after each addition. Add the golden syrup, orange rind, and molasses. Add the fruit alternately with the sifted dry ingredients. Add the rum. Pour into the prepared tin and bake in a slow oven for 3 to 3½ hours.

OLD ENGLISH WEDDING CAKE

8 oz (250 g) plain flour
6 oz (185 g) butter
6 oz (185 g) brown sugar
4 eggs
½ cup milk
1 tbsp treacle
½ tsp baking powder
1 lb (500 g) currants
8 oz (250 g) mixed candied peel
finely grated rind of 1 lemon
¼ tsp mace
cinnamon
grated nutmeg
4 oz (125 g) ground almonds
½ cup brandy

Grease a 9-inch (23-centimetre) cake-tin and line with two layers of greased greaseproof paper. Tie two thicknesses of brown paper around the outside of the tin. Pre-heat the oven to moderate. Sift the flour into a mixing bowl; rub in the butter until the mixture resembles breadcrumbs. Mix in the sugar, eggs, milk, treacle, and baking powder. Stir in the currants, peel, lemon rind, mace, cinnamon, nutmeg, ground almonds, and brandy. Pour into the prepared tin and bake for 3 hours.

CHRISTMAS CAKE

1 lb (500 g) seeded raisins
1½ lb (750 g) sultanas
8 oz (250 g) currants
4 oz (125 g) chopped candied peel
4 oz (125 g) chopped dates or figs
8 oz (250 g) chopped glacé cherries
4 oz (125 g) chopped blanched almonds
1 lb (500 g) butter
1 lb (500 g) sugar
9 eggs, well beaten
4 tbsps rum or brandy
1 tsp glycerine
¼ tsp vanilla essence
1½ lb (750 g) plain flour
a pinch of salt
½ tsp cinnamon
½ tsp mixed spice
½ tsp grated nutmeg
¼ tsp bicarbonate of soda
2 tbsps hot water

Wash the raisins, sultanas, and currants and leave to dry. Mix in the peel, dates, cherries, and almonds. Line a 10-inch (25-centimetre) square or 11-inch (28-centimetre) round cake-tin, or two smaller tins, with three layers of thick brown paper and two layers of white paper. Pre-heat the oven to hot. Cream the butter and sugar. Gradually add the eggs, beating well. Add the rum, glycerine, vanilla essence, and fruits. When evenly blended, add the sifted flour, salt, cinnamon, spice, and nutmeg. Mix well. Dissolve the soda in the hot water and stir evenly into the cake mixture. Pour the cake mixture into the prepared tin. Bake for 15 minutes, then lower the temperature to slow and bake for 4 to 5 hours, or 2½ to 3½ hours for two small cakes. Test before removing from the oven.

NEW-STYLE CHRISTMAS CAKE

1½ cups halved Brazil nuts
1½ cups halved walnuts
8 oz (250 g) chopped dates
⅔ cup mixed candied peel
½ cup green glacé cherries
½ cup red glacé cherries
½ cup seeded raisins
¾ cup plain flour
½ tsp baking powder
½ tsp salt
¾ cup sugar
3 eggs, lightly beaten
1 tsp vanilla essence

Grease a loaf-tin and line with greased greaseproof paper. Pre-heat the oven to slow. Place the nuts and fruit in a large mixing bowl. Sift the flour, baking powder, and salt three times and add with the sugar to the nuts and fruit; mix well. Add the eggs and vanilla essence to make a stiff consistency. Transfer to the prepared tin and press down well with the back of a spoon. Bake for 1½ to 2½ hours. Leave in the tin to cool. When cold, wrap securely, place in an airtight container, and store in the refrigerator.

GINGER AND DATE CAKE

1 cup chopped dates
½ cup butter
1 dsp ground ginger
1 tsp bicarbonate of soda
1 cup boiling water
2 tbsps golden syrup
1½ cups plain flour
½ tsp bicarbonate of soda

Grease a cake-tin and line it with greased greaseproof paper. Pre-heat the oven to moderate. Put the dates, butter, and ginger in a mixing bowl. Sprinkle over the teaspoon of soda. Pour in the boiling water, then the golden syrup, and allow to stand for a time. Beat the mixture well. Sift the flour with the ½ teaspoon of soda; stir into the mixture. Pour into the prepared tin. Bake for 1 to 1¼ hours.

EGGLESS CAKE

1 cup sugar
1 cup water
1 cup sultanas
1 tbsp dripping
a pinch of salt
2 cups plain flour
1 dsp baking powder
½ tsp mixed spice
½ tsp cinnamon
½ tsp grated nutmeg

Boil the sugar, water, sultanas, dripping, and salt, stirring until the sugar has completely dissolved; leave to cool. Stir in the sifted flour, baking powder, spice, cinnamon, and nutmeg. Pour into a well-greased cake-tin. Bake for 1½ hours in a moderate oven. Allow to cool.
Slice and spread with butter before serving.

HONEY ROLL

20 oz (625 g) honey
4 oz (125 g) butter
a pinch of salt
3 eggs
12 oz (375 g) plain flour
a pinch of ground ginger
a pinch of mixed spice
1 dsp bicarbonate of soda
2–3 tbsps milk
¼ pt (150 ml) cream, whipped

Warm the honey, butter, and salt. Remove from the heat and stir in the eggs. Add the sifted flour, ginger, and spice. Dissolve the soda in the milk, and add, mixing until smooth. Divide the mixture into three equal parts and spread evenly on greased, paper-lined oven trays. Bake in a moderately hot oven for 10 to 15 minutes. Turn out on to dampened tea-towels covered with greaseproof paper sprinkled with sugar. Roll up tightly. When cold, unroll, spread with the cream and roll up lightly.

HONEY GINGERBREAD (without eggs)

½ cup honey
½ cup boiling water
½ cup lightly packed brown
    sugar
1 cup plain flour
½ cup self-raising flour
1 tsp bicarbonate of soda
3 tsps ground ginger
¼ tsp salt
4 oz (125 g) butter

Grease a loaf-tin and line with greased greaseproof paper. Pre-heat the oven to moderate. Melt the honey in the water in a mixing bowl, and mix in the sifted dry ingredients. Melt the butter and beat into the mixture. Pour into the prepared tin. Bake in a moderate oven for 1 hour, or until cooked. Test with a skewer. Turn out on a wire rack to cool.

OLD-FASHIONED GINGERBREAD

1 cup butter
1 cup sugar
3 eggs, beaten
1 cup treacle
1 cup milk
3 cups plain flour
1 tsp cinnamon
1 tsp grated nutmeg
1 dsp ground ginger
a pinch of salt
1 dsp bicarbonate of soda
a little extra milk

Grease a large roasting tin and line with greaseproof paper. Cream the butter and sugar; beat in the eggs. Heat the treacle and milk; stir into the butter mixture. Sift the flour, cinnamon, nutmeg, ginger, and salt into the mixture. Mix well. Add the soda dissolved in a little milk. Pour the mixture into the prepared tin. Bake in a slow oven for about 1 hour. Cool for a little while then turn out on a wire rack.

PIONEER'S SPONGE CAKE

5 eggs
1 cup sugar
1 cup plain flour
1 tsp baking powder
juice of 1 lemon

Beat the eggs and sugar for half an hour. Fold in the sifted flour and baking powder and the lemon juice. Pour into a greased tin and bake in a moderately hot oven for about 17 minutes. Turn out on a wire rack to cool.
Cover with whipped cream and decorate as you wish.

SPONGE CAKE

5 eggs
the weight of the eggs in plain
    flour
the weight of 3 of the eggs in
    sugar
1 tsp cornflour
3 tbsps water
1 tsp butter

Grease two 8-inch (20-centimetre) round sandwich tins. Pre-heat the oven to moderate. Beat the eggs, salt, and sugar in a large mixing bowl until thick. Fold in the sifted flour and cornflour. Heat the water and butter until boiling and fold into the mixture. Pour the mixture into the prepared tins and bake for 20 minutes. Turn out on a wire rack to cool.
Fill and ice (see the chapter 'Luscious Icings and Fillings').

SPONGE SANDWICH

4 large eggs
¾ cup sugar
1 cup self-raising flour
a pinch of salt
vanilla essence or lemon
    essence

Grease two large sandwich tins. Pre-heat the oven to moderate. Beat the eggs and sugar until the sugar has dissolved and the mixture is thick and light. Carefully fold in the flour, which has been sifted three times with the salt. Add essence. Pour into the prepared tins and bake for about 25 minutes. Turn out on a wire rack to cool.
Fill and ice (see the chapter 'Luscious Icings and Fillings').

Greasing a cup in which syrup or treacle is to be measured will prevent it from sticking.

COFFEE SPONGE

4 *eggs, separated*   2 *tbsps milk*
1 *cup sugar*   2 *tbsps coffee essence or strong*
1 *cup plain flour*   *black coffee*
1 *tsp baking powder*   2 *tbsps melted butter*

Grease two sandwich tins. Pre-heat the oven to moderate. Beat the egg-whites until stiff; add the sugar and beat until stiff again. Add the egg-yolks and beat. Fold in the sifted flour and baking powder, then the milk, coffee essence, and butter. Pour the mixture into the prepared tins and bake for 20 minutes. Turn out on a wire rack to cool.

Fill and ice (see the chapter 'Luscious Icings and Fillings')

Add a pinch of salt to egg-whites before beating them; when they become foamy add a pinch of cream of tartar and continue beating swiftly until they are stiff. Use at once.

GINGER FLUFF SANDWICH

3 *eggs*   1 *tsp cream of tartar*
½ *cup sugar*   1 *tsp ground ginger*
½ *cup arrowroot*   1 *tsp cinnamon*
1 *level tbsp plain flour*   1 *tbsp warmed golden syrup*
½ *tsp bicarbonate of soda*

Grease two sandwich tins. Pre-heat the oven to moderate. Beat the eggs for 5 minutes, then add the sugar and beat for another 5 minutes until thick and pale. Sift the arrowroot with the flour, soda, cream of tartar, ginger, and cinnamon four times. Fold the sifted ingredients carefully into the egg mixture. Fold in the syrup. Pour into the prepared tins and bake for 15 to 20 minutes. Turn out on a wire rack to cool.

Sandwich the cakes together with whipped cream and sprinkle with icing sugar.

If a cake is browning too quickly, cover it with greased paper.

FEATHER SPONGE

4 *eggs*   1 *dsp cinnamon*
1 *cup sugar*   2 *oz (60 g) butter*
1 *cup plain flour*   6 *tbsps boiling milk*
1 *tsp baking powder*
1 *dsp cocoa*

Beat the eggs and sugar together for 15 minutes until thick and light. Carefully fold in the flour, which has been sifted with the baking powder, cocoa, and cinnamon. Melt the butter in the boiling milk and fold into the mixture. Pour into greased sandwich tins and bake in a moderate oven for about 20 minutes. Turn out on a wire rack to cool.

Fill and ice (see the chapter 'Luscious Icings and Fillings').

Remove sponges from the oven with a dry cloth and turn out to cool in a place where there are no draughts.

CINNAMON SPONGE

4 *eggs*   1 *dsp cinnamon*
1 *cup sugar*   1 *dsp ground ginger*
1 *cup plain flour*   *a pinch of salt*
1 *tsp baking powder*   1 *tsp butter*
1 *dsp cocoa*   4 *tbsps hot water*

Grease two sandwich tins. Pre-heat the oven to moderate. Beat the eggs and sugar until thick and light. Carefully fold in the flour, which has been sifted with the baking powder, cocoa, cinnamon, ginger, and salt. Melt the butter in the water and fold into the mixture. Pour into the prepared tins and bake for about 20 minutes. Turn out on a wire rack to cool.

Fill and ice (see the chapter 'Luscious Icings and Fillings').

SWISS ROLL

3 *large eggs*   3 *tbsps boiling water*
4 *oz (125 g) sugar*   *jam*
4 *oz (125 g) self-raising flour*   *extra sugar*

Grease a Swiss-roll tin and line with greased greaseproof paper. Pre-heat the oven to hot. Beat the eggs and sugar together for 15 minutes, until thick and light. Sift the flour three times and fold into the mixture. Fold in the water. Pour into the prepared tin and bake for 8 to 10 minutes. Turn out on to paper sprinkled with sugar, and peel off the lining paper. Spread quickly with warmed jam and roll up tightly. Trim and dust with sugar.

JAM ROLL

4 *eggs*   ¾ *cup plain flour*
¾ *tsp baking powder*   *extra sugar*
¾ *cup sugar*   *jam*

Grease a Swiss-roll tin and line it with greased greaseproof paper. Pre-heat the oven to hot. Beat the eggs and baking powder until light and fluffy. Gradually beat in the sugar until pale and thick. Fold in the sifted flour. Pour into the prepared tin and bake for 10 to 15 minutes. Sprinkle a dampened tea-towel with sugar and turn the cake out on it. Roll the cake up in the towel and leave for 2 minutes. Unroll and spread with warmed jam. Roll up firmly and cool on a wire rack. Sprinkle with sugar.

THREE-MINUTE SPONGE

1 *cup sifted plain flour*   3 *tbsps milk*
¾ *cup sugar*   1 *dsp cream of tartar*
3 *eggs, well beaten*   1 *tsp bicarbonate of soda*
2 *tbsps melted butter*

Grease two 7-inch (18-centimetre) sandwich tins. Pre-heat the oven to moderate. Put all the ingredients in a mixing bowl in the above order. Beat with a fork for 3 minutes. Pour the mixture into the prepared tins and bake for 15 to 20 minutes. Turn out on wire racks to cool.

Fill and ice (see the chapter 'Luscious Icings and Fillings').

Use dark sugar for fruit cakes and castor sugar for sponges and other light cakes.

CHOCOLATE SIMPLICITY CAKE

4 oz (125 g) butter, melted
2 tbsps cocoa
1 cup self-raising flour
1 cup sugar
½ cup milk
2 eggs
½ tsp vanilla essence
grated ginger and walnuts
(optional)

Grease a 7-inch (18-centimetre) cake-tin. Pre-heat the oven to moderate. Put all the ingredients in a mixing bowl and beat for 5 minutes. Pour into the prepared tin and bake for 45 minutes to an hour. Leave to cool.

Ice with chocolate icing (see the chapter 'Luscious Icings and Fillings').

To measure quantities of fat expressed as parts of a cup: if, say, ½ cup of butter is specified, half-fill a cup with water and then add enough butter to bring the water-level to the top of the cup.

LEMON CAKE

1½ cups self-raising flour
2 eggs
1 cup sugar
½ cup milk
4 oz (125 g) butter, melted
1 tsp grated lemon rind

Grease a 7-inch (18-centimetre) cake-tin. Pre-heat the oven to moderate. Beat all the ingredients in a mixing bowl for about 5 minutes. Pour the mixture into the prepared tin and bake for 45 minutes to an hour. Turn out on a wire rack to cool.

Ice with lemon icing (see the chapter 'Luscious Icings and Fillings').

WONDER CAKE

2 oz (60 g) butter, melted
2 eggs
milk
1 cup plain flour
1 small cup sugar
a pinch of salt

Grease a cake-tin. Pre-heat the oven to moderate. Pour the melted butter into a cup, add the eggs, and fill up with milk; mix gently. Pour into a mixing bowl with the dry ingredients and beat for 5 minutes, until smooth. Pour into the tin and bake for 20 to 30 minutes. Add orange or lemon rind and juice or mixed dried fruit to the basic mixture if you like.

FIVE-MINUTE CAKE

¾ cup sugar
1 cup plain flour
1 heaped tbsp softened butter
2–3 eggs
3 tbsps milk
vanilla essence
1¼ tsps baking powder

Grease a 7-inch (18-centimetre) cake-tin. Pre-heat the oven to moderate. Put the sugar, flour, butter, eggs, milk, and essence in a mixing bowl. Beat well for 4 minutes. Add the baking powder and beat again for 1 minute. Pour into the prepared tin and bake for 45 minutes to an hour. Turn out on a wire rack to cool.

Ice as you wish (see the chapter 'Luscious Icings and Fillings').

To keep a fruit cake moist, add a slice of fresh bread or an apple to the cake-tin.

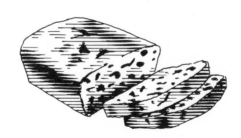

Luscious ICINGS and FILLINGS

Basic Types of Icing

Glacé Icing: This is a simple, economical kind of icing that is made by combining a little warm liquid and optional flavouring and colouring with sifted icing sugar. It needs to be of a fairly runny consistency and should be poured at once over the cake on a wire rack; do not smooth it with a knife. Do not move the cake until the icing has set or it will crack. When the icing sets it has a smooth, glossy appearance but tends to harden with long keeping.

Butter Icing, or Cream: This is a soft icing, made by creaming the icing sugar with butter and then adding liquid and flavourings to achieve a suitable spreading consistency. It is spread over the cake with a knife dipped in hot water. Butter icing does not set quickly and has a slightly rough, mat appearance. It stays moist for a reasonable time, depending on the amount of butter used, and is equally suitable for fillings.

Almond Icing: This is generally used to cover rich fruit cakes before they are frosted with royal icing. It is made from ground almonds, icing sugar, eggs, and lemon juice.

Royal Icing: This is a good icing for wedding cakes and Christmas cakes, piping, and so on, because of its smooth, shiny appearance. It is made by combining egg-whites with well-sieved, fine icing sugar; it is important not to over-beat, or air bubbles will form. It must be used at once or the surface will begin to harden and set. Royal icing sets hard and keeps well.

GLACE ICING

8 oz (250 g) icing sugar
2 tbsps warm water

*flavouring and colouring
(optional)*

Sift the icing sugar into a mixing bowl. Gradually add the water, beating until the icing is thick enough to coat the back of a spoon. Add flavouring and colouring if you wish and use at once, pouring over the cake.

CHOCOLATE GLACE ICING

2 oz (60 g) plain chocolate
1 tsp butter
1–2 tbsps warm water

1 tsp vanilla essence
4 oz (125 g) icing sugar

Melt the chocolate with the butter and water in a mixing bowl over simmering water. Add the vanilla, then gradually beat in the icing sugar. Use at once.

COFFEE GLACE ICING

8 oz (250 g) icing sugar
2 tbsps warm water

1 tbsp coffee essence or strong
black coffee

Sift the icing sugar into a mixing bowl. Beat in the liquid until the icing will coat the back of a spoon. Use at once.

FRUIT GLACE ICING

2–3 tbsps strained, warmed
fruit juice

8 oz (250 g) icing sugar

Sift the icing sugar into a mixing bowl. Beat in the liquid until the icing will coat the back of a spoon. Use at once.

VIENNA ICING

3 oz (90 g) butter
8 oz (250 g) icing sugar

approx. 2 tbsps sherry,
brandy, or liqueur

Cream the butter in a mixing bowl. Sift in the icing sugar gradually, beating thoroughly. Add the liquid and beat until soft and creamy.

VIENNA CHOCOLATE ICING

6 oz (185 g) butter
8 oz (250 g) icing sugar
1 tbsp cocoa

approx. 2 tbsps sherry,
brandy, or liqueur

Cream the butter in a mixing bowl. Sift in the icing sugar and cocoa gradually, beating thoroughly. Add the liquid and beat until soft and creamy.

VIENNA FRUIT ICING

approx. 2 tbsps passionfruit
pulp, or strained orange or
other fruit juice

3 oz (90 g) butter
8 oz (250 g) icing sugar

Cream the butter in a mixing bowl. Sift in the icing sugar gradually, beating thoroughly. Add the liquid and beat until soft and creamy.

BUTTER CREAM

4 oz (125 g) butter
8 oz (250 g) icing sugar
1–2 tbsps warm milk or water

*flavouring or colouring
(optional)*

Cream the butter in a mixing bowl. Gradually beat in the sifted icing sugar, alternately with the warm liquid. Beat in flavouring or colouring. This is enough to fill and cover the top of an average sandwich cake.

CHOCOLATE BUTTER CREAM

2 oz (60 g) cooking chocolate
or 1 tbsp cocoa
4 oz (125 g) butter

8 oz (250 g) icing sugar
1–2 tbsps warm milk or water

Melt the chocolate over a pan of simmering water; if you are using cocoa instead, sift it with the icing sugar. Cream the butter in a mixing bowl. Gradually beat in the icing sugar, alternately with the liquid. Beat in the melted chocolate.

FRUIT BUTTER CREAM

4 oz (125 g) butter
8 oz (250 g) icing sugar
1–2 tbsps passionfruit pulp or
strained fruit juice

½ tsp finely grated orange or
lemon rind (optional)

Cream the butter in a mixing bowl. Carefully beat in the sifted icing sugar, alternately with the liquid. Beat in the grated rind.

ALMOND ICING

1 lb (500 g) icing sugar or
8 oz (250 g) icing sugar and
8 oz (250 g) castor sugar
8 oz (250 g) ground almonds

2 egg-yolks
2 tbsps sherry, brandy, or fruit
juice
egg-white

Sift the icing sugar into a bowl with the ground almonds. Mix to a firm paste with the egg-yolks and liquid. Turn on to a surface dusted with icing sugar and knead well until smooth and pliable. Divide into three portions. Roll one into a circle the size of the top of the cake and roll each of the other pieces into strips to cover half the sides of the cake. Brush the icing with egg-white before pressing on to the cake. The icing must be very dry before using, so if necessary leave it for 24 hours before covering the cake. Leave to harden on the cake, then ice with royal icing (see page 125).

ROYAL ICING

1 lb (500 g) icing sugar   juice of 1 lemon
2 egg-whites   food colouring (optional)

Sift the icing sugar. Beat the egg-whites in a mixing bowl and then beat in the icing sugar and the lemon juice. Beat vigorously for about 5 minutes until stiff and snowy. Beat in a few drops of colouring if you wish. Use the icing at once or cover with a damp cloth until you are ready.

FUDGE ICING

1 oz (30 g) butter   ½ pt (315 ml) milk
8 oz (250 g) sugar   flavouring

Heat all the ingredients in a saucepan, stirring until the sugar has dissolved and boiling-point is reached. Boil to the soft-ball stage (see page 128). Remove from the heat and beat to a spreading consistency. Flavour as required.

TRANSPARENT ICING

1 lb (500 g) sugar   1 dsp vanilla essence
½ pt (315 ml) water

Heat the sugar in a saucepan with the water and vanilla essence. Boil the mixture until it becomes thick, like transparent glue. Rub the sugar against the sides of the pan with a wooden spatula until it has a white milky appearance. Pour into a bowl and beat until it thickens. Pour over the cake while hot, to cover completely.

MARSHMALLOW ICING

½ cup water   1 dsp gelatine
½ cup sugar

Put all the ingredients in a saucepan, whisk to combine, and bring to the boil without stirring. Boil for 3 minutes. Pour into a mixing bowl and leave to cool until a skin forms on top. Beat vigorously until thick and snowy. Use at once.

BOILED FROSTING

1 lb (500 g) sugar   a pinch of cream of tartar
¼ pt (150 ml) water   1 tsp vanilla essence
2 egg-whites

Heat the sugar and water gently, stirring until the sugar has dissolved. Bring to the boil. Cover and boil for 1 minute. Remove the lid and boil for another 5 minutes, to the soft-ball stage (see page 128). In the meantime, beat the egg-whites with the cream of tartar until stiff. Remove the syrup from the heat, leave for a moment to settle, then gradually pour it on to the egg-whites, beating constantly. Add the vanilla and continue beating until the frosting is thick and cool. Use at once, working quickly and covering the top and sides of the cake.

TOFFEE TOPPING

1 cup sugar   chopped nuts

Heat the sugar in a saucepan over gentle heat until melted, boiling, and golden, stirring occasionally. Cool slightly, then pour over the cake. Sprinkle the nuts over. Leave to set.

ALMOND AND HONEY FILLING

4 oz (125 g) ground almonds   4 oz (125 g) honey
4 oz (125 g) butter

Cream all the ingredients together in a mixing bowl.

HONEY BUTTER FILLING

2 oz (60 g) butter   2 oz (60 g) honey

Beat the honey and butter until fluffy.

APRICOT FILLING

4 oz (125 g) icing sugar   3 tbsps apricot jam
2 oz (60 g) ground almonds   1 tbsp lemon juice

Sift the icing sugar into a mixing bowl. Stir in the almonds then beat in the jam and lemon juice vigorously until smooth.

BANANA FILLING

1 banana   ½ tsp vanilla essence
2 oz (60 g) butter   4 oz (125 g) icing sugar

Mash the banana in a mixing bowl then beat to a cream with the other ingredients.

DATE FILLING

1 cup chopped dates   4 tbsps milk
1 tbsp butter   1 tbsp brown sugar

Heat the dates with the butter and the milk, stirring to combine. Cook for a few minutes. Remove from the heat, beat the sugar in vigorously, and leave to cool before using.

PASSIONFRUIT FILLING

1 oz (30 g) butter   1 tbsp passionfruit pulp
4 oz (125 g) icing sugar

Cream the butter then gradually beat in the sifted icing sugar. Mix to a spreading consistency with the passionfruit pulp.

MOCK CREAM

2 oz (60 g) butter   1 tbsp cold water
1 tbsp boiling water   approx. 1 tbsp milk.
3 oz (90 g) icing sugar
½ tsp vanilla essence

Melt the butter in the boiling water. Beat in the sifted icing sugar to form a cream. Beat in the vanilla and the cold water. Gradually beat in a little milk. Use as a filling for sandwich cakes.

CUSTARD FILLING

1 oz (30 g) cornflour   1 egg, separated
1 oz (30 g) sugar   1 tsp vanilla essence
a pinch of salt
½ pt (315 ml) milk

Mix the cornflour, sugar, and salt to a smooth paste with a little of the milk. Heat the rest of the milk to boiling-point then pour it on to the blended ingredients, beating well. Pour back into the saucepan and return to the heat. Stir constantly, heating to boiling-point. Remove from the heat, pour a little custard over the egg-yolk, beat, and pour back into the saucepan. Heat gently until the custard thickens. Remove from the heat when smooth and thick and fold in the egg-white, which has been stiffly beaten. Add the vanilla, strain, and leave to cool before using.

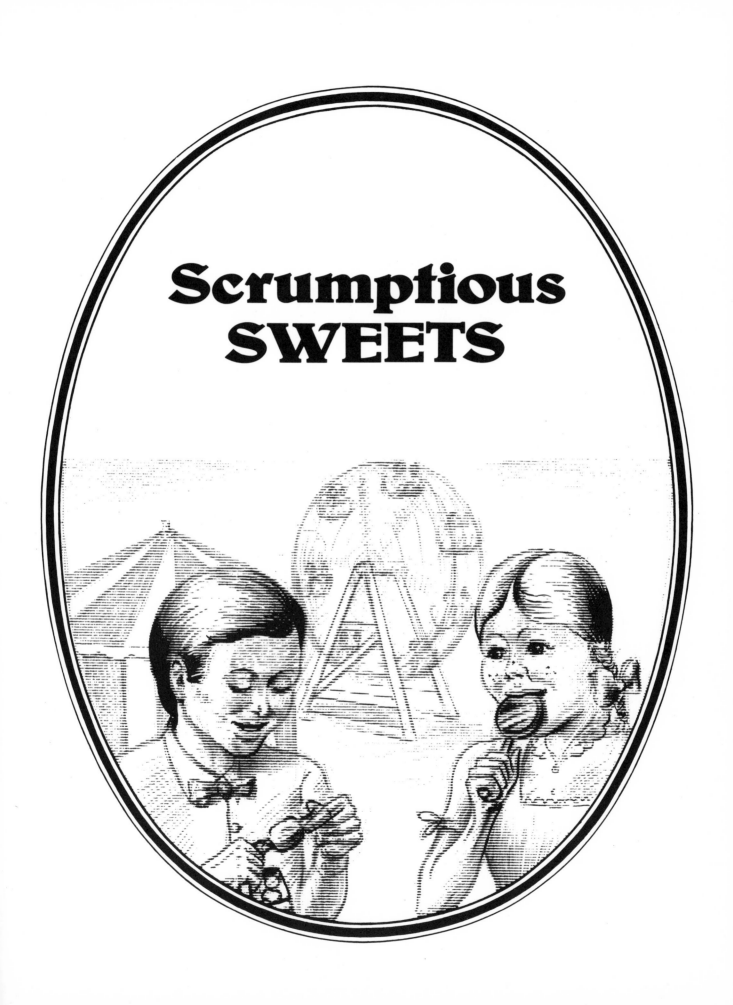

Scrumptious SWEETS

Many kinds of sweets are made by boiling sugar and water together at different temperatures. Use a strong, heavy-based saucepan and make sure to boil to the temperature recommended in the recipe; a sugar thermometer is very helpful for this.

Syrup-based sweets must have the sugar dissolved before boiling-point is reached; do not stir, however, or crystals will form. The boiling syrup will often splash on to the sides of the saucepan and form crystals, which should be washed down with a clean pastry brush dipped in cold water. Otherwise, sweets that should look clear and smooth may be sugary and rough when set. Some recipes include cream of tartar, glucose, golden syrup, or lemon juice, which also helps to prevent the sweets from becoming crystalline.

Exceptions are fudge and some caramel mixtures, which need to be stirred towards the end of the cooking time, or sometimes after they have been left to cool for a time. This prevents burning and helps to achieve the right 'grained' consistency.

Allow the syrup to 'settle' before creaming or beating it. Add colouring and flavouring to lukewarm fondant at the beginning of the beating period, if one colour and flavour is to be used for the entire batch. Otherwise, divide the fondant into portions and colour each as you wish.

The Main Stages of Sugar-boiling

Thread Stage 220°–235°F (104°–112°C): At this stage the mixture begins to look syrupy and a little dropped from a spoon will form a fine thread.
Soft-ball Stage 235°–245°F (112°–118°C): When a little syrup poured into cold water forms a soft ball. This is the stage for fudges and fondants.
Hard-ball Stage 245°–265°F (118°–130°C): When a little syrup poured into cold water forms a hard ball. This is the stage for caramels, nougats, and marshmallows.
Soft-crack Stage 270°–290°F (132°–143°C): When a little syrup poured into cold water separates into threads that are hard but not brittle. This is the stage for toffees and butterscotch.
Hard-crack Stage 300°–320°F (149°–160°C): When a little syrup poured into cold water separates into threads that are hard and brittle. This is the stage for hard toffees and brittle.
Caramel Stage 340°–350°F (170°–177°C): When the syrup turns golden. This is the stage for caramels and pralines.

This is the basis of all but the most simple sweet-making. The sugar is dissolved in the liquid, which is then heated to boiling-point and boiled to whichever stage beyond that is required for the particular sweet. The syrup thickens and darkens until the maximum temperature of 350°F (177°C) is reached—if the syrup is boiled to a higher temperature, it will burn.

CANDIED FRUIT

Prepare the fruit: prick apricots or plums with a fork; stone cherries; peel and halve large fruits such as peaches and pears. Bring to the boil just enough water to cover the fruit, *then* add the fruit. Simmer until tender, from 3 to 15 minutes, according to the type of fruit; drain. For every pint (625 millilitres) of water add 12 ounces (375 grams) of sugar. Heat in a saucepan, stirring until the sugar has dissolved, and bring to the boil; boil for 2 minutes. Pour the boiling syrup over the fruit in a bowl; if the fruit floats, press it down with a plate. Leave for 24 hours.

Next day, drain the syrup off the fruit, add another 2 ounces (60 grams) of sugar for each original pint (625 millilitres) of water, and bring again to the boil. Pour the boiling syrup over the fruit and leave for 24 hours. Repeat this process for three days.

On the sixth day, after again adding the extra sugar, add the fruit to the boiling syrup and boil for 5 minutes. Return to the bowl and leave for 48 hours. Again add the sugar, add the fruit to the syrup, and boil for 5 minutes, by which time the syrup should be thick. Let the fruit stand in the syrup for four days. Drain off the syrup, then dry the fruit in a very cool oven. This drying process must be thorough and should take 3 to 6 hours, which can be spread over several days. The fruit, when dried, will not be sticky. Remove from the oven and leave to cool. Pack in greaseproof paper in wooden or waxed boxes.

CRYSTALLISED FRUIT

Make a syrup by boiling 3 pounds (1·5 kilograms) of sugar for each pint (625 millilitres) of water until it reaches 220°F (104°C), the thread stage, see page 128. Remove from the heat and allow the syrup to cool a little. Arrange the fruit in single layers on wire trays or shallow dishes. Pour over the cooled syrup and leave undisturbed until a thin crust of sugar forms on top (about 10 to 12 hours). Drain the fruit well and put in a cool oven until dry, when it should be covered with clear crystals.

CRYSTALLISED PEARS

small pears
loaf sugar
water
1 egg-white, stiffly beaten
icing sugar

Thinly pare the fruit, taking care not to break the stalks. Allow 1½ pounds (750 grams) of sugar and ¾ pint (475 millilitres) of water for each pound (500 grams) of pears. Heat sugar, water, and egg-white to boiling-point; let it boil up until it is about to boil over, then pour on a little cold water. When it rises the second time, remove from the heat, and set aside for 15 minutes. Skim gently and pour the syrup into a bowl, leaving any sediment behind. Heat the pears to boiling-point in some slightly salted boiling water; remove from the heat and allow to stand in the water for 20 minutes. Transfer the pears to a sieve to drain, then place them in the syrup in a saucepan and bring again to the boil. Remove and drain the pears, and roll in icing sugar until quite white. Set on a wire rack in a warm place to dry slowly.

Any fruits may be crystallised in this way—apricots, pineapples, and cherries are all most suitable.

ORANGE MATCHES

pared peel of 2 oranges
8 oz (250 g) sugar
¼ pt (150 ml) hot water
castor sugar

Cut the peel in narrow strips. Place in a saucepan, cover with cold water, and bring to the boil; drain. Repeat this process five times. Heat the sugar and hot water, stirring until the sugar has dissolved; add the peel. Cook slowly until nearly all the syrup has been absorbed; drain. Roll the orange strips in castor sugar.

APRICOT SWEET

1 lb (500 g) dried apricots
1 lb (500 g) castor sugar
extra castor sugar

Pour boiling water over the apricots and leave to soak for a couple of minutes. Drain and mince with the castor sugar. Mince again. Pour into a buttered shallow tin and leave to set overnight. Cut into squares and roll in castor sugar.

BOILED FONDANT

1 lb (500 g) sugar
¼ pt (150 ml) water
1 oz (30 g) glucose or a pinch of cream of tartar

Put the water in a saucepan, add the sugar, and dissolve, heating slowly. Bring to the boil, add the glucose or cream of tartar, and boil to 240°F (115°C, the soft-ball stage, see page 128). Pour on to a marble slab and leave to cool for a few minutes, until a skin starts to form; alternatively, pour into a bowl and leave to cool. Work the cooled fondant with a spatula, using a backwards-and-forwards movement, until it becomes firm and opaque. Scrape it up and knead until it is of an even texture throughout. Use as required.

The basic fondant can be coloured to taste, flavoured with essences, fruit juice, liqueurs, chocolate, or coffee; and moulded into various shapes.

UNCOOKED FONDANT

1 egg-white
1 lb (500 g) sieved icing sugar
1 tsp lemon juice
a pinch of cream of tartar

Whisk the egg-white stiffly and gradually beat in the icing sugar. Add the lemon juice and cream of tartar. Knead for 5 minutes and leave for an hour before using. Roll out on a surface sprinkled with icing sugar. Knead and use as required.

EASY UNCOOKED FONDANT

1¼ cups sieved icing sugar
2 tbsps condensed milk

Blend the icing sugar into the condensed milk. Knead and use as required.

CHOCOLATE CREAMS

8 oz (250 g) fondant (see page 129)
vanilla essence

4 oz (125 g) chocolate
butter

Work the essence into the fondant on a surface generously dusted with icing sugar. Roll into small balls or roll out and cut into small rounds. Melt the chocolate with a small knob of butter in a bowl over simmering water. Allow the chocolate to cool until warm and dip the fondant pieces in it to coat thoroughly. Place on a buttered tin or plate to set and store in an airtight tin.

PEPPERMINT CREAMS

1 quantity fondant (see page 129)

a few drops of peppermint essence

Knead a few drops of peppermint essence into the fondant. Roll out and cut into rounds.

DATE CREAMS

½ quantity fondant (see page 129)

dates, stoned

Divide the fondant into two or three pieces and colour or flavour each as you wish. Break off small pieces of fondant to fill the spaces where the stones were removed from the dates.

PRUNE CREAMS

Follow the instructions for date creams (see above).

NUT CREAMS

1 quantity fondant (see page 129)

whole blanched almonds or walnut halves

Divide the fondant into several portions and colour and flavour as you wish. Break into small pieces and roll into balls, or roll out and cut into rounds; press a nut into the top of each ball or round.

COCONUT ICE

¼ pt (150 ml) milk
1 lb (500 g) sugar
4 oz (125 g) desiccated coconut
½ tsp vanilla essence
cochineal

extra coconut

Heat the milk and sugar gently, stirring to make sure that the sugar has dissolved. Bring to the boil. Boil for about 5 minutes to 240°F (115°C, the soft-ball stage, see page 128). Remove from the heat and stir in the coconut and vanilla. Beat until the mixture is thick and white. Pour half into a buttered shallow dish or tin. Quickly colour the rest of the mixture pink with cochineal and pour over the white layer. Sprinkle with extra coconut. When partly set, mark into bars or cubes. Cut when cold and set.

UNCOOKED COCONUT ICE

12 oz (375 g) icing sugar
1 cup condensed milk
6 oz (185 g) desiccated coconut
cochineal

extra coconut

Mix the icing sugar and condensed milk together. Stir in the coconut to make a very stiff consistency. Press half the mixture into a buttered shallow tin. Colour the remaining mixture pink and press on to the white layer. Sprinkle with extra coconut. When partly set, mark into bars or cubes. Cut when set.

MARSHMALLOWS

2 tbsps gelatine
1 lb (500 g) sugar
2 cups hot water
½ tsp cream of tartar

vanilla essence or other flavouring

Heat all ingredients (except for the flavouring), stirring until the sugar has dissolved. Bring to the boil and boil for 2 or 3 minutes. Leave to cool until a skin begins to form, then beat vigorously until the mixture is thick and white. Flavour and colour to taste and pour into a slab-tin that has been greased and dusted with icing sugar. Leave to set then cut into squares and roll in icing sugar, coconut, toasted coconut, or coloured sugar.

The mixture may be varied by adding chopped nuts, cherries, or dried fruit with the flavouring.

TURKISH DELIGHT

1 lb (500 g) sugar
3 tbsps gelatine
½ pt (315 ml) hot water
¼ tsp citric acid or 1 dsp lemon juice

food colouring
2 oz (60 g) icing sugar
1 oz (30 g) cornflour

Heat the sugar, gelatine, water, and citric acid gently, stirring until the sugar has dissolved. Bring to the boil and boil for 2 or 3 minutes. Colour as you wish. Pour into a shallow tin that has been rinsed with cold water. When set, cut into squares with a sharp knife dipped in hot water and roll in the icing sugar mixed with the cornflour.

FRENCH JELLIES

4 tbsps gelatine
1 cup cold water
1 cup boiling water
2 lb (1 kg) sugar
colouring and flavouring

icing sugar or castor sugar

Soak the gelatine in the cold water for about half an hour. Pour over the boiling water and transfer to a saucepan. Add the sugar, stir until it has dissolved, and bring to the boil. Boil for 2 or 3 minutes. Colour and flavour. Strain into a slab-tin rinsed with cold water. Leave to set overnight. Cut into squares with a wet knife and roll in icing sugar or castor sugar; leave to dry and then store in airtight tins.

FUDGE

1 lb (500 g) sugar
¼ pt (150 ml) milk
2 oz (60 g) butter
1 tsp vanilla essence

Heat the sugar, milk, and butter, stirring until the sugar has dissolved. Bring to the boil. Boil to 240°F (115°C, the soft-ball stage, see page 128). Remove from the heat and stir in the vanilla. Leave to cool for a few minutes, then beat until it is thick and creamy. Pour into a buttered shallow tin. When partly set, mark into squares. Cut when cold.

ALMOND FUDGE

8 oz (250 g) sugar
1 oz (30 g) butter
1 dsp golden syrup
2 tbsps milk
½ tin evaporated milk
2 drops of vanilla essence
2 oz (60 g) halved blanched almonds

Put the sugar, butter, golden syrup, and milk in a large pan. Place over a very low heat and stir until the sugar has completely dissolved. Slowly bring to the boil and boil fast for 5 minutes, stirring all the time. Remove from the heat and stir in the evaporated milk. Return to the heat and stir with a wooden spoon until the mixture thickens and reaches 240°F (115°C, the soft-ball stage, see page 128); this will take 10 to 15 minutes and the fudge will have become darker. Remove from the heat and add the vanilla essence and almonds. Leave to cool for 5 minutes, then beat vigorously for 5 to 8 minutes, until thick. Pour into a buttered tin, allow almost to set, then cut into squares. Store in an airtight tin or jar.

CHOCOLATE FUDGE

1½ lb (750 g) sugar
4 oz (125 g) butter
2 tbsps cocoa
¼ pt (150 ml) milk
1 tsp vanilla essence

Heat the sugar, butter, cocoa, and milk, stirring until the sugar has dissolved. Bring to the boil. Boil to 240°F (115°C, the soft-ball stage, see page 128). Remove from the heat and stir in the vanilla. Beat until it is thick and creamy. Pour into a buttered shallow tin. When partly set, mark into squares. Cut when cold.

RUSSIAN TOFFEE

3 oz (90 g) butter
1 cup sugar
2 tbsps golden syrup
1 tin condensed milk
chopped nuts
1 tsp vanilla essence

Melt the butter, stir in the sugar and golden syrup, and heat slowly, stirring until the sugar has dissolved. When boiling-point is reached, add the condensed milk and nuts; stirring constantly, boil for 12 to 15 minutes to 240°F (115°C, the soft-ball stage, see page 128). Add the vanilla and pour into a buttered shallow tin. Mark into squares when cool. Wrap the toffees individually in greaseproof paper if you wish.

DIVINITY CANDY

10 oz (315 g) sugar
1 tbsp golden syrup
a pinch of cream of tartar
5 tbsps hot water
1 egg-white, stiffly beaten
3 oz (90 g) chopped nuts

Heat the sugar, golden syrup, cream of tartar, and hot water gently, stirring until the sugar has dissolved. Bring to the boil and boil without stirring to 250°F (121°C, the hard-ball stage, see page 128). Pour the mixture very slowly in a thin stream over the egg-white, stirring all the time, or the egg-white will coagulate (if this does happen, quickly pour the mixture through a coarse mesh strainer). Beat constantly with a wooden spoon until the mixture thickens and stands up in peaks, about 10 minutes. Stir in the nuts gently. Using a teaspoon, put small rocky heaps on waxed paper. Leave to dry in a warm place overnight before packing into airtight tins. The candy hardens with keeping.

NOUGAT

¼ pt (150 ml) water
12 oz (375 g) sugar
2 oz (60 g) glucose
4 oz (125 g) honey
3 egg-whites, stiffly beaten
2 oz (60 g) chopped glacé cherries
4 oz (125 g) sliced blanched almonds
vanilla essence

Heat the water and sugar, stirring to make sure that the sugar has dissolved. Add the glucose and bring to the boil. Boil to 270°F (132°C, the soft-crack stage, see page 128). Meanwhile, melt the honey in a bowl over simmering water; add the egg-whites and beat until the mixture is thick and white. Stir in the syrup, beating constantly over simmering water to 250°F (121°C, the hard-ball stage, see page 128). Remove from the heat and add the cherries, nuts, and vanilla. Pour into a buttered shallow tin and leave to set. Cut into bars or cubes.

TOFFEE

1 cup sugar
½ cup vinegar
¼ cup butter

Heat all ingredients in a small saucepan, stirring until the sugar has dissolved. Bring to the boil. Boil without stirring for about 10 minutes, to 270°F (132°C, the soft-crack stage, see page 128). Pour into paper patties or a buttered shallow tin.

HONEY TOFFEE

1 tbsp butter
2 cups sugar
2 tbsps vinegar
1 tbsp water
1 cup honey
icing sugar

Melt the butter in a saucepan. Add the other ingredients and heat to boiling-point, making sure that the sugar has dissolved; boil for about 15 minutes, to 270°F (132°C, the soft-crack stage, see page 128). Pour into a buttered dish. When cool, cut into squares and dust with icing sugar.

VANILLA CREAM TOFFEE

2 oz (60 g) butter
2 tbsps cold water
8 oz (250 g) loaf sugar
2 tbsps golden syrup

1 small tin sweetened
condensed milk
a few drops of vanilla essence

Melt the butter with the water in a saucepan over low heat. Add the sugar and golden syrup. Heat slowly without boiling, stirring occasionally, until the sugar has dissolved. Remove from the heat and stir in the condensed milk. Return the pan to the heat and bring to the boil. Boil quickly for 20 minutes, stirring well all the time, to 270°F (132°C, the soft-crack stage, see page 128). By this time the toffee will have darkened and will leave the sides of the pan. Remove from the heat and add the vanilla essence, stirring in well. Pour into a greased 7-inch (18-centimetre) tin. When nearly cold, mark the toffee into squares with a knife and cut into pieces with scissors. Wrap each piece of toffee in waxed paper and store in an airtight tin.

HONEYCOMB TOFFEE

4 oz (125 g) sugar
2 large tbsps golden syrup

1 oz (30 g) butter
1 tsp bicarbonate of soda

Put the sugar, syrup, and butter in a deep saucepan and heat, stirring until the sugar has dissolved. Bring to the boil and boil rapidly without stirring until the syrup begins to turn brown, the hard-crack stage (see page 128). Remove from the heat and stir the soda in thoroughly. The toffee will froth up immediately; pour at once into a greased 6-inch (15-centimetre) square and 2-inch (5-centimetre) deep tin. Mark the toffee into squares when cool, but not quite set, or leave till brittle, then crack into pieces.

ALMOND TOFFEE

3 oz (90 g) halved blanched
almonds
1 lb (500 g) brown sugar
¼ pt (150 ml) water

2 oz (60 g) butter

Arrange the almonds in a buttered shallow tin. Heat the sugar, water, and butter, stirring until the sugar has dissolved. Bring to the boil. Boil without stirring to 300°F (149°C, the hard-crack stage, see page 128). Pour over the almonds and leave to set.

BUTTERSCOTCH

6 oz (185 g) sugar
2 tbsps water
1 tbsp vinegar
1 heaped tbsp golden syrup
2 oz (60 g) butter

¼ tsp salt
vanilla or peppermint essence
chopped nuts or a little grated
coconut (optional)

Put all the ingredients except for the vanilla essence and nuts in a large saucepan. Bring slowly to the boil, stirring to make sure that the sugar has dissolved. Stirring constantly, boil rapidly for 8 minutes to 300°F (149°C, the hard-crack stage, see page 128). Quickly stir in a few drops of vanilla or peppermint essence and the nuts. Remove from the heat and pour into a well-greased tin. When the mixture begins to harden, mark into squares with a strong, buttered knife. Leave for 1 hour. Turn the tin upside-down and tap in several places to empty the toffee out. Store in an airtight jar.

BARLEY SUGAR

1 lb (500 g) loaf sugar
¼ pt (150 ml) water

juice and rind of ½ lemon
a pinch of cream of tartar

Heat the sugar and water, stirring until the sugar has dissolved. Add the lemon rind and cream of tartar. Bring to the boil. Boil to 240°F (115°C, the soft-ball stage, see page 128) then remove from the heat and add the lemon juice. Return to the heat and boil to 300°F (149°C, the hard-crack stage, see page 128). Strain into a buttered dish. When it has cooled a little, cut it into strips with scissors and form into twists. Store in an airtight container.

PEANUT BRITTLE

4 oz (125 g) roasted peanuts
1 lb (500 g) sugar
2 tbsps water

a pinch of cream of tartar

Arrange the peanuts in a buttered shallow tin. Heat the sugar, water, and cream of tartar, stirring until the sugar has dissolved. Bring to the boil. Boil for about 10 minutes, to 300°F (149°C, the hard-crack stage, see page 128). Pour over the peanuts. Leave to set, then crack into pieces.

PRESERVES
For Your Pantry

Jam-making

Use only fresh, unflawed, barely ripe fruit for jam and make sure to weigh and measure it accurately. The average proportions to allow are 1 pound (500 grams) of sugar for each pound (500 grams) of fruit. Cook the jam in a large heavy-based aluminium or copper pan and avoid having it more than half full. The simplest jams are made with fruit, sugar, and water. In the case of some fruits (for example, strawberries, blackberries, and rhubarb), which are deficient in pectin, or acid, it is necessary to add citric or tartaric acid, lemon juice, or redcurrants, blackcurrants, or gooseberries.

The jam must be stirred with a wooden spoon after the sugar has been added and not allowed to boil until the sugar has dissolved. It should then be boiled rapidly until setting-point is reached. There are two ways of testing for setting-point:

* Using a sugar thermometer: the thermometer should register between 220° and 222°F (104°–106°C).
* Dropping a little jam on a china plate: leave to cool for a minute and then touch lightly—if the jam wrinkles it is ready. For this method of testing, the pan should be removed from the heat or the jam may cook for too long.

Remove scum from the top of the jam just before the end of cooking time. Let the jam cool for a time in the pan before pouring into jars, to prevent separation of the fruit from the syrup. Using a jug, pour the jam into clean, dry, heated jars; fill them to the top. Cover the jars when the jam is hot or when it is quite cold. Store the jam in a cool, dark, airy place.

Marmalade is made in much the same way as jam but longer cooking is needed to soften the peel; because of the extra cooking time, considerably more water is needed.

APRICOT JAM

4 lb (2 kg) apricots
¾ pt (475 ml) water

juice of 1 lemon
4 lb (2 kg) sugar

Wash the apricots, cut in halves, and remove the stones. Crack a few of the stones, blanch them, and remove the kernels. Put the apricots, water, lemon juice, and kernels in a pan. Bring to the boil and simmer until the fruit is tender, then add the sugar and stir until it has dissolved. Boil until setting-point is reached (see page 134). Bottle and seal.

DRIED APRICOT JAM

3 qt (3·75 litres) water
2 lb (1 kg) dried apricots
6 lb (3 kg) sugar

3 oz (90 g) almonds,
  blanched and chopped

Pour the water over the apricots and leave to soak for 24 hours. Next day, boil until tender. Add the sugar and almonds and stir over low heat until the sugar has dissolved. Boil until setting-point is reached (see page 134). Skim the jam. Bottle and seal while still hot.

BLACKBERRY AND APPLE JAM

3 lb (1·5 kg) blackberries
3 lb (1·5 kg) peeled, cored,
  and sliced apples

1 pt (625 ml) water
6 lb (3 kg) sugar

Pick over the blackberries and put in a pan with the apples and water. Bring to the boil then simmer gently for about 15 minutes, or until the fruit is soft. Add the sugar and heat slowly, stirring until it has dissolved. Bring to the boil and boil briskly until setting-point is reached (see page 134). Skim if necessary. Bottle and seal while still hot.

BLACKCURRANT JAM

4 lb (2 kg) blackcurrants
3 pt (1·8 litres) water

6 lb (3 kg) sugar

Pick over and wash the blackcurrants. Put them in a pan with the water. Heat until boiling-point is reached then cover and simmer gently until the fruit is tender. Add the sugar and stir until it has dissolved. Boil briskly until setting-point is reached (see page 134). Skim if necessary. Bottle and seal while still hot.

PLUM JAM

6 lb (3 kg) plums
1½ pt (940 ml) water

6 lb (3 kg) sugar

Wash the plums then put them in a pan with the water. Heat slowly until boiling-point is reached then simmer steadily for about 15 minutes. Add the sugar and stir until it has dissolved. Bring to the boil and boil briskly until setting-point is reached (see page 134). Remove stones as they rise to the surface. Skim if necessary. Bottle and seal while still hot.

RASPBERRY JAM

5 lb (2·5 kg) raspberries
5 lb (2·5 kg) sugar

Pick over the fruit carefully then put in a pan and heat gently. Slowly bring to the boil then simmer for a few minutes, until tender. Add the sugar, stirring until it has dissolved, and bring to the boil. Boil until setting-point is reached (see page 134). Bottle and seal while still hot.

STRAWBERRY JAM

4 lb (2 kg) strawberries
4 lb (2 kg) sugar

¼ pt (150 ml) lemon juice

Put all the ingredients in a pan and heat, stirring until the sugar has dissolved. Boil for about 15 minutes, or until setting-point is reached (see page 134). Skim if necessary. Bottle and seal when cold.

PERSIMMON JAM

persimmons
sugar
lemons

finely shredded preserved
  ginger

Scoop the pulp from the persimmons and weigh. For every pound (500 grams) of fruit add 12 ounces (375 grams) of sugar; leave to stand for 4 to 5 hours, or overnight. Grate the rind of 1 lemon for every pound (500 grams) of pulp and squeeze the juice; add to the fruit with 1 ounce (30 grams) of ginger for every pound (500 grams) of pulp. Cook for about 45 minutes, or until setting-point is reached (see page 134). Bottle and seal.

Passionfruit may be added instead of ginger: the pulp of one large passionfruit for every pound (500 grams) of fruit.

LIME JAM

6 large limes
3 pt (1·8 litres) water

3 lb (1·5 kg) sugar

Slice the limes finely, cover with water, and leave for 12 hours. Drain, and again cover with fresh water and leave for 12 hours. Drain and add the 3 pints (1·8 litres) of water. Boil until tender and then add the sugar. Stir until the sugar has dissolved then boil until setting-point is reached (see page 134). Bottle and seal.

FIG JAM

6 lb (3 kg) figs
4½ lb (2·25 kg) sugar
3 oz (90 g) blanched almonds

6–8 oz (185–250 g) preserved
  ginger

Wipe the figs, cut in halves, and remove the stones. Sprinkle over half the sugar and leave to stand overnight. Next day heat slowly, stirring constantly and without adding water, until the sugar has dissolved. Bring gently to the boil then add the rest of the sugar and stir constantly until it has dissolved. Cook until the figs are tender. Add the ginger and continue boiling until setting-point is reached (see page 134). Stir in the almonds. Bottle and seal while still hot.

135

PINEAPPLE JAM

1 *large ripe pineapple*   *juice of 1 lemon*
sugar

Peel and weigh the pineapple. Allow 1 pound (500 grams) of sugar for every pound (500 grams) of fruit. Chop the pineapple and let it stand overnight with the sugar. Next day, add the lemon juice and heat gently, stirring until the sugar has dissolved. Bring to the boil and boil until the pineapple is transparent and setting-point is reached (see page 134). Skim if necessary. Bottle and seal when cold.

LEMON AND CARROT JAM

4 *large carrots, finely sliced*   3 *pt (1·8 litres) water*
3 *lemons, thinly sliced*   4 *lb (2 kg) sugar*

Stand the carrots and lemons overnight in the water. Next day, boil until tender. Add the sugar, stir until it has dissolved, then boil until setting-point is reached (see page 134). Bottle and seal.

GRAPEFRUIT JAM

3 *grapefruit*   1 *lemon*
1 *orange*   5 *lb (2·5 kg) sugar*

Slice the fruit thinly, removing the pips, and stand in a little water overnight. Next day, strain off the water and replace with 5 pints (3·1 litres) of fresh water. Boil the mixture until soft. Add the sugar, stir until it has dissolved, then boil until setting-point is reached (see page 134). Bottle and seal.

TWO, FOUR, SIX ORANGE MARMALADE

2 *lb (1 kg) oranges*   6 *lb (3 kg) sugar*
4 *pt (2·5 litres) water*   1 *lemon*

Slice the oranges and lemon very thinly, removing the pips; put in a large pan. Cover with the water and leave to stand overnight. Next day, boil until the fruit is tender. Add the sugar, stir until it has dissolved, then boil rapidly until setting-point is reached (see page 134). Bottle and seal.

LEMON MARMALADE

lemons   *sugar*
water

Slice the lemons finely, removing the pips. Put them in a pan, pour over 1 cup of water for each lemon, and soak overnight. Next day, bring to the boil and simmer for 45 minutes. Measure and add 1 cup of sugar for each cup of lemon and water. Stir until the sugar has dissolved, then boil for 1½ hours, or until setting-point is reached (see page 134). Bottle and seal.

CHOKO LEMON MARMALADE

12 *chokos*   2 *oz (60 g) preserved ginger,*
juice of 4 lemons   *sliced*
3½ *lb (1·75 kg) sugar*   *shredded rind of 2 lemons*
1 *cup water*

Peel the chokos and cut into small squares. Sprinkle with the lemon juice and 1 cup of the sugar and leave to stand overnight. Next day, put into a preserving pan with the water, ginger, and shredded rind. Heat gently to boiling-point, stirring until the sugar has dissolved. Boil for 1½ hours. Add the remaining sugar, stir until it has dissolved, and boil briskly until setting-point is reached (see page 134), about 1 hour. Bottle and seal when cold.

GRAPEFRUIT MARMALADE

grapefruit   *sugar*
water

Slice the grapefruit finely, removing the pips. Weigh the fruit, transfer to a pan, and add 3 pints (1·8 litres) of water for every pound (500 grams); leave to stand overnight. Next day, boil until clear and tender. Measure the fruit and water and for every cup allow 1 cup of sugar. Bring the fruit to the boil, add the sugar, and stir until it has dissolved. Boil quickly until setting-point is reached (see page 134). Bottle and seal.

Jelly-making

The fruit must be in perfect condition and a little under-ripe. The best kinds of fruit to use are those with a high pectin content, such as redcurrants, gooseberries, and cooking apples. The fruit should be washed and chopped but it is not necessary to peel or core it or to remove stalks. It should then be cooked slowly with water for about an hour, until it is a pulp. The fruit should be transferred to a jelly bag and left to drip overnight. If you do not have a jelly bag, there are several alternatives:
* Put several layers of muslin over a bowl.
* Use a fine sieve over a bowl.
* Attach a coarse cloth to the legs of an upside-down chair with a bowl underneath.

Whatever is used for a jelly bag, the material must first be scalded with boiling water. The fruit must be left to drip at its own rate, no matter how slow, or the jelly will be cloudy. The juice should then be measured and heated gently in a saucepan with 1 pound (500 grams) of sugar for every pint (625 millilitres) of juice. Stir until the sugar has dissolved then bring to the boil and boil rapidly until setting-point is reached (see page 134). Skim off any scum on the surface and pour at once into clean, dry, heated, small jars. Cover at once or when the jelly is quite cold.

APPLE JELLY

6 lb (3 kg) green apples   lemons
water
sugar

Wash the apples and chop roughly without peeling. Put in a pan and cover with water; heat until boiling-point is reached. Simmer until the fruit is soft. Strain through a jelly bag or thin muslin overnight. Next day, measure the liquid and add 1 pound (500 grams) of sugar and the juice and peeled rind of one lemon for each pint (625 millilitres); put the rind in a muslin bag and heat with the other ingredients, stirring until the sugar has dissolved. Boil until setting-point is reached (see page 134). Skim if necessary. Remove the bag of rind. Bottle and seal while still hot.

MINT JELLY

2 lb (1 kg) green apples   a bunch of mint, washed and
2 pt (1·25 litres) water   chopped
juice of 2 lemons   green food colouring (optional)
sugar

Wash the apples and chop roughly without peeling. Put the apples in a pan with the water and lemon juice. Bring to the boil and cook until the fruit is soft. Strain through a jelly bag or thin muslin overnight. Next day, measure the juice and return to the pan; add 1 pound (500 grams) of sugar for every pint (625 millilitres) of juice. Add the mint and heat, stirring constantly until the sugar has dissolved. Bring to the boil and boil briskly until setting-point is reached (see page 134). Add a little green food colouring. Bottle and seal while still hot.

DELICIOUS FRUIT JELLY

4 large cooking apples,   1 cup water
   roughly chopped   lemons
2 cups strawberries   sugar
1 cup passionfruit pulp

Simmer the apples, strawberries, passionfruit pulp, and water gently for 1 hour. Strain through a jelly bag or thin muslin overnight. Next day, measure the juice and for each cup add the juice of one lemon, and 1 cup of sugar. Return to the pan and heat, stirring until the sugar has dissolved. Boil for 1 hour, or until setting-point is reached (see page 134). Bottle and seal.

REDCURRANT JELLY

4 lb (2 kg) redcurrants   sugar
1½ pt (940 ml) water

Wash the redcurrants. Put them in a pan with the water. Heat slowly until boiling-point is reached. Simmer gently until tender. Strain through a jelly bag overnight. Next day, measure the juice and allow 1 pound (500 grams) of sugar for every pint (625 millilitres). Return to the pan and heat, stirring until the sugar has dissolved. Boil for about 10 minutes, or until setting-point is reached (see page 134). Skim if necessary. Bottle and seal while still hot.

QUINCE JELLY

quinces   sugar
water

Wipe the quinces and remove the cores and pips. Put the fruit in a pan, cover with water, and heat slowly to boiling-point; simmer until the quinces are soft. Strain through a jelly bag or thin muslin overnight. Next day, measure the liquid and add 1 pound (500 grams) of sugar for each pint (625 millilitres). Return to the pan and heat, stirring until the sugar has dissolved. Bring to the boil and boil steadily until setting-point is reached (see page 134). Bottle and seal.

ORANGE CURD

4 oz (125 g) butter   juice and finely grated rind of
8 oz (250 g) sugar   1 lemon
3 eggs
1 extra egg-yolk
juice and finely grated rind of
   2 oranges

Melt the butter in the top of a double saucepan, or over a pan of simmering water. Add the sugar, eggs, egg-yolk, and the rind and juice. Cook gently without boiling, stirring until the sugar has dissolved. Stir occasionally until the mixture thickens enough to coat the back of a spoon, about 20 to 30 minutes. Bottle and seal.

LEMON CURD

4 lemons   4 oz (125 g) butter
8 oz (250 g) loaf sugar
2 eggs, beaten

Wash the lemons, and then rub them with the sugar to extract the flavour. Cut the lemons and squeeze the juice. Put the eggs, sugar, lemon juice, and butter in the top of a double saucepan and cook over simmering water, stirring until the sugar has dissolved and the butter melted. Continue cooking, stirring occasionally, until the mixture thickens enough to coat the back of a spoon. Bottle and seal.

PASSIONFRUIT CHEESE

8 oz (250 g) butter   pulp of 12 passionfruit
1 lb (500 g) sugar
4 eggs

Put all the ingredients in the top of a double saucepan and stir constantly over simmering water until the sugar has dissolved and the butter melted. Continue cooking and stirring until the mixture thickens enough to coat the back of a spoon—do not allow to boil. Bottle and seal.

PINEAPPLE CHEESE

1 pineapple   4 egg-yolks
¼ pt (150 ml) water   1 tbsp butter
1 lb (500 g) sugar
1 tbsp cornflour

Peel and shred the pineapple and heat with the water and sugar. Bring to the boil and simmer until tender. Blend the cornflour with a little water and add to the pineapple to thicken. Cook through for a few minutes then remove from the heat and allow to cool slightly. Beat in the egg-yolks and butter and cook gently until thick. Bottle and seal.

PASSIONFRUIT PRESERVE

4 large Granny Smith apples.   3 lb (1.5 kg) sugar
3 pt (1.8 litres) water
pulp of 10–12 passionfruit

Chop the apples and put them in a saucepan with the water. Partly cover with a lid and boil for about 2 hours. Strain and measure the liquid—there should be about 4 cups. Pour back in the saucepan and return to the heat. Add the passionfruit pulp and the sugar. Stir until the sugar has dissolved, bring to the boil, and boil briskly for about half an hour, or until setting-point is reached (see page 134). Bottle and seal.

MINCEMEAT

3½ lb (1.75 kg) currants   1 dsp mixed spice
1¾ lb (875 g) finely chopped   juice and finely grated rind of
   beef suet   2 oranges
1¾ lb (875 g) finely chopped   juice and finely grated rind of
   apples   2 lemons
4 oz (125 g) finely chopped   ½ bottle brandy
   mixed candied peel   ½ bottle ginger wine
1 lb (500 g) fine moist sugar

Mix together the currants, suet, apples, peel, sugar, mixed spice, and rind. Mix the brandy with the ginger wine and orange and lemon juices. Pour this liquid over the mincemeat and press down hard with the hand. Pack into prepared jars and seal tightly.

   Half the currants may be replaced with an equal weight of chopped seeded raisins.

INDIAN CHUTNEY

12 large apples, peeled, cored,   4 oz (125 g) chopped seeded
   and chopped   raisins
1 qt (1.25 litres) vinegar   1 tsp dry mustard
1 lb (500 g) finely chopped   ½ oz (15 g) cayenne pepper
   dates
1 lb (500 g) sugar
4 oz (125 g) salt
2 oz (60 g) ground ginger
4 oz (125 g) finely chopped
   onions

Put all the ingredients in a large pan. Boil slowly until soft. Bottle and seal.

ENGLISH MINT CHUTNEY

3 cups vinegar
2 cups sugar
1 dsp salt
2 tbsps dry mustard
1 lb (500 g) ripe tomatoes,
  peeled and chopped
1 lb (500 g) sour apples,
  peeled, cored, and chopped

8 medium onions, peeled and
  chopped
½ cup chopped mint leaves
1½ cups seeded raisins
2 red chillies, chopped

Bring the vinegar to the boil. Add the sugar, salt, and mustard.
Allow to cool. When cold, add the remaining ingredients, mixing
well. Boil the mixture until soft. Bottle and seal when cold.
   Allow to stand for ten days. This chutney will keep for months,
and improves with age.

PLUM CHUTNEY

4 lb (2 kg) ripe plums, peeled
  and stoned
1 lb (500 g) apples, peeled,
  cored, and chopped
1½ lb (750 g) brown sugar
2 lb (1 kg) seeded raisins,
  chopped

1 oz (30 g) garlic, crushed
1 oz (30 g) ground ginger
½ oz (15 g) dried chillies,
  crushed
1 qt (1·25 litres) vinegar

Boil the plums, apples, and brown sugar for 15 minutes, stirring
until the sugar has dissolved. Add the raisins, garlic, ginger, and
chillies, and boil for 10 minutes. Add the vinegar and boil again
for 10 minutes. Bottle and seal.

PEACH CHUTNEY

2 cups vinegar
1½ lb (750 g) sugar
4 large cups peeled and
  chopped peaches
3 pieces preserved or candied
  ginger, chopped

1 clove of garlic, chopped
8 oz (250 g) currants

Heat the vinegar and sugar, stirring until the sugar has dissolved,
until a clear syrup is formed. Add the peaches, ginger, garlic, and
currants. Simmer slowly for 3 to 4 hours, stirring occasionally.
Bottle and seal. Store in a cool dry place.
   Ginger roots may be substituted for the preserved or candied
ginger, but remove them before pouring the chutney into jars.

DATE AND BANANA CHUTNEY

12 bananas, sliced
2 lb (1 kg) finely chopped
  onions
1 lb (500 g) chopped dates
1 pt (625 ml) vinegar
1 dsp curry powder

½ oz (15 g) finely chopped
  crystallised ginger
1 tbsp salt
1 lb (500 g) treacle

Put the bananas, onions, dates, and vinegar in a saucepan and cook
until tender. Beat to a pulp. Add the curry powder, crystallised
ginger, salt, and treacle; return to the heat and cook until the
mixture is a rich brown colour. Bottle and seal.

GRANDMA'S CHUTNEY

2 lb (1 kg) apples, peeled,
  cored, and chopped
1 lb (500 g) sugar
1 lb (500 g) onions
1 lb (500 g) seeded raisins
2 oz (60 g) garlic, crushed

1 tsp ground ginger
1 tsp cayenne pepper
salt and pepper
1 qt (1·25 litres) vinegar

Heat the apples and half the sugar in a pan, stirring until the sugar
has dissolved; boil to a pulp. Put the onions and raisins through a
mincer and add to the pan, with the garlic, ginger, cayenne, salt,
pepper, and vinegar. Add the remaining sugar, stir until it has
dissolved, and boil until tender, about 1 hour. Bottle and seal.

TOMATO CHUTNEY

6 lb (3 kg) ripe tomatoes,
  peeled and chopped
4 lb (2 kg) brown sugar
2 lb (1 kg) onions
½ pt (315 ml) vinegar
1 clove of garlic
6 large Granny Smith apples,
  peeled, cored, and chopped
½ oz (15 g) dried chillies,
  crushed
1 dsp cloves

1 tsp pepper
3 dsps salt
juice of 3 lemons
1 small tsp mixed spice

Put all the ingredients in a large pan. Bring to the boil, stirring
until the sugar has dissolved, and boil slowly for 4 to 5 hours.
Strain. Bottle and seal.

TOMATO RELISH

3 lb (1·5 kg) ripe tomatoes,
  peeled and chopped
2 large onions, chopped
brown vinegar
2 cups sugar
1 dsp dry mustard
1 dsp curry powder

1 tsp salt
½ cup cornflour
2 cups white vinegar

Put the tomatoes and onions in a large pan and cover with brown
vinegar. Bring to the boil and simmer for half an hour. Add the
sugar, mustard, curry powder, and salt; simmer for a further 20
minutes. Thicken with the cornflour, which has been blended
with the white vinegar. Bottle and seal.

CUCUMBER RELISH

4 lb (2 kg) cucumbers	1⁄4 oz (10 g) ground ginger
4 lb (2 kg) apples, chopped	1⁄2 tsp cayenne pepper
4 lb (2 kg) onions, sliced	vinegar
2 lb (1 kg) sugar	
12 oz (375 g) seeded raisins or sultanas	
1 oz (30 g) cloves	
1 oz (30 g) peppercorns	

Cut up the cucumbers, sprinkle with salt, and leave to stand overnight. Next day, strain off the liquid and put the cucumbers in a large pan; add the other ingredients, cover with vinegar, and bring to the boil, stirring until the sugar has dissolved. Boil for 1 hour. Bottle and seal.

SPICED VINEGAR

1 qt (1·25 litres) vinegar	1⁄4 oz (10 g) mace
1⁄4 oz (10 g) cinnamon	1⁄4 oz (10 g) allspice
1⁄4 oz (10 g) cloves	
1 dsp peppercorns	

Tie the spices in a piece of muslin. Bring the vinegar slowly to the boil, add the bag of spices, and boil for 10 minutes. Leave to get cold, then remove the spices and use as required.

PICKLED BEETROOT

Wash beetroot and put in a pan of boiling salted water. Boil for about 1 1⁄2 hours, until tender. Remove from the water and leave to get cold. Peel and slice or dice. Pack into prepared jars, pour over spiced vinegar (see above), and seal.

PICKLED ONIONS

6 lb (3 kg) small pickling onions	3 pt (1·8 litres) spiced vinegar (see above)
salt	

Peel the onions and leave to stand for 24 hours in water with 1 tablespoon of salt for each pint (625 millilitres) of water. Drain and pack into jars, to three-quarters fill. Pour over the spiced vinegar. Cover and seal.

PICKLED RED CABBAGE

1 large red cabbage	2 qt (2·5 litres) spiced vinegar (see above)
salt	

Remove the coarse outer leaves of the cabbage. Cut the cabbage into four, removing the central core and the thick stalks. Slice thinly and place in layers in a bowl, sprinkling salt between each layer. Cover and leave to stand for 24 hours. Drain off the water and fill prepared jars with the cabbage. Pour over enough spiced vinegar to cover. Cover and seal.

Allow to stand for a fortnight before using. If the cabbage is kept for longer than a few months it will become soggy.

PICCALILLI

4-lb (2 kg) mixture of cauliflower, cucumber, firm green or red tomatoes, French beans, small pickling onions, celery, and marrow	1 oz (30 g) turmeric
	1 oz (30 g) plain flour
	1 oz (30 g) dry mustard
salt	
1 qt (1·25 litres) vinegar	
4 chillies	
2 oz (60 g) sugar	
ground ginger	

Prepare the vegetables, leaving the onions whole. Spread them on a large dish, sprinkle with salt, and leave to stand for 24 hours. Drain then heat to boiling-point in salted water; boil for 5 minutes then drain. Heat the vinegar with the chillies, sugar, ginger, and turmeric in a large pan; stir until the sugar has dissolved, then bring to the boil. Blend the flour and mustard with a little vinegar and stir into the hot vinegar. When boiling, add the vegetables and simmer for a few minutes. Leave to cool slightly then bottle and seal.

MELON PICKLE

8 lb (4 kg) melon	1 tsp curry powder
1 cup salt	1 dsp turmeric
2 lb (1 kg) onions, sliced	2 lb (1 kg) brown sugar
2 lb (1 kg) apples, sliced	1 lb (500 g) seeded raisins
2 qt (2·5 litres) vinegar	
1 cup plain flour	
a little extra vinegar	
1⁄4 tsp cayenne pepper	
1 tbsp dry mustard	

Cut up the melon, pour over the salt, and leave to stand overnight in a large pan. Next day, boil with a little water until soft. Add the onions and apples. Cook until soft, then drain and set aside. Boil the vinegar, and thicken with the flour, which has been mixed to a smooth paste with a little cold vinegar. Add the cayenne, mustard, curry powder, and turmeric, then the sugar, raisins, and the cooked melon, onion, and apple. Cook for about 1 hour. Bottle and seal.

PICKLED WALNUTS

walnuts	salt
vinegar	allspice
black peppercorns	shallots
bruised ginger	

Choose walnuts that are quite young; they must not be woody or hard. Prick with a steel fork and place in strong brine. Leave for a week or more, changing the brine once or twice. Lay on dishes or trays in the sun for two days until the walnuts turn black. When the walnuts are ready, boil the vinegar with the spices; for every quart (1·25 litres) of vinegar allow 1 ounce (30 grams) of peppercorns, ginger, salt, allspice, and shallots. Put the walnuts in dry jars and cover with the hot spiced vinegar. Bottle, seal when cool, and keep in a cool dry place.

Allow to stand for five to six weeks before using.

SPICED PEACHES

1 qt (1·25 litres) white
  vinegar
2 lb (1 kg) sugar
1 tsp cloves
1 tsp peppercorns

1 stick of cinnamon
4 blades of mace
1 dsp salt
3 lb (1·5 kg) firm peaches,
  peeled, halved, and stoned

Put the vinegar and sugar in a pan. Tie the cloves, peppercorns, cinnamon, and mace in a muslin bag and add to the pan. Bring slowly to the boil. Boil for 5 minutes. Add the salt and the peaches and simmer gently until the peaches are almost transparent. Remove the peaches and transfer carefully to jars. Let the vinegar boil until it is reduced and thick; pour on to the peaches. Seal immediately.

Allow to stand for several weeks before using.

PICKLED EGGS

8 hard-boiled eggs, shelled
$\frac{1}{4}$ oz (10 g) black peppercorns
$\frac{1}{4}$ oz (10 g) allspice

$\frac{1}{4}$ oz (10 g) whole ginger
1 pt (625 ml) vinegar

Put the eggs in one large or two medium-sized jars. Boil the peppercorns, spice, and ginger in the vinegar for 10 minutes. Immediately pour over the eggs. When cold, cover closely, and store in a cool, dry place.

Leave for two weeks before using.

DRINKS
For All Seasons

TEA

Keep tea stored in a tightly covered container. Use fresh water from the cold-water tap; bring to the boil and pour some into the teapot to heat. Pour off the water, add 1 teaspoon of tea per person, plus one extra, pour over boiling water and leave to stand for 3 to 5 minutes.

ICED TEA

crushed ice
1 tsp sugar
juice of 1 lemon

¼ pt (150 ml) orange juice
1 pt (625 ml) strong tea

Put the ice, sugar, and fruit juices in a jug. Strain over the freshly made tea. Chill.
Serve with sugar and slices of lemon.

COFFEE

Store coffee in an airtight container to preserve its flavour. Preferably, keep a store of coffee beans and grind them as required. Coffee can be made in a number of ways and without special equipment but it is essential that the coffee is fresh and that the coffee pot is kept well scrubbed. It is difficult to recommend an exact amount of coffee to be used, as tastes vary so widely that 2 tablespoons of ground coffee per pint (625 millilitres) of water is sufficient for some whereas those with a preference for a stronger brew will use 8 tablespoons per pint (625 millilitres) of water. Serve with heated milk.

Following are two simple methods of making coffee. If you have a percolator or a filter, the maker's accompanying instructions should be followed.

Making Coffee in a Jug
Heat the jug and add the required amount of ground coffee. Pour over fast boiling water, stir well, cover, and leave to stand in a warm place for 10 minutes. Strain the coffee into a heated coffee pot, or directly into cups, and serve at once.

Making Coffee in a Saucepan
Heat the required amount of ground coffee in the water in a saucepan. Bring almost to boiling-point, then remove from the heat, stir well, cover, and leave in a warm place for about 5 minutes. Strain the coffee into a heated coffee pot, or directly into cups, and serve at once.

FROTHED COFFEE

5 cups strong black coffee
5 cups boiling milk

3 egg-whites
1 tbsp sugar

Pour the hot coffee into the boiling milk. Cover and leave to stand for 5 minutes. Meanwhile, beat the egg-whites until frothy, then stir in the sugar. Pour the coffee into cups, and add a large tablespoon of froth to each cup.

ICED COFFEE

1 qt (1·25 litres) milk
½ pt (315 ml) sweetened strong
  black coffee

¼ pt (150 ml) cream, whipped
cinnamon

Beat the milk and coffee together. Chill. Serve in tall chilled glasses and top with whipped cream and a sprinkling of cinnamon.

COCOA

Allow 1 dessertspoon of cocoa per ½ pint (315 millilitres) of milk, and sugar according to taste. Heat the milk, or half milk and half water, to just below boiling-point; meanwhile blend the cocoa and sugar to a paste with a little cold milk or water. Pour the hot milk over slowly, stirring vigorously. Return to the saucepan for a minute or so. Beat with an egg-whisk for a frothy effect.

CHOCOLATE NECTAR

2 oz (60 g) unsweetened
  chocolate
½ cup black coffee
½ cup sugar

3 cups water
1 tsp vanilla essence
whipped cream

Melt the chocolate over gentle heat; stir in the coffee and cook for 2 minutes, stirring constantly. Add the sugar and water, then simmer for 5 minutes. Remove from the heat and stir in the vanilla essence. Serve in hot cups or mugs with a teaspoon of whipped cream on top.

HOT CHOCOLATE

Melt 2 ounces (60 grams) of cooking chocolate in a double saucepan, or over very low heat. Stir in 4 tablespoons of sugar and a pinch of salt. Gradually stir in 1 cup of boiling water, stirring until smooth. Blend in 3 cups of hot milk, beat well, and serve.

CHOCOLATE MILK WHISK

1 tbsp cocoa
1 qt (1·25 litres) milk
1 egg

1 dsp malt
1 dsp honey

Blend the cocoa to a paste with a little of the milk. Boil the rest of the milk, add the cocoa, and simmer for 1 minute. Leave to cool. Whisk the egg well, beat in the milk, malt, and honey, and whisk again.

MILK AND HONEY

1 cup milk

1 tbsp honey

Heat the milk and stir in the honey. Serve hot.

PEPPERMINT MILK

1 cup milk

2 strong peppermints

Heat the milk with the peppermints, stirring until they have dissolved.

MILK POSSET

2 slices of stale white bread
a pinch of salt
a pinch of grated nutmeg
1 dsp sugar

3 cups milk
1 tbsp brandy or sherry
  (optional)

Cut the bread into small squares. Put the cubes in a bowl and sprinkle with the salt, nutmeg, and sugar. Heat the milk until nearly boiling then pour over the bread. Allow to swell. Add the brandy or sherry.

SPICED MILK PUNCH

1 qt (1·25 litres) milk
rind of 1 orange
½ stick of cinnamon

2 cloves
3 tbsps sugar

Heat the milk, orange rind, cinnamon, cloves, and sugar to boiling-point. Strain into a jug. Mix and serve. A little brandy may be added if you wish.

HONEY MILK GINGER

1 pt (625 ml) milk
rind of 1 lemon
3 sprigs of mint

2 tbsps honey
thin slices of preserved ginger

Heat the milk with the lemon rind and the mint. Strain and sweeten with the honey; add the ginger. Serve hot.

EGG-FLIP

1 cup milk
1 egg, separated

1 tsp brandy or sherry
a pinch of sugar

Warm the milk and mix with the egg-yolk. Add the brandy or sherry and sugar. Beat the egg-white until slightly frothy; fold into the yolk mixture.

EGG-NOG

1 egg
1 dsp sugar
1 cup hot or cold milk

vanilla essence
grated nutmeg (optional)

Beat the egg and sugar together thoroughly. Beat in the milk and flavour to taste with vanilla. Beat until frothy. Pour into a glass. Sprinkle with a little nutmeg if you wish.

PINEAPPLE EGG-NOG

1 egg, separated
½ cup pineapple juice

a pinch of salt
a pinch of grated nutmeg

Beat the egg-yolk well, and mix with the pineapple juice. Fold in the egg-white, which has been stiffly beaten with salt. Pour into a glass. Sprinkle with nutmeg.

GINGER AND LEMON NOG

1 egg
juice of 1 lemon
1 tbsp sugar

ice
ginger ale

Beat the egg, lemon juice, and sugar with an egg-whisk. Strain into a glass. Add a little ice, then fill up with ginger ale.

BARLEY WATER

4 tbsps pearl barley
4 cups water
juice and thinly pared rind of
  2 lemons

sugar

Wash the barley in a colander. Put the barley, water, and lemon rind in a saucepan; bring slowly to the boil. Cook gently for 2 hours; strain. Sweeten to taste and add the lemon juice. Cool.

QUICK LEMONADE

juice and thinly pared rind of
  4 lemons

½ cup sugar
4 cups boiling water

Put the lemon rind in a jug with the sugar. Pour in the boiling water and stir until the sugar dissolves. Leave until cold. Strain and add the lemon juice.
  Serve with ice.

LEMONADE

3 lemons, halved
1 gal (5 litres) water

1 lb (500 g) sugar
1 dsp cream of tartar

Heat the lemons in the water; when boiling-point is reached add the sugar and stir until it has dissolved. Pour the liquid over the cream of tartar in a large bowl, stir well, and leave to cool. Strain into bottles and secure tightly. Leave for two weeks before using.

STRAWBERRY LEMONADE

½ punnet strawberries, chopped
juice of ½ lemon
1 dsp sugar

¾ glass crushed ice and water
1 egg-white, stiffly beaten

Shake the strawberries vigorously, with the lemon juice, sugar, ice, and water; strain and fold in the egg-white.

ORANGEADE

4 tbsps sugar
juice of ½ lemon

juice of 4 oranges
4 cups cold water

Dissolve the sugar in enough boiling water to cover. Add the strained lemon and orange juices and the cold water. Leave to cool.
  Serve with ice.

ORANGE DRINK BASE

3 pt (1·8 litres) boiling water
juice and grated rind of 6
  oranges
5 lb (2·5 kg) sugar

2 oz (60 g) citric acid
1 oz (30 g) tartaric acid
1 oz (30 g) Epsom salt

Pour the boiling water over the orange rind and juice, the sugar,
the acids, and the Epsom salt; stir until the sugar has dissolved.
Leave for one day, then strain into bottles.

RASPBERRY VINEGAR

2 lb (1 kg) raspberries
1 pt (625 ml) vinegar

sugar

Mash the raspberries in a large bowl; pour over the vinegar and
leave to stand for 24 hours. Strain and add 1 pound (500 grams) of
sugar for every pint (625 millilitres) of liquid; boil for about 20
minutes. Pour into bottles when cold.

FIFTY-FIFTY SUMMER DRINK

juice and grated rind of 3
  lemons
juice and grated rind of 3
  oranges
1 oz (30 g) tartaric acid

½ oz (15 g) citric acid
1 oz (30 g) Epsom salt
4 lb (2 kg) sugar
3 pt (1·8 litres) boiling water

Mix together the lemon and orange rind and juice, the tartaric
acid, citric acid, and Epsom salt, and the sugar. Pour the boiling
water over and stir to dissolve the sugar. Bottle when cold.

PASSIONFRUIT CORDIAL

2 cups sugar
2 cups water

pulp of 9 passionfruit
1 dsp citric acid

Heat the sugar and water to boiling-point, stirring until the sugar
has dissolved. Pour over the passionfruit and acid in a bowl,
stirring well. Pour into bottles when cold.

MIDSUMMER PUNCH

1½ cups orange juice
1 tbsp lemon juice
1 cup sugar
4 cups ginger ale

½ cup cherries
soda water
ice

Pour the orange and lemon juices over the sugar in a bowl. Leave
to stand for 4 hours. Turn into a glass jug. Add the ginger ale and
cherries; top up with soda water and add ice.

CIDER FRUIT CUP

1 qt (1·25 litres) cider
½ pt (315 ml) orange squash
1–2 lemons, sliced thinly

a few slices of cucumber
mint leaves
ice

Put the cider in a large glass jug or bowl; add the orange squash.
Add the lemons, cucumber, and mint leaves, which have been cut
in strips. Add ice and stir.

PARTY FRUIT CUP

1 large pineapple
juice and thinly pared rind of
  3 lemons
1 apple, sliced and cored
1 lb (500 g) loaf sugar
juice of 6 oranges

2 bananas, sliced
8 oz (250 g) stoned cherries
pulp of 6 passionfruit
a few strawberries
5 pt (3·1 litres) lemonade,
  ginger beer, or soda water

Peel and core the pineapple; reserve the peel and the core and
shred the flesh finely. Put the lemon rind, sliced apple, and
pineapple rind and core in a saucepan; cover with cold water.
Simmer for 20 to 30 minutes to extract the flavours. Strain
through muslin or a fine sieve, pressing to extract all juices; add
enough water to make 1 quart (1·25 litres) of liquid. Return to the
saucepan, and add the sugar; heat slowly, stirring until the sugar
has dissolved. Bring the syrup to the boil and simmer for 10
minutes. Add the shredded pineapple and simmer for 5 minutes;
leave to cool. Add the strained orange and lemon juices, the
bananas, cherries, passionfruit pulp, and strawberries to the cold
liquid. Leave on ice or in the refrigerator until required. Just
before serving, pour in the lemonade, ginger beer, or soda water.

FRUIT PUNCH

2 cups sugar
4 cups water
6 oranges
3 lemons
2 bananas, sliced

1 cup small green grapes
1 cup stoned red cherries
2 cups ginger ale
1 cup cold tea
4 cups soda water

Boil the sugar and water together for 10 minutes, stirring until the
sugar has dissolved. Leave to cool. Peel three of the oranges and
slice thinly, removing as much white pith as possible; add to the
syrup. Add the strained juice of the remaining oranges and the
lemons. Add the bananas, grapes, and cherries. Chill thoroughly.
Add the ginger ale, tea, and soda water.
  Serve with ice.

ORANGE AND GRAPEFRUIT CUP

1 cup castor sugar
1 cup tinned grapefruit juice
2 cups tinned orange juice
¼ cup lemon juice

1 pt (625 ml) water
2 sprigs of fresh mint
1–2 ice-cubes

Dissolve the sugar in the fruit juices, stirring all the time. Add the
water. Bruise the mint leaves and add, with the ice-cubes.

CLARET CUP

2 lemons, sliced
sugar (optional)
grated nutmeg
ice

6 bottles lemonade
3 bottles soda water
2 bottles claret

Place the sliced lemons in a large serving bowl. Sprinkle with
sugar and nutmeg, add plenty of cracked ice, then pour over the
lemonade, soda, and claret.

NEGUS

½ bottle brown sherry or port
1 lemon
1 pt (625 ml) boiling water

sugar
grated nutmeg
1 tbsp brandy

Warm the wine. Slice the lemon into a heated jug. Add the wine, then the water, sugar, and nutmeg. Stir, add the brandy, and serve piping hot.

MINT JULEP

fresh mint
juice and pared rind of 2
  lemons

4 tbsps icing sugar
ginger ale
ice

Bruise mint leaves in a jug. Add lemon rind, juice, and sugar. Chill for 1 hour. Fill the jug with ginger ale and cracked ice.

COLD WATER GINGER BEER

2 lb (1 kg) sugar
1 dsp citric acid
2 tbsps ground ginger
1 tbsp cream of tartar
1 tsp lemon essence

¼ oz (10 g) yeast or 3 tbsps
  brewer's yeast
1 egg-white, stiffly beaten
1 egg-shell, crushed
2 gal (10 litres) cold water

Dissolve the sugar in a little hot water in a large bowl. Mix together the acid, ginger, cream of tartar, lemon essence, yeast, egg-white, and egg-shell; add to the sugar and pour over the cold water; stir, then leave overnight. Strain and bottle.

ORANGE WINE

12 oranges
2 lemons

1 gal (5 litres) water
4 lb (2 kg) sugar

Wash the oranges and lemons. Cut into slices and put in a large bowl. Add the water. Stir well each day for fourteen days, then strain well. Return the liquor to the bowl and add the sugar. Stir well each day for four days until the sugar has dissolved. Strain again and put into a cask or a 1-gallon (5-litre) jar. Bottle and cork lightly until fermented. Cork tightly.

CHILLI WINE

25 chillies, bruised
8 oz (250 g) brown sugar
2 lb (1 kg) white sugar
½ oz (15 g) citric acid

1 gal (5 litres) boiling water
8 oz (250 g) burnt sugar
1 small bottle lemon essence

Put the chillies, brown and white sugar, and acid into a large bowl. Add the boiling water. When nearly cold, add the burnt sugar and lemon essence.

ORANGE BRANDY

1 gal (5 litres) brandy
4 lb (2 kg) loaf sugar

6 oranges
rind and juice of 6 lemons

Pour the brandy into a large jar with the sugar, the juice of all the oranges and the rind of four, and the lemon rind and juice. Let stand for three weeks, stirring regularly. Strain and bottle.

CHERRY BRANDY

2 cups water
1 cup sugar
1 cup brandy

1 dsp almond essence
cochineal

Boil the water and sugar together for 5 minutes. When cool, add the brandy and almond essence. Colour lightly with cochineal.

RASPBERRY LIQUEUR

1 qt (1·25 litres) gin
2 large cups raspberries

1 lb (500 g) sugar
1½ pt (940 ml) water

Put the gin and fruit in bottles that cork closely. Leave to stand for a fortnight. Heat the sugar and water, stirring until the sugar has dissolved; boil to make a clear syrup. Leave to cool. Pour the syrup over the gin and fruit. Filter through blotting paper and pour into small, well-corked bottles.

CREME DE MENTHE

3 cups water
1 cup sugar
1 cup brandy

peppermint essence
a few drops of green food
  colouring

Heat the water and sugar, stirring until the sugar has dissolved; boil for 15 minutes. Add the brandy, peppermint essence, and colouring.

Index